the poetic
image
in **6** genres

david madden

Southern Illinois University Press
Carbondale and Edwardsville

Feffer & Simons, Inc., *London and Amsterdam*

to

robert daniel,

margaret myers,

and my students.

may they thrive, prosper,

and, above all, soar

Acknowledgments

For permission to reprint essays and essay-reviews, I want to thank the editors of the journals in which they first appeared.

The Louisville *Courier-Journal* for reviews of *Under Twenty-Five, New Voices '64, It Is Time, Lord, A Multitude of Sins,* in "A Gallery of First Novels" and for reviews of *Making It* and *The Armies of the Night* in "Approaching Autobiography as Art"; *The Kenyon Review* for the short story, "The Singer," and sections of "A Gallery of First Novels." Reviews of Joyce Carol Oates' *By the North Gate* and *Upon the Sweeping Flood* are reprinted from *Studies in Short Fiction* (Newberry College, Newberry, S.C.) Volume I, 169–70 and Volume IV, 369–72. Acknowledgment is made for the use of the following essays: "Form and Life in the Novel: Toward a Freer Approach to an Elastic Genre," *The Journal of Aesthetics and Art Criticism,* XXV, Spring 1967, 323–33; "The Fallacy of the Subject-Dominated Novel," *The English Record,* XVIII, April 1968, No. 4, 11–19; "Harlan, Kentucky ... Sunday ... Things At Rest," *Appalachian Review,* I, No. 2, 24–27; "*The Virgin Spring*: Anatomy of a Mythic Image," *Film Heritage*; "Wright Morris' *In Orbit*: An Unbroken Series of Poetic Gestures," *Critique*; "Gene Derwood: Cassandra Sane," *Approach,* Fall 1966, 27–33; "Cassandra Singing — On & Off Key: or, How Not to Write a Play," *Drama Critique,* X, Spring 1967, No. 2, 58–70.

Sections of "Theater without Walls" first appeared in *Shenandoah*; most of the essay is reprinted from "The Theatre of Assault," *The Massachusetts Review,* © 1967, The Massachusetts Review, Inc.

"Elegy on Gordon Barber" by Gene Derwood from *The Poems of Gene Derwood,* © 1955 by Oscar Williams, reprinted by permission of October House, Inc.

D.M.

Contents

"Once upon a time and a very good time it was there was a moocow coming down along the road and this moocow that was down along the road met a nicens little boy named baby tuckoo . . . ." So most stories, and thus most writers, begin. Stephen Dedalus' father, in *Portrait of the Artist as a Young Man*, told him that one. My grandmother, looking, I often thought, like Wallace Beery, told me one about an old man who used the money his wife saved for their twelve children's Christmas presents to buy himself a handsome tombstone. My grandmother's voice was like the sound track of a movie (or "show," as we called them), and as she gestured, her body was like a stage. At age four, I began to pass my own version of that story, along with my renditions of the adventures of Buck Jones and Zorro (accompanied by throaty simulations of symphonic background music) and the escapades of Laurel and Hardy (Straighthair and Fatsy) for comic relief, to my two brothers, curled under the quilts, to neighborhood kids, huddled on our high front steps, and later to classmates during recess in grammar school. What began as play has metamorphosed through many stages. The suspicion that the essays in your hand are play under yet another guise delights me. As Joyce brought *Finnegans Wake* to an esoteric close, with "Till thousendsthee. Lps. The keys to. Given! A way a lone a last a loved a long the," wasn't he still at play? Wasn't the infant still listening inside the adult "punrambler"?

Telling stories as a child, acting out all the parts, doing all the voices, I was an actor on a stage, my spectators within reach. When I wasn't telling stories, I was daydreaming them. No wonder the movies appealed to me so powerfully, inducing passive dreaming in fitful images. From age four until fifteen, I saw about three "shows" a week, usually twice each; I worked as an usher at the age

of twelve — an immersion verging at moments on immolation. I wanted to be able to affect people the way the
movies affected the spectators around me; but the only
way I could deal in the magic powers of the movies was to
write down my own versions of such films as *A Song to
Remember* (a technicolor biography of Chopin, starring
Cornel Wilde), *Frenchman's Creek*, and *Our Vines Have
Tender Grapes*. So it was not written stories but moving
picture stories that inspired me, at age ten, to write my
first story, and thus, I discovered, quite accidentally, the
private, lonely thrill of affecting individual, absent readers
— a relationship remote from the public, communal
transaction of movies. But by absorbing and transmuting
movie techniques, I made the images in my stories more
vivid, the action more immediate; most of my early
writing read like screen scenarios. Comic books offered a
more purely visual stimulation; like sound movies and
radio drama, comics had, in the thirties, all the raw impact
of technological novelties. Early in junior high, I drew my
own comic books, using my stories as scenarios.

Between these two extremes — my grandmother and
Hollywood — another influence was radio drama, which
demanded that listeners see through their ears. Just as the
silent moving image was the basis of the art of early films,
the purblind aural image was the basis of the craft of
radio drama; technological "improvements" suddenly
prevented both these media from developing their own
peculiar techniques to full maturity; thus, the crudeness
of much of even the best silent movies and of old-time
radio plays makes us chuckle condescendingly. But the
English and the Europeans — Beckett, Dylan Thomas,
Harold Pinter, for instance — never abandoned the
difficult and unique radio medium, knowing that in art
one achieved maturity by cultivating limitations. Following the recent camp-nostalgia for radio drama ("The
Shadow," for instance), a revival of serious radio has gotten
underway; one hopes that its special aesthetic characteristics will be developed to a much higher level of sophisti-

cation. I began writing radio plays in junior high, and in high school directed and acted in my own plays on a commercial station in Knoxville, Tennessee.

Long before I read many stories, I began writing them. I read no children's books, none of the classics; in grammar school, I read only what I couldn't avoid. At thirteen, I read a book all the way through for the first time — *God's Little Acre*; enticed by the sex, I was seduced by the storytelling. Another stimulation to my interest in writing was *The Saturday Evening Post* and *Liberty*, which I sold from door to door. (I have always had some practical, workaday involvement with media for which I've written; I've been a radio announcer — fired for trying to uplift the masses by playing Tchaikovsky's "Romeo and Juliet Overture" on a hillbilly disc-jockey show; an actor and a director; an editor.) Clarence Budington Kelland, I declared in my ninth grade "career book," was a great writer. Thus, I came in on the commercial level, writing pulp cowboy stories; at fourteen, I had the same agent as Raymond Chandler and MacKinlay Kantor. Ironically, not until I had passed through a long period of contempt for commercial writing and had published in a number of literary quarterlies did I sell to commercial magazines. After a high school exposure to the theater, I wrote a play which won a state play contest and was produced at the University of Tennessee. Louis Untermeyer's and Oscar Williams' anthologies stimulated me to write poetry, and John Gassner's anthologies inspired me to continue to write for the stage. So I entered the university having written in all six genres, except the movies.

Soon after I stumbled onto Caldwell, I discovered Hemingway, and began to write more seriously — even about my own life, for up to then that had not occurred to me, although life seemed overwhelmingly rich in fascinating people and episodes. In key with my early receptivity to media, my first responses to Thomas Wolfe and to James Joyce were superficial, romantic, and non-literary. I often went to the drugstore just to look at the picture of Thomas Wolfe (I had read nothing by him) on the back of the Penguin edition of his short stories — the shadowed, marble head, resting on the Promethean fist. This was how a writer should look! Although I could afford to buy the paperback, I deliberately stole it — the risk enhanced the book's value for me. Wolfe became my hero, as my first published story, "Imprisoned Light," shows (*Coraddi*, 1952, The Woman's College of the University of North Carolina at Greensboro). In a dirty, secondhand bookstore window, I often saw a picture of Joyce on the back of the Penguin edition of *Portrait of the Artist*; hand to brow, wearing his eyepatch and white coat, he epitomized for me the esoteric, bohemian artist-exile. For a year, I delayed buying the novel (I had read nothing by Joyce); such self-denial was a move away from Wolfean self-indulgence. Though I have continued to love Wolfe the man (who was once very real to me), Joyce, a remote, godlike, aesthetic inspiration, replaced him within a few years as mentor. More in my own fiction perhaps than in my criticism, I am always in the act of trying to resolve the conflict between my natural Wolfean (or dionysian) inclinations in life and literature and my need of Joycean (or apollonian) discipline and technique.

In the past few years, I have re-evaluated those early enthusiasms in popular and high culture from various points of view. While writing a book about Wright Morris, one of the most subtle and therefore most neglected writers in America, I took a nostalgic look at James M. Cain, master of the hard-boiled popular novel of the thirties. My essay describing his work grew into a book, and my explorations into works of other tough writers culminated in not one book, but two; for as I examined Hammett, Cain, Chandler, and Horace McCoy, I discovered affinities between their novels and the otherwise contrasting type, the proletarian novel. My teaching has quite naturally reflected my various interests. An honors seminar for non-English majors, which I conducted at Ohio University in 1968, examined various types of popular novels. We were able to see certain literary techniques at work on a low level. But, more important, we were startled to discover that so-called trash achieved some purposes and insights more effectively than serious literature; the similarities between popular and serious fiction were not always flattering to the latter; we discovered gross hypocrisies in some serious literature as opposed to relative honesty in some "bad" fiction. To writers, students, and teachers nurtured almost exclusively on serious literature, and who are weary of their own snobbery and hyper-sophistication, I recommend such a venture as being mysterious, dangerous, but eventually enlightening. (I would like to see a textbook for freshmen that contains "good" and "bad" "commercial" writing in all genres alongside "good" and "bad" "serious" writing.)

During this same period, I experienced such startling juxtapositions as receiving in the same mail copies of *The Kenyon Review* and *Adam* magazines containing my stories. I haven't written any stories with *Cad*, *Knight*, and *Adam Bedside Reader* in mind, but I have submitted stories that I enjoyed writing and they wanted to publish (including a detective novel, *Hair of the Dog*, in *Adam* April–November, 1967, and two stories about "Big Bob," a radio announcer). These I call, imitating Graham Greene, "entertainments" as opposed to serious stories — although I didn't begin them with that distinction in mind. With reputable writers like J. P. Donleavy, Bernard Malamud, and William Golding appearing in *Playboy*, the barriers between popular and high culture are falling and shifting. Nine chapters of my "serious" novel, *Cassandra Singing*, have appeared in literary quarterlies, but *Knight* also published a chapter; "The Master's Thesis" was accepted by *Story*, which folded, then by *Genesis West*, an avant-garde quarterly, which folded, and finally appeared in *Fantasy and Science Fiction* (July, 1967) — another example of blurred distinctions. Out of snobbery (until recently), I seldom look at such magazines. I have been amazed to learn that many of my scholarly colleagues, including "a Milton man," not only read them but aspire to write for them. Reaction to my story "The Day the Flowers Came" (September, 1968) made me wonder whether *anybody* misses reading *Playboy*.

A final example in my own writing of cutting across genres and culture levels. I became excited by commedia dell'arte while I was an undergraduate, and for five years a play about a troupe of Renaissance commedia actors germinated; but I conceived it more in terms of the theater of Pirandello, Beckett, and O'Neill than of the overtly popular theater of Harlequin's day. A year before I finally wrote the play, I began a study of the movies and saw rich parallels between commedia dell'arte and silent slapstick comedy; an article for *Film Quarterly* germinated for the next five years. Meanwhile, just as the play, *Fugitive Masks*, was being performed at Ohio University, *Playboy*, a genuinely popular medium, published my version of a commedia scenario, "The Virgin of Venice," in its Ribald Classics department. Then in the fall of the same year (1968), the essay "Harlequin's Stick, Chaplin's Cane," appeared; it is a scholarly approach to manifestations of a basic set of stock characters and comic routines in two popular media, theater and movies. In this shifting from one perspective to another on the same material, over several genres, I have learned more about writing, about my own interests, and about the teller-listener relationship.

I sense that my grandmother was aware of the effects her storytelling had on me, and, even as a child, I was aware of another part of myself that stood at a distance, observing the dynamic interplay between teller and listener. But not until I had written "The Singer" (a short story included here) did I realize consciously that I had been fascinated all my life by the teller's compulsion to tell a story. "The Singer" itself is a dramatization of various kinds and levels of response between teller and listener — a mysterious collaboration in which both, for a moment, transcend time and place, and the listener humanizes the teller, the teller humanizes the listener. Looking back, I see that my own compulsion to tell a story, on one or another level of sophistication, has always, consciously and unconsciously, reached out to explore every possible medium in which to express what has always been a rich and abundant raw material. Each medium and genre had its own special attraction, offered its peculiar way into the relationship between teller and listener. My reactions since childhood to movies, radio, magazines, books, and theater, purely as media, explain my experiences as a writer. Thus, to Marshall McLuhan's formula — The Medium Is The Message — I made a déjà vu response. Since 1958, when I began writing criticism, I have felt impelled to comment on facets of this teller-listener process in essays that examine works in more than six genres. I use "genre" in the very broadest sense of the Latin *genus* to mean "class" — novel, short story, poetry, autobiography; for convenience, I use the term even more broadly to absorb drama and film, two media that usually start with a written script.

It was as a young writer of fiction that I read the novels of Wright Morris; studying his techniques, especially his unique style, I learned a great deal about writing. But it was as a student of literature that I began to write criticism, because I wanted "to point out" (James's phrase for the critic's function) what makes Morris' fiction excellent. Neither entirely by accident nor entirely by design have my essays and fiction explored many genres; I have simply followed my interests in living, reading, seeing plays and movies, writing, and teaching. But looking back over a decade of writing criticism, I see quite clearly that my critical pieces parallel my fiction in the various genres. (While I haven't written for the movies, my study of cinematic techniques has affected my fiction, as "The Singer" demonstrates.) For instance, while working with Walter Van Tilburg Clark for a master's in writing at San Francisco State College (in the halcyon days of the beat renaissance), I began writing essays about Morris (who, appropriately enough, now teaches writing — between riots — at San Francisco State); then I wrote a book about Morris while working in a contrasting genre at Yale Drama School. It is as a teacher, critic, poet, playwright, writer of novels and short stories, aware of my work in relation to the writings of others, that I have composed these and other essays.

Again looking back, I see that I have been inclined to explore possibilities *within* genres. For instance, I have written both poetic and realistic, urban and rural plays; a modern verse adaptation of *Medea* for radio; a libretto adaptation of *The Trojan Women*, performed on educational TV; a cantata about Saint Paul; a modern, musical version of Plautus' *Casina*; stage adaptations of my own fiction and of *Look Homeward, Angel* (before Ketti Frings), *The Heart Is a Lonely Hunter*, and Morris' *The Deep Sleep*. This pattern becomes even more complex when I discover that in the genre of criticism itself, I have published essays across disciplines in philosophical, psychological, scholarly, belletristic, offbeat, and religious journals; and written book and drama reviews for mass circulation magazines, literary quarterlies, and newspapers (including *Kentucky Labor News*). Thus, critical commentary, it turns out, has been another genre for realizing possibilities in the teller-listener relationship, and the very makeup of this collection is yet another exploration.

I sense that the reader's patience may be waning, for what writer, critic, or teacher of literature growing up in the thirties and forties *wasn't* strongly affected by massive and varied exposure to these media and genres? Indeed, in one way or another, my own story reflects the drama of creativity among many of my contemporaries. However, actual practice in and critical comment on all these forms is not common — and that is probably a good thing. Autobiographical background comes into this preface to a collection of critical essays because the interplay of tensions between popular culture and high culture, between one medium, one genre and another, has to some extent

determined my choice of raw material and the techniques I
have used to transform that material (this continuing
interplay may explain seeming inconsistencies among the
attitudes and principles enunciated in these essays); and,
of course, the impact of media is expressed in the essays
themselves. If I went into each of these genres, including
criticism (a seventh), out of sheer interest in the genres
themselves, as well as in the subject matter which seemed
best expressed in each, I see now that my involvement has
been a process of self-education. Thus, especially appropriate to this collection is the truism that all writing is
autobiography, even criticism — think of D. H. Lawrence,
Wright Morris, Anaïs Nin, Norman Mailer, Henry Miller,
William Carlos Williams, Edward Dahlberg, Ezra Pound,
Wyndham Lewis, Colin Wilson, Gertrude Stein, Leslie
Fiedler, as extreme examples. While these essays range
from the formal to the informal, the theoretical to the
anecdotal, from evaluation to appreciation, from scrutiny
of the works of others to self-scrutiny, both content and
conception reveal a strong preoccupation with my own
problems as a writer.

I sense, at thirty-five, that this sort of exploration is
ending, and probably should end. For somewhere, some-
time, maturity must wag a cautionary finger. So I resolve
(at a time when four new critical books are in preparation)
to confine myself to one or two media and practice in-
tensively what I've learned and preached during this process. There ought to be much less criticism, and perhaps
less teaching. But since what attracted me originally to
these media was sheer love of teaching and criticism and
the teller-listener opportunities they provided, I know
that word cannot easily be forced to become flesh.

But at some point in one's self-education, codification,
at least, is necessary. After I had selected these essays I
discovered that in all my critical pieces and recently in my
fiction, I have been preoccupied with the concept of the
poetic image, a way of talking about coherence and
synthesis in a work of art. (In fact, it is here that I already

break my resolution, for I plan another book in which the poetic image concept is more deliberately examined — a bibliographical essay will appear first.) The poetic image concept is more apparent in some of these pieces than in others; it hovers, though, even over those essays in which the term isn't mentioned. Students of writing may find that this approach encourages the reader's active participation more than one which spells everything out, step by step.

Since I am interested here in the function of the image in six genres, why do I use the term "poetic image"? Because the dominant image or image-nucleus in a work that is organically unified has the potency of a poetic image, discharging its power, as the work reveals itself, into every part, retaining its power, after the work is fully perceived, in a picture. This poetic image is not necessarily a single picture. The symbolic image of the green light at the end of Daisy's dock in *The Great Gatsby* becomes a condensation and abstraction of many other images. The developing elements in a novel (or aspects of a character in a play or in a film) become integrated finally, Croce tells us, in an image, and "what is known as an image is always a tissue of images."

It is too early in my study of the poetic image for anything but a working definition: *In a work of art, a poetic image focuses some element which in its prepared context is highly expressive, and is evocative of the work's important themes and experiences, and these are condensed and compressed finally into the poetic image. The image is, therefore, highly charged with meaning, both experiential and symbolic.* (Prose-poetry and poetic prose style have nothing to do with this conception.)

From forty essays and some fifty essay-reviews published in the past ten years, I have made choices out of my basic intention to represent six genres; in various versions these pieces were written over the past five years, published over the past three. In most instances, it is the individual work itself that excites me, and to that extent

I reveal the influence of the New Critics. I am, in these essays at least, less interested in what I sometimes call "theme-mongering" than in technique. And because I want especially to speak to other writers who are in the midst of self-education, as I am, I think it appropriate to blend into the following description of the design of this collection a bibliography of some of my other essays and noncritical work that parallel and augment elements discussed in the ones I have included here.

The newspaper review form is a special challenge: how not only to be fair but somehow to serve the author, and also to fulfill one's responsibility to the reader and to one's own criteria — in space as uncomfortable as the little-ease. While conducting writing workshops at the University of Louisville and Kenyon College, I deliberately chose to review first novels to gain insight into the creative process in early stages. The piece that opens this volume, "A Gallery of First Novels," is a medley of essays and reviews written over the past seven years, devoted to collections of the writing of new writers and to first novels (arranged on a scale of quality in ascending order): *Under Twenty-five; New Voices '64; Early Summer* by Anna Sevier; *A Multitude of Sins* by J. A. Cuddon; *It Is Time, Lord* by Fred Chappell; *The Orchard Keeper* by Cormac McCarthy; *The Long Voyage* by Jorge Semprun; and *The Garden* by Yves Berger. (Cuddon, Chappell, and McCarthy have since published second novels.) An unfavorable review of my own first novel, *The Beautiful Greed*, is quoted.

"The Violent World of Joyce Carol Oates" is a compilation of several essays and reviews dealing with the short stories and novels of a single young writer from the beginning of her phenomenal career to the present. In the essay I note that Miss Oates never uses the first person; however, *Expensive People*, published too recently to be discussed in the essay, does employ the first person, but, characteristically, it is a boy who tells the story. For other studies in the short story see "Katherine Mansfield's 'Miss Brill,'" *University Review*, December, 1964;

"Organic Unity in James Joyce's 'Clay,'" *University Review*, Spring, 1967; and "Kafka's 'In the Penal Colony,'" *Ann Arbor Review*, Winter, 1967.

Alluded to in the first two essays, the poetic image concept is discussed more deliberately in "Form and Life in the Novel: Toward a Freer Approach to an Elastic Genre," a philosophical examination of general theories about the techniques for dealing with the raw material of a novel, citing traditional and contemporary examples. An early draft of this essay, dating back to the beginning of my interest in criticism, was almost a young fiction writer's reaction against formal criticism. As a bias for the purely aesthetic approach developed, I moved away from the position presented in this essay. But in the spirit of a statement by Fitzgerald that I have always striven to live and write by — "The test of a first-rate intelligence is the ability to hold two opposed ideas in the mind at the same time and still retain the ability to function" — I decided in 1965 to publish the essay anyway; however, I revised it a little so that it did not conflict too severely with the beliefs I held then. (Some important books on theories of fiction have appeared in the past seven years: Wayne C. Booth's *The Rhetoric of Fiction*; Susan Sontag's *Against Interpretation*; Frank Kermode's *The Sense of an Ending*; and Richard Poirier's *A World Elsewhere*.)

"Form and Life in the Novel" warns against over-emphasis on technique at the expense of the "life" of a novel; several years before that essay appeared "The Fallacy of the Subject-Dominated Novel" was written; its thesis is that the writer's and the reader's awe of a particular subject matter or raw material in life can blind them to the necessity for artistic shaping and control; an attack is made on the notion that implicit in this subject matter is an appeal and an importance that transcends technical failures. (My own novel, *The Beautiful Greed*, is cited as falling victim to this fallacy.) Thus, these two theoretical essays exhibit the Wolfe-Joyce conflict in my work, resolved, momentarily at least, in "The Singer";

later, my study of popular literature modified the positions
discussed in the two essays. In the popular fiction course
described earlier, some of the novels discussed in this essay
were studied; it was published while the course, which was
contradicting some of the attitudes expressed, was in
progress. For a close textual comparison of a masterpiece
of the popular tough guy novel, James M. Cain's *The
Postman Always Rings Twice*, with a masterful example of
the philosophical novel, Albert Camus' *The Stranger*
(which Camus testified was influenced by Cain's novel),
see my essay which is to appear in *Papers in Language and
Literature*, Winter, 1970. For more on Cain and the tough
writers, see *James M. Cain*, projected for the Twayne
series in 1970; "James M. Cain and the Tough Guy
Novelists of the Thirties" in *The Thirties*, edited by
Warren French, Everett / Edwards Press, 1967; *Tough
Guy Writers of the Thirties*, Southern Illinois University
Press, 1968; "James M. Cain, Twenty-Minute Egg of the
Hard-Boiled School," *Journal of Popular Culture*, Winter,
1967. For more on the thesis, exposé, propaganda, or
sociological novel, see *Proletarian Writers of the Thirties*,
Southern Illinois University Press, 1968; although I
edited this volume, I have written no fiction in the
ideological vein. For more on the concept of the "pure
novel," see "James M. Cain and the Pure Novel," *University Review*, December, 1963 and March, 1964.

"Harlan, Kentucky . . . Sunday . . . Things at Rest"
relates to the two theoretical essays that precede it,
especially to "The Fallacy of the Subject-Dominated
Novel," because it deals with sensational raw material:
impoverished Eastern Kentucky. But I try in this lyrical,
personal essay to reveal, without exposing, facets of life
there — thus, my purpose is the opposite of journalistic
social consciousness; reading Mailer's new books about the
march on the Pentagon and the 1968 political conventions
makes me see that this essay, too, was an attempt to work
within, while transcending, the province of journalism. I
try to use the techniques of imaginative literature to make

the reader see this raw material in a balanced way, so that he feels and understands without being aroused to reform conditions and without being merely titillated by the exotic in Eastern Kentucky. The effect of the people and the landscape caused me to shift the locale of my novel and play, *Cassandra Singing*, from my home town, Knoxville, to Harlan; and I am working on a new story set in Eastern Kentucky. For more on Eastern Kentucky as an intriguing raw material area, see Harry Caudill's *Night Comes to the Cumberlands* and Harriette Arnow's *Seedtime on the Cumberland*, and her novels, *Mountain Path* and *Hunter's Horn*. "Harlan" is directly related to "The Singer," the short story that follows it; they are included here as specimens of my own noncritical writing, and they illustrate some of the general principles enunciated in the essays in this collection. At the time I wrote the piece, I did not realize that the lyrical essay technique was acting as an agent of exploration for the story I had longed for five years to write. But later, images and passages from the essay were consciously carried over (almost verbatim) into the story. Thus, within the context of this collection, a comparison of the styles and of the consequences of point-of-view techniques amounts to a study of the short story and the lyrical essay genres. The "Harlan" essay is also related to "Approaching Autobiography as Art," the essay that concludes this collection.

The poetic image concept is more overtly at work in "The Singer" than in any of my other noncritical writing. Usually, experimentation should begin and end in the privacy of the writer's study. While "The Singer" is probably unique in its structural and point-of-view techniques it is not included here as an example of technically avant-garde writing. The sensational Eastern Kentucky raw material and the singer's simple story posed serious problems; inspired by a singer in real life, the story languished while I searched and waited for a technical inspiration. It is the best illustration in my own work of what Mark Schorer is talking about in his brilliant essay

"Technique as Discovery" (discussed in "Form and Life in the Novel," Schorer's essay is reprinted in his new book, *The World We Imagine*, which it will profit every writer to read). The technique that solved the story's problems also enabled me to discover almost everything, as it turned out, that was effective in the story.

Three entwined themes in "The Singer" link it with two recent novellas — "Traven," *Southern Review*, Spring, 1968, and "Nothing Dies But Something Mourns," *Carleton Miscellany*, Fall, 1968 — as well as several stories unpublished or in progress: Mann's idea of the confidence man as artist, the artist as confidence man; the relationship between a hero and his witness; and the compulsion to tell a story. Giving dramatic readings of this story through the United States, I have experienced kinetically the relationship between the teller and his listeners. Surrendering to this compulsion to tell a story has been another way of going back to the place from which I started: the burden of making up a story without any introduction or asides, so that I must, like an actor, sustain the illusion of being, at once, both Pete and Wayne, the characters who tell the story simultaneously. The relationship between a performer and his audience parallels that between the story-teller and his listeners; the obligations entailed are sacred, the experience at best quasi-religious. This has been the decade of the poet as performer; audiences are eager now to hear more prose writers read their work. While I am moved to make a more thorough critical study of the hero-witness relationship and the compulsion to tell a story in such novels as *Don Quixote*, *Moby Dick*, *Wuthering Heights*, *The Great Gatsby*, *Requiem for a Nun*, *Absalom, Absalom!*, Glenway Wescott's *The Pilgrim Hawk*, Robert Penn Warren's *All the King's Men*, Morris's *The Field of Vision*, and in several Salinger stories, my only essay on the subject is "Romanticism and the Hero-Witness Relationship in Four Conrad Stories" ("Youth," "The Secret Sharer," "Heart of Darkness," *Lord Jim*), *Ohio University Review*, Fall, 1968.

"The Singer" is related to the essay that follows it. Originally, I wanted to tell the simple story of a legendary singer with the purity of Bergman's film, *The Virgin Spring*. But what is convincing on the screen threatened to appear vacuous and sentimental in a story. The poetic image concept operates directly in "*The Virgin Spring:* Anatomy of a Mythic Image." This is the first of three detailed analyses of individual works in three genres. For more on the poetic image concept in film, see Sergei Eisenstein's *Film Form and Film Sense*, a Meridian paperback. In my involvement with movies, I have gone from collecting thousands of stills (steals, in some instances) and magazines to serving as associate editor of *Film Heritage* and writing articles and reviews on films. See "James M. Cain and the Movies of the Thirties and Forties," *Film Heritage*, Summer, 1967; "Toward Film Criticism," *Antioch Review*, Spring, 1966; and "Film as Educator," *Antioch Review*, Spring, 1967.

Wright Morris' novels illustrate again the wisdom of Schorer's declaration that "technique is discovery." In "Wright Morris' *In Orbit:* An Unbroken Series of Poetic Gestures," the poetic image concept functions even more specifically. A short novel, *In Orbit* is discussed in the context of the author's other fifteen novels. *In Orbit* is available as a Signet paperback. For further comment on his work, see *Wright Morris*, Twayne, 1964; and "Letter to a Young Critic" (my correspondence with Morris) in *Massachusetts Review*, Autumn-Winter, 1964–65. For other close studies of single novels see "Chapter 18 in Emily Brontë's *Wuthering Heights*," *The English Record*, February, 1967; "Camus' *The Stranger:* An Achievement in Simultaneity," *Renascence*, Summer, 1968; "The Paradox of the Need for Privacy and the Need for Understanding in Carson McCullers' *The Heart Is a Lonely Hunter*," *Literature and Psychology*, Numbers 2–3, 1967; and "Ambiguity in Camus' *The Fall*," *Modern Fiction Studies*, Winter, 1966–67.

In high school and during the first years of college, I

read and wrote an enormous amount of poetry; then,
having decided that I was not a poet, I stopped writing
poetry for about ten years. Teaching Yeats at Kenyon, I
began to write again, and a dozen or so poems have appeared in such journals as *Southern Poetry Review*,
Wormwood Review, *Ante*, and *Northwest Review*. I have
written only a few essays about poetry. In "Gene Derwood: Cassandra Sane," the poetic image concept is now
applied to a poem, "Elegy on Gordon Barber." A minor
poet, Gene Derwood never was in fashion, but I like this
poem and want to talk about it. My desire to call attention
to such neglected writers as Miss Derwood has resulted in a
book called *Rediscoveries*, in which well-known novelists
comment informally on their favorite novel by a little-
known writer of fiction.

    Although the poetic image concept does not dominate
"*Cassandra Singing* — On and Off Key," it is at work
indirectly behind other concepts that explain my problems in writing and rewriting *Cassandra Singing* as a play
and as a novel over fifteen years. (Crown will publish the
novel version in the early fall of 1969.) This essay relates
to the first in the volume and anticipates "Theater without Walls."

    In the spring of 1967, I gave a lecture at the Univer-
sity of Dayton on new American playwrights. When
Anthony Macklin, editor of *Film Heritage* and himself a
writer, challenged me for basing my judgments more on
reading such plays than on seeing them, I flew straight to
New York and saw six. Focusing upon five off-off-Broadway plays by young playwrights, "Theater without Walls"
analyzes some of the faults and virtues of the new theater
in America; thus it relates to "A Gallery of First Novels."
For extended comment on the new theater see "Happenings Off-Off-Broadway," *Shenandoah*, Fall, 1967.

    Literary critics, and practitioners of the form as
well, have long neglected the aesthetic possibilities of
autobiography. "Approaching Autobiography as Art" is a
discussion of Willie Morris' *North Toward Home*, Norman

Podhoretz's *Making It*, Frank Conroy's *Stop-time*, and Norman Mailer's *The Armies of the Night* (1969 National Book Award winner); these books take a fresh approach to autobiography and suggest some fascinating possibilities for the future — a future in which the genre may break out of strict chronology and use more aesthetic techniques — ones which are implied in the poetic image concept — making autobiography an art form, rather than simply a report. This essay is an exploration for a book on American autobiography.

The most difficult struggle for many young writers is to escape from the me-rack of subjectivity. For a long time, influenced by Wolfe, I wrote too much about my own life, out of what I now call the "it-really-happened" fallacy. *The Beautiful Greed* was based on my experiences in the Merchant Marine; but even then I was moving in the opposite direction — a deliberate avoidance of subjectivity and the show of real, external events as being too easy compared with the difficulties of pure art. "Traven" was the first indication of a turning back to a rich raw material that I have, I now feel, unnecessarily neglected. As I plunge now into the most dangerous waters of all — my days as a twelve-year-old aspiring writer, working as a uniformed usher in a movie palace in Knoxville — I do not know whether the result will be an autobiographical novel or a new sort of autobiography. Another work in progress, based on my two years in the army as a private who refused to sign Senator Joseph McCarthy's loyalty oath, is definitely autobiography.

My interest in autobiography as a genre has gone through several mutations. A few years ago, partially inspired by William Bolitho's *Twelve Against the Gods*, I decided that someday I would write a book about famous young men who burned themselves out before they reached forty: Alexander, Marlowe, Chatterton, Rimbaud, Keats, Billy the Kid, Jesse James, Sam Davis, James Dean, Dylan Thomas, Thomas Wolfe, James Agee, Montgomery Clift, Icarus, among others. Then, in 1968,

teaching a colloquium at Ohio University on the theme of
the American Dream-turned-Nightmare in literature, I
deliberately chose to review four new autobiographies by
writers who came out of the same period in which I grew
up: Willie Morris, Podhoretz, Frank Conroy, Mailer. My
intuition that they would express some facet of American
Dreams and Nightmares was justified. Inspired by these
books, I conceived another course — American Lives:
Studies in American Character. It deals with autobiographies by Americans whose lives offer perspectives on the
spirit and character of their times, with an emphasis on
the twentieth century, one of the purposes of the course
being to stimulate self-scrutiny in the student within the
context of his own time. Out of this experience was to
come the student's own autobiography, covering only the
period in which he is taking the course, so that he will
talk about his life as it relates to the autobiographies he is
studying, to his contemporaries, to his past life and future
aspirations, and to immediate events — which included
that spring the assassination of Martin Luther King; then
the threat of a nonacademic employees' strike that would
have closed the University, followed by a student riot
when the strike failed to occur; a major flood; and then
the assassination of Robert Kennedy.

I have brought these essays together on the assumption that an involvement in many genres might interest
students and teachers of literature, critics, and, perhaps
above all, students of writing. While few young writers
will work in all these areas, perhaps this collection, by
employing some of the same critical concepts in various
genres, will suggest alternatives, new combinations, new
approaches. Given my background and temperament, it is
quite natural that I have worked in diverse areas; but I
certainly don't recommend this struggle to all developing
writers. On the other hand, some exploration of genres
other than the one in which the young writer feels most
comfortable, competent, and productive will stimulate new
perspectives on his raw material and on the possible

techniques for discovering its facets and its meanings. So I offer this volume as a demonstration of the values — positive and perhaps negative as well — of working in and writing about various genres. Self-discipline and vigilance may overcome the anarchical dangers of eclecticism.

David Madden

Louisiana State University
January 1, 1969

a gallery of first novels

A year after the unenthusiastic reception in 1961 of my own novel *The Beautiful Greed* (actually billed on the jacket as a Random House First Novel — a bit like sending a girl into the world with a note pinned to her blouse: "I Am A Virgin"), I moved to the University of Louisville to conduct the writers' workshop that Harvey Curtis Webster had made successful. I had not taught a workshop full time before. Having failed to write a good novel, being engaged in writing a better one (*Cassandra Singing*), attempting to *advise* others about some of the problems involved, I requested only first novels to review (reviewing also was a new activity for me). Looking back over these reviews of new writing — stories, poetry, novels — I detect a preoccupation with techniques of writing which at the time I was not only discussing with my students but exploring in my critical writing and my own stories, plays, novels, poems.

Some of the basic problems and achievements of first novels are seen in two collections of stories and poems produced in university workshops. Campus literary magazines perform a worthy function: student writing is tested among a limited audience of friends and fellow students in what remains a kind of workshop situation. But the current trend toward hardcover collections for the general market ought not, as a rule, to be encouraged. The "New Campus Writing" series succeeds because it collects the best from the nation's workshops. (*Intro*, a new venture from Bantam Books, follows a similar principle of selection).

But isn't it presumptuous of a single school to offer its own collection? The excellence of the recent Duke anthology is exceptional. The short stories in *Under Twenty-Five: Duke Narrative and Verse, 1945–1962* (edited by William Blackburn, Duke University Press, 1963) are fine and memorable. If the poetry by James Carpenter and Guy Davenport is not as praiseworthy, none of it is "student work." The writing was done in college or within a year after graduation by students under twenty-five; most of it first appeared in Duke's literary magazine, *Archive*. William Blackburn's creative writing course has turned out some notable writers: William Styron, whose essay "Writers Under Twenty-five" is a witty attack on the claim that no original writing has appeared since World War I; Reynolds Price, whose "A Chain of Love" introduces Rosacoke, the heroine of the highly praised *A Long and Happy Life*; Mac Hyman (*No Time For Sergeants*), whose "The Dove Shoot" is a serious story of a boy's first profound exposure to racial prejudice; and Fred Chappell, whose "Inheritance" compares well with the best writing in his first novel *It Is Time, Lord*, a sketch for which appears here, along with ten good poems that explore some of that book's themes and characters. While some stories and sketches indicate promising talent, the rest have a control and ring of authority that give them a firmly professional stance. Of these, the best three are James Applewhite's "Water in a Dry Place," about a boy who understands his grandfather's faith in religion and the past; Thomas R. Atkins's "Island Summer," whose flowing, lyrical style creates an atmosphere of natural and human fecundity; and Elinor Divine's "The Onlooker," in which a boy is profoundly affected by the drowning of the family's hero. (This story, by the way, appeared in *Coraddi*, literary magazine of the University of North Carolina at Greensboro, in the same issue in which my own first story was published; re-reading it, I realized that my own novel *Cassandra Singing* had been influenced by Elinor Divine's story.) These stories deserve a wide readership. The "Southern" stories seem to be in a new tradition. None are avant-garde or precious; that only four are in the first person indicates a certain remove from subjectivity.

But in exposing his thirty New School students — prematurely in almost every instance — Hayes B. Jacobs exhibits a reckless eagerness and a rather embarrassing vanity. Listening to *New Voices '64* (Macmillan, 1964), one hears the squeaks of voices still braving the transition to creative maturity.

Only two of the five poems and three of the twenty-five stories are memorable. With poignant irony, Nancy Spraker scrutinizes the "water-resistant, shock-proof" watch on the arm of a drowned friend. In "Summer 1943," Eva Miodownik gracefully walks a tightrope of clichés, without a net. Conceptual audacity and a unity of subject, theme, and style distinguish Nat Esformes' "The Guitars of Third Avenue." By a kind of psychological osmosis, the narrator (unborn child of a Puerto Rican) experiences the world's misery so intensely that it entreats its mother to join it in the security of the womb. In "Memorial Day, 1961" Bedros Najarian attempts something difficult and original. He aims pointlessly satirical darts at Hemingway and Faulkner; he spews both sentimentality and bitterness out of the side of his mouth, reminding one of Michael Gold, angry young man of the thirties; but Najarian's is a personal and passionate voice that cries out for a larger stage. "Paradis 4" by Zelda Dietze is not an unusual story, but her control is firm, she has a feeling for language, and she evokes a sense of place admirably well. A few of the others may put up a good fight against obscurity.

Too often in the stories irony belongs to the "great-hairy-foot-trampling-the-flower-bed" department. Stylistically, the few attempts at humor rely upon such lead-ins as "who could have known" and "so my fate was sealed." Forced phrasing suggests a sleeping teacher-editor: "The window-panes ... played a game of hide-and-seek with the golden sunbeams." Mawkish effusions got by the teacher also: "since then ten years have passed — too quickly ... a prophetic vapor rises from the volcano of my increasing age." Subtlety is a technique some have yet to learn; for instance, in the three-page sketch "Silence," the word "silence" is repeated seven times.

Most of the writers demonstrate little natural or acquired talent for style, technique, or even storytelling. Some exhibit a craven submission — in concept, style, and incident — to the cliché. Others are misled by a conceptual notion; even when conception is interesting, style is often flat. These "new" voices show a preference for old themes: the futility of effort in an absurd modern world dehumanized by technology. ("We were sitting around in the loft of this painter we know," begins one narrator, a victim of ennui.) Several commit the subject matter fallacy: for instance, in one pointless, egocentric testimonial, the character upchucks "Naked Lunch." Many of these writers have heeded too literally the good advice, "write about what you know," and have thus committed the "it-really-happened" fallacy. Adolescent fantasies find a home in the volume, too: "There was something about her ..." one narrator begins, and Holden Caulfield rides again. An unjustified brevity typical of beginning writers characterizes most of the pieces; they are mere sketches of character, place, or situation impersonating stories.

The teacher-editor who gives his overreaching Icaruses an opportunity to take flight with wax wings does no one a favor.

Plot is almost nonexistent in *Early Summer* (Atheneum, 1963) by Anna Sevier. Grey Anderson, twenty, having lived six months in Paris, persuades her parents to let her say a five-day farewell, alone, to France. In the first half of *Early Summer* the only developing element is Grey's personality and sensibility, both predictable, unfortunately, after page 15. By telling the story in the present tense Miss Sevier gives Grey's story some effective immediacy, but the barebones structure of conflict emerges from the prolonged scene-setting too late to give the total work the resolution it needs from the beginning. While the writer achieves at times a fresh and poetic style, too often she strains to be smart and sophisticated but becomes merely affected and literary. A few of the scenes are sharply presented; however, because so little is happening, the action often lapses into woolgathering description and revery.

With youthful overstatement, every detail is given

cosmic overtones. Pseudo-witty, sand-sifting, beach-party talk is presented as philosophy. The characters quiz each other with all the adolescent questions about Life. But with these great waves of overblown emotion, Miss Sevier seems to have cleared the beach for a good, perhaps fine, second novel.

Bitten by the rabid, red ape of his childhood guilts and fears, James, the narrator of *It Is Time, Lord*, by Fred Chappell (Atheneum, 1963), presents the spectacle of a young man in the near-fatal convulsions of remorseful nostalgia. "I remember," James constantly repeats. The patient reader may discover the conception that shapes these recollections. But does an intellectual realization of the author's design ever substitute for empathy? Having informed us that "there is no story to tell ... only a story to look for," James argues convincingly that he is "uninteresting." Enter, limping, once again the anesthetized antihero, with his inverted egotism, his pseudo self-hatred and self-effacement; and once again we are invited to scrutinize the facelessness of a faceless character.

"Something mean and stupid squats in my brain," James says. Whether in his "study," littered with the debris of childhood, where he pursues the desperate therapy of writing about his past, or out drinking with promiscuous women, James's hope is finally to obey the command: "Take yourself up." A starving cannibal faced with tomorrow, he gnaws the bones of yesterday for sustenance and revelation.

Is the failure of the novel in its hyper-literary conception or its fitful execution? Jarringly, Chappell refracts an authentic North Carolina rural milieu through the sensibility of a combined literary scholar and arrested juvenile. To seize upon whatever experiences and perceptions James is struggling to order we must plod through a proliferation of literary quotations and allusions, pretentious astrological profiles of the characters, inert description, an equivocal, crocheting style, a ponderous, polyglot rhetoric. The unreliable, prevaricating narrator creates many problems, but we suspect James's mask is partly an excuse for the author's self-indulgence.

The scenes between James and his father and several of the terse, present-tense episodes are brilliant. Thus it is not difficult to imagine, at least to hope, that the talented writer who could write them will produce, in spite of some deadly blunders, a masterful second novel.

Writing in *The Kenyon Review*, Thomas Williams found in my own first novel faults similar to those I have cited thus far in others.

The Beautiful Greed by David Madden is a novel about going to sea to find self-knowledge. So is *What Ship? Where Bound?* by Shepard Rifkin. Rifkin's novel is a professional job of storytelling; Madden's is highly serious, but in places awkwardly talky. At the very end of the novel for instance, he literally dangles his two main characters on and about the side of the ship and the long boat that will take one of them away, while they philosophize, in awfully literary language, about the meaning of the book. Suddenly they are not two real men on a real ocean, but a couple of explainers. This is a first novel, but even so, after seeing some of Mr. Madden's other work, I was disappointed. It is a novel about a young man on his first ship, and an older man — a scapegoat who has been paid to serve a sadistic, rebellious crew. At the end the paid scapegoat leaves the ship and the young man will be the unpaid scapegoat for the next leg of the voyage.

The older man is mysterious; in fact he is so mysterious I had trouble believing in him. His mysteriousness, however, is absolutely necessary to the author's theme. Like most shipboard novels this is a kind of allegory, and odd things happen to allegorical characters; but it seems to me that in order to be believable these odd things had better happen in a very special atmosphere. They cannot be superimposed upon what I can only call standard realism. The writer of such basically artificial stuff must be prepared to render it with precision — even with brilliance. It's not enough to depend upon the interesting, even the weird details of shipboard life; to prove, merely, that the writer has his union card. It's not enough to take the reader once again to the sailors' whorehouses (the whorehouse scenes in these two novels, by the way, are interchangeable), to point out the homosexual, the wino, the sadist, the joker. The cataloguing of these usual freaks will not supply life to any novel. I think of Calvin Kentfield's *The Alchemist's Voyage*, which is quite similar in its near-fantasy and its highly deliberate, intellectual plotting. The difference is that Kentfield has a particular joy in finding the precise, startling metaphor that makes such brittle material, if not quite real, at least as fascinating as, say, a collection of brilliant, exotic, stuffed birds.

Reviewing my novel along with Peter Matthiessen's *Raditzer* in *The Partisan Review*, Martin Greenberg stresses the importance of a fundamental element in fiction which many young writers seem to lack — the compulsion to tell a story. He asks, What makes the two otherwise quite different novels so flat? "I think the answer is quite simple: their authors' lack of talent as storytellers. These men may be writers, but they aren't story writers, not in these books. It is often said that there is never any lack of talent, every generation has as much of it as another; the difficulty is to bring the talent to fruition...."

The title of David Madden's novel, *The Beautiful Greed*, is from *Lord Jim* (the greed that is meant is for sea adventure) and the hero also carries a copy of *Lord Jim* in his duffle. The story concerns a young fellow who must find the courage, with the help of a world-weary old hand who is the ship's scapegoat, to possess his own manhood. So the general intention of the novel, as well as the title, is Conradian. But the style and quality of the narrative are the opposite of Conradian. Instead of long reflective sentences, a rich commentary on the action and slowly ripening significances, Mr. Madden's story has short declarative sentences and abrupt transitions, few observations, and a significance so little realized as hardly to exist without the title and the epigraph. I don't of course accuse Mr. Madden of failing to write like Conrad. Any author may come to his subject matter through a master and take his title and even the intention of his work from him, and still be free to produce his own very different kind of story. You can write just as well with short declarative sentences as with long reflective ones, maybe even better. But Mr. Madden's short sentences are bald and jejune, catching only the surface of things, and so is his story. After invoking the name of Conrad which stands for the magic of storytelling if any name does, Mr. Madden proceeds to rattle the dry knucklebones of a narrative style that is about as unmagical as one could be.

A Multitude of Sins (Sheed and Ward, 1963), an apprenticeship novel by a thirty-four-year-old Englishman, is a casebook of the strivings of a certain kind of nascent talent. The Miltonic intention of J. A. Cuddon's novel is, roughly, to justify the ways of God to man.

Garrard, ex-monk, ponders the divine mystery of the sin-ensnarled lives of some representative Londoners. In the compassionate vision of Raeside, apostate priest, these people are being tortured by an "inspired lunatic" (God). As workers in a Home for the reclamation of the scum of society, the two men meet, and their effect on each other is a reversal of conscience: Raeside returns to the priesthood; Garrard discovers, a short while before he is due to enter another monastery, that his faith is unfounded.

Inadequate preparation makes both recognitions unconvincing. Unfortunately, most of the book is devoted to the musings and maunderings of Garrard, a boring, self-righteous ass, not enough to Raeside, the more interesting, sympathetic character. Their spiritual progress is enhanced by the spiritual dilemmas of a number of potentially fascinating characters, both believers and nonbelievers, who, in their sinning, alter each other. All the raw plot, thematic, and character ingredients exist, well-stirred, for a novel of scope and importance.

But the author is inept and lacks control in almost every aspect of the art of the novel. How conceptualize and transform, meaningfully and dramatically, such rich, complex raw material? Mr. Cuddon seems to have considered few, if any, of the possibilities.

Instead of focusing his vision through the point of view of one or several characters, Cuddon jumps erratically among most of them, including minor ones. A reader is willing to shift from one consciousness to another, even within a single sentence, if he can rely on the technical control and engaging personality of the omniscient author to help him keep his bearings. In the hands of masters this method worked well during the early phases of the development of the novel. Regrettably, Cuddon's novel won't inspire a revival of that rich technique.

Blindness to opportunities and failure to imagine possibilities fully are typical faults in first novels. With greater technical awareness and imaginative effort, the author might have exploited some of the means of control inherent in his own material: the point-counter-point relationship between the monk and the priest; the symbolic fact that all men are monks; the priest and the prostitute as persons to whom secret thoughts are confided.

Instead, Cuddon relies upon crude devices to carry forward his story and explore its meaning: authorial intrusions in the form of epigrams, axioms, truisms ("There are times when we forget to conceal ourselves"); hysterical discovery of the obvious; crude foreshadowings ("He could hardly have forseen the effects ..."); mechanical tying up of loose ends; moralizing (the novel ends with: "And would there not be rejoicing over two that were found?"); and narrative summary overbalancing the author's talent for creating scenes. Generally, the style is amateurish and affected. It seesaws between clichés and unrestrained rhetoric, turgid with Miltonic metaphors. "From the lees of love he wrung a drop of hope" is typical.

In *The Orchard Keeper* (Random House, 1965), Cormac McCarthy does not tell a story; he shows relationships, develops patterns, using the now rather conventional method of juxtaposition, or cinematic montage. For instance, the novel begins with Kenneth Rattner's departure from the Smoky Mountains for Atlanta. Then the Green Fly Inn is described, and Marion Sylder, who has been gone five years, returns, well-dressed, driving a new car. McCarthy cuts to Rattner leaving Atlanta years later, stopping at Jim's Hot Spot. Cut to: Marion and a friend picking up two girls and a boy on the road (one of the women may be Rattner's wife, the boy, his son); they make love to the girls. Cut to: old man seeing them pass by; then to Marion and his friend talking it over. Cut to: Rattner in Jim's Hot Spot; he recalls an incident at the Green Fly Inn, when the back porch, loaded with men, accidentally collapsed into a dark ravine and he robbed the injured and fled to Atlanta. Having set up these parallels (along with an intricate pattern of minor ones), McCarthy brings us to the intersection where these paths will accidentally cross. Even about the central events the reader is, for a long time, only a little more informed than the characters. The separate scenes and images are intensely fascinating, and while the reader may be generally bewildered, he senses that he is participating in a process of unification, and that if it is to succeed, he must contribute attention and imagination. The author is perhaps too concerned with creating the compelling moment to guide the reader as surely as he might. The aura of mystery itself is a little bogus, since the omniscient author deliberately withholds information and covers his tracks between one point and another. So everything depends upon the successful expression of his theme through the accumulation of meaningfully juxtaposed images.

Finally, the separate events and characters do converge through the method of juxtaposition, a method appropriately expressive of the theme: in a common natural setting that changes with the seasons, men and animals cross paths, ignorant in the darkness of partial knowledge of the elusive pattern of relationships in which chance and coincidence are the agents of coherence. This is a theme that demands to be *shown*, and McCarthy's technique enables him to discover the form and meaning of his raw material. We are fascinated by his demonstration of man's pathetic ignorance of his participation in intricate relationships. We perceive the pattern gradually; the characters, overwhelmed by the isolated moment, never perceive it at all. Patterns of animal behavior and processes in nature parallel developments among humans; sometimes these patterns mesh, paths cross on all three levels. In the larger context, we see the death, from one perspective after another, of the old mountain way of life, invaded by technology. A government installation exists beside the decaying orchard; in the orchard pit a corpse decomposes.

McCarthy is the best Faulkner mimic to come on the scene with a first novel in a long time. He fragments time and narrative and seems to write in a Faulknerian trance, describing in the master's manner the very kinds of things Faulkner would describe in such a way. His prose has Faulkner's rhythm, syntax, even his diction ("purlieus," "avatar," "an air transient and happenstantial"); it reeks of exotic words, as though he has read Faulkner as a young writer might read the dictionary. Here are typical passages: "[The] face of some copper ikon, a mask, not ambiguous or inscrutable but merely discountenanced of meaning, expression." "Then Sylder stood, still in that somnambulant slow motion as if time itself were running down, and watched the man turn, seeming to labor not under water but in some more viscous fluid, tortuous slow, and the jack itself falling down on an angle over the dying forces of gravity." When his own voice comes through, it is unsure of itself, but relatively without faults. He works best in scenes that require dialog and straight action and don't allow much cosmic contextualizing. While his dialog is consistently superb, it is difficult to determine what effect the omission of quote marks achieves, but it does no harm. If the style is sometimes good Faulkner, it is sometimes bad public domain rhetoric: "candywrappers pressed furtively into the brown wall of weeds"; "a ballet of gnats rioted in the path of the headlights"; bullets enter a room like "malevolent spirits," then like "vermin." A buckshot style is bound to hit something, but careful aim with a rifle is more admirable. McCarthy's extreme style, which tends to give everything equal value, often claims an importance which the experience being depicted can't justify.

But what he chooses to see survives his rhetoric; like Joyce Carol Oates, he has a sense of life so strong it struggles through all the molasses. And many of the passages describing the old man moving, as keeper, through the orchard, Marion moving, as whiskey runner, over landscapes and cityscapes, and young John moving, as trapper, along the river are unforgettable.

In *The Long Voyage* (Grove Press, 1964), the classic night-journey form has a profound twentieth-century validity. Jorge Semprun's autobiographical hero, Gerard, survives a five-day train trip with 119 other prisoners in a padlocked boxcar. Gerard's journey, like Marlow's, becomes a quest into "the heart of darkness," and Gerard is greeted at the gates with the cry of that disillusioned idealistic imperialist, Kurtz: "Exterminate the brutes!" Like Conrad, Semprun feels that it is not enough merely to chant, "The horror! The horror!" Unlike the shadowy, reticent stand-ins of much modern fiction, Gerard is forceful, vibrant, and resourceful, and he earns the name of hero.

Beginning on the long fourth day of the journey, the novel is carefully executed in relation to its spinal image, the moving train. The conception and the structural device arise naturally out of the situation: night trains are expressive of the encompassing reality of Gerard's experience as exile and saboteur. As in the movie *Hiroshima, Mon Amour*, intricate and meaningful juxtapositions of past and present and significant anticipations of the post-liberation future are done with acute relevance of detail. Transitions are smooth. We are in the prison, then suddenly in the boxcar.

Gerard's unnamed, ordinary neighbor in "the little-ease" of the boxcar asks many times, "Will this night never end?" His dying words are, "Don't leave me, pal." This enforced voyage obliges Gerard to venture upon a second sixteen years later, compelled by a knowledge that the night has never ended, that he has never left his comrade, that the millions of prisoners, and thus the so-called survivors, have not been liberated. "I forgot this voyage while realizing full well that I would one day have to take it again.... It was all there, waiting for me." Past and future are now, and the train is still moving. While one of the novel's strengths is the apparent spontaneity of these juxtapositions, a more controlled fusion of theme and form could have evoked even more profound and awesome intuitions of inevitability and eternity.

Twenty when he makes the voyage, the narrator wisely waits sixteen years for the talk to die down so that his more controlled voice may be heard. He realizes that while he remembers perfectly the relatively uneventful voyage itself, it is difficult to recall the memories and dreams which sustained him in the period of greatest extremity, the long final night of the journey that killed the man from Semur next to whom he happened to be standing. The boxcar is already a tomb, crammed with future corpses; herded into boxcars, they are later herded into the barracks, then into the shower stalls to be gassed, then stuffed into the furnaces. As the train moves over the peaceful landscape, we sense the dead-aliveness of them all. Gerard's personal tactic of endurance is to reconstruct certain books, like *Swann's Way*, in his head and to evaluate the life he is liable to lose. Gerard can see the absurdity of some of the Allies' notions and he finally achieves compassion for the enemy. While the man from Semur contains the voyage within his death, Gerard's life is devoted to expanding that voyage; thus, in a sense, the man from Semur never dies. In Gerard's arms, his body becomes infinitely heavy, an eternal burden. When he lays the man down, he lays down his own past, as told to the man; but sixteen years later he takes it up again by telling us the same story. The burden becomes lighter with every moment that Gerard's life justifies itself in thought and action. The dead "need a pure, fraternal look. What they need, quite simply, is for us to live, to live as fully as we can." And Gerard does live, imaginatively and actively, with a fullness that is heroic.

To achieve distance from his experience, Gerard seizes spontaneously on many devices. He conducts two beautiful French nurses on a tour of the liberated camp; to tell about the camp is to see it from the outside, that is, for the first time. He tries to understand the mind of a lovely German girl who, like him, strives, though out of guilt rather than suffering, to "will into oblivion" the facts of the camps. Viewing the crematorium chimneys from the living room window of a German housewife who mourns the loss of her sons in the war, Gerard feels not hatred but compassion for her.

The Long Voyage has the kind of fictive life only a preoccupation with death can evoke. Although there is little sequential story, many moments are memorable. Just as Gerard is often caught off guard as Melville was, suddenly remembering images of the Encantadas in the midst of a polite dinner party, the reader will one day be smitten by his memory of Semprun's description of the way the Polish Jewish children were killed. They emerged from a frozen mass of standing corpses, that had to be pried loose from a boxcar, only to be slaughtered by dogs and SS guards as they ran, expecting some haven, toward the gates of the camp. "Beneath the empty gaze of the Hitlerian eagles" above the entrance, the Jewish children were cut down, "their hands clasped for all eternity." Imagination enabled him to survive; now, sensibility demands that he understand his experience.

Semprun has a tendency to cavort with language somewhat in the manner of Günter Grass, but with less justification. And we find the sort of clowning in dialog that Jake and Bill exhibit in *The Sun Also Rises*. But repetition as a device is not displayed in language alone; dictated by the nature of his experience, it is essential to Semprun's theme as well as to his technique. He is adroit in his use of clichés; his experiential context moves Gerard to examine such clichés as "go up in smoke." This is only one way in which he attempts to reify the mysteries of his experience. No rhetorical passages obtrude, and Semprun's lyricism is earned because it never approaches the self-indulgence one might expect and possibly forgive in such a book.

Striving rigorously for focus, Semprun excludes memories of Gerard's childhood before the war and of his life after the liberation, except as they relate to the war. The absence of chapter breaks emphasizes the continuity of the experience and the simultaneity of all moments relevant to it. That the reader may identify more intensely with the evaluating Gerard, Semprun shifts to the third person for a last impression of the hero; this shift also sets off the voyage, with its mingling of memory and imagination, from the pure reality of the arrival at camp. Gerard speaks in the present tense most of the time; Semprun shifts to past tense as he senses opportunities for emphasis; but the shift also has thematic relevance: all time is one in the consciousness that evaluates and shapes its own raw material.

Semprun overcomes the subject matter fallacy (heavy reliance on the inherent interest of a subject to the neglect of artistic considerations) that must threaten anyone who writes about concentration camps. In *The Long Voyage* craft and subject join. In Gerard, the victim's compulsion to testify is combined with the artist's impulse to prevent it all from slipping into oblivion as some mere matter of record. Years after the war, Gerard hears from an eye-witness the story of the Taboo massacre in which his comrades were killed; but this man, in contrast to Gerard, tells a very dull, disordered story, intent as he is upon simply purveying the facts. Although Gerard is annoyed that he himself is unable to "seize completely" his experience, "to provide a second-by-second account," it is Semprun's refusal to try that helps make him an artist, rather than an impassioned reporter only.

Amid the many fictionalized reports, only a work of art embodying the significant shape, essence, and meaning of that massive experience can ultimately concern us as

both life and as literature. Assailed though he is by
"absolutely vivid memories that arose from the willed
oblivion of this voyage," Semprun is no slave to the
extraordinary; while he acknowledges the banality as well
as the incredibility of the most human of history's massive
atrocities, he defies oblivion with form and speaks in a
passionate, authoritative voice, alive with rage and conviction. Like Stephen Crane in "The Open Boat," Semprun
fulfills the obligation of the survivor to be an "interpreter,"
not merely one who testifies.

Twenty-seven-year-old Yves Berger's first novel, *The
Garden* (George Braziller, 1963), in many ways resembles
Susan Sontag's first novel, *The Benefactor*, which appeared
the same year. But while Berger, a Frenchman, assimilates
beautifully certain American raw material and literary
elements, Miss Sontag has less control over the European
elements in her otherwise exceptionally good philosophical
comedy, though she perhaps attempts, intellectually and
imaginatively, much more. Berger has two stories to tell,
the one enhancing the other, and together they constitute
a composite, highly expressive poetic image. Both are
paradoxical, for the first conveys the extensive reality of
the subjective imagination, and the second projects the
intensive exoticism of objective reality itself. Berger limits
his characters, action, and locale, shutting out all else, to
focus intensely on the eternal values embodied in these
abstracted elements. *The Garden* is virtually barren of
social and historical details; for instance, World War II
is merely a background disturbance.

The narrator opens and closes with brief descriptions
of his immediate situation, thus setting the novel in a
time-present frame. Two years after the major events in
his story occurred, he lives in solitude on his deceased
father's estate. As mayor, his father fought the technological progress which the town desired; he strove to
cleanse his children "of school, of the age, of time," so
that they might "grow up together in Virginia about
1842." In the Virginia estates, man achieved "the small

amount of civilization which we need." In a single year "the dreams of mankind during a million years were consummated and consumed." The father reads to the boy and his sister, Virginie, about the Golden Age from historical documents, travel books, the writings of de Tocqueville, de Crèvecoeur, Lewis and Clark, Parkman, and a legion of obscure commentators. Describing the Garden of Eden in America, his father's sentences soar: "Once the monologue was interrupted, we were a long time coming back to earth." But Virginie, with her fervor for practical learning and immediate experience, rejects the garden of images; only the self-effacing narrator is seduced by the father's sensuous words. Having lost Virginie (an ironically symbolic name), the father sees his "immortality" in the boy. The external conflict between Virginie and her father, between two ways of living in time and space, is internalized in the boy.

The father and the sister initiate the boy into the life of the imagination and the life of action. First, he achieves complete felicity with his father in the garden of innocence. The father had inherited the house from his own father and transformed it into a facsimile of the Virginian estates, but now he feels he has made "an error of principle and of method." He should have been satisfied with "an inner Virginia," resurrected within his imagination rather than reconstructed with "the expedient of things." Thus, he tells the boy: "I can never warn you sufficiently against the things which can be seen," heard, touched. "Nobody ever dreams enough." To the learning of languages there is no end; he teaches the boy the languages of the Hebrew and Hellenic cultures and the dialects of Indians now extinct. In the past "words — inhabited things," enabling men to "steep themselves at the same time in the vision and the meaning of things." In the modern age, however, words have departed from things, and chaos reigns.

If man's enduring obsession is to cheat time, it is only in his imagination, the boy's father persuades him, that he can achieve temporal immortality. They take long drives after midnight, pretending to move through Virginia estates, seeming often to be one with the ground as the earth turns. Lying on a hill, they conjure up sounds and images out of eternity. Phrases from books, chanted ritualistically, give impetus to their visions of the sublime: "They hoisted me with halters up an otter path." Together, they reach Virginia about 1842, "time and evil overwhelmed." They experience again the expulsions of the Acadians from Nova Scotia and the long march of the Cherokees; the invasion of Virginia by the Burnt Woods half-breeds; the fall of the Golden estates; the extermination of the teeming bison. The Indians and the Virginians almost prevented "time from undoing its tapestry." After their failure, "men ought to have been created all over again." Whatever lives at the foot of the hill where they dream has "its roots and strength in putrefaction." Down there, "because of the passing of time, mankind lost its memory." As they emerge from Berger's splendid conception, the vivid dream details of American history before 1862 seem exotic and evoke an aura of surrealistic nostalgia. The only disruptions in this dreamworld are Virginie's visits home from the lycée in Avignon.

Certain poetic techniques enhance the novel's intuitive insights. For instance, one day, when he returns to the room he shares with his sister in Montpellier, the boy senses that his father has been there, has seen their things "mixed up together," and has perceived that they are having an incestuous affair. Immediately, the boy is inside his suffering father, and the narrator becomes a "we" as the discovery is re-experienced: himself and his father, discovering himself and his sister. "He shakes pensively the head which I hang in despair."

The novel's poetic rhythm and its time concept forbid chapter breaks. The first seventy pages are especially poetic; the image montages create impressions similar to the movies of Resnais, *Last Year at Marienbad* and *Hiroshima, Mon Amour*. For instance, the boy experiences a presentiment of the future when he discovers his sister sitting in the grass, her thighs and bloomers exposed; Berger's description of the grass springing back up with phallic vigor is one of the novel's most vivid symbolic images. In these first pages, the novel moves from image to image, rather than from motive to act. While the style is fragile and lyrical in the first part and relatively tough and explicit in the second, Berger manages to create the impression of even texture for the whole novel.

The boy achieves an equally complete felicity with his sister in the garden of experience. When the mother, a mere shadow on the estate, dies, Virginie, seeing her chance to rescue her brother, persuades her father that the boy, with no one to tend to him at home, should go to school in Montpellier and take a room next to hers while she attends medical school. Appropriately, from this point on the novel has a more dramatic or narrative structure. The style, too, changes. In the first part, under his father's influence, the boy writes long, flowing sentences, strung together with commas, for the father's Faulknerian style is appropriate to a rendering of the past; but under Virginie's spell in the immediate present, the boy obeys her command to use short, Hemingwayesque sentences. Into the best of all possible worlds Virginie endeavors to introduce various other possibilities. She urges the boy to make friends and allows him to witness the passions and erratic behavior of her own student acquaintances as they come and go constantly. "She revealed in surprises, impulsive actions, whims, caprices" that "time with her was always trembling at the end of the line." The boy detests his sister's use of obscenity, and his adamant solitude enrages her. But slowly she comes between father and son; for example, she convinces her father that his frequent visits, during which the exchange of images continues, distract the boy from his studies. The boy becomes aware of his sister's body; during a vacation, he misses his life with her in Montpellier. Thus Berger enables us to witness the assault of the life of action upon the imaginative life.

In the first phase of their Montpellier relationship Virginie tells the boy, with a gentle anxiety, her own view of life: all men die; one must live in harmony with time; the boy must grow up and grow old. "'You must live your life' and I translated 'You must die your death.'" Virginie announces that he should write a book. But Virginie insists that he include memories of childhood which she will recognize; as they recall the past he discovers he has led an earth-bound existence on the fringe of his ethereal life in Virginia about 1842. His father, when he hears of the project, declares his trust in the boy to fill it with experiences they shared from other books. But Virginie has deeply immersed the boy in "time-passing"; for instance, his life now follows a timetable: homework, the book, the languages. Eventually he discovers that in his creative fervor he has forgotten his father. Each of his attempts to assert the supremacy of the imagination is met by her lively response to the immediate present: his sister offers him liquor, lends him pornographic novels, allows him to stroke her body, takes him to nightclubs, to movies, and into Nature. She loves only what exists, sees everything, retains very little.

Immersed in the life of action, Virginie's body represents time, love, and death; luxuriating in the imagination's light, the father's garden is eternity: solitude, and cyclical recurrence. One night Virginie runs her hands over the boy's body and he discovers that "there are dreams in the tips of Virginie's fingernails." In their flow of words, the imaginations of father and son mingled incestuously; the affair between the boy and his sister begins wordlessly and moves into erotic lethargy and comas of bliss. Until Virginie revealed it to him, he hated his body. The boy tries to surrender to Virginie's concept of life as separate little moments, as "time passing at breakneck speed." His mortal embrace with her releases Time from its captivity in him, and him from his captivity in Time. In their languorous conversations Virginie teaches the boy the meaning of mortality. Threatened by death, one must seize life as it flies. "Living is taking life against the current.... And if you are to keep me, I shall have to feel that you know me to be mortal," for it is death that makes her young and beautiful, it is the awareness that each moment is irrecoverable that gives urgency and fulfillment to their desires.

Berger demonstrates the power of the imagination to thwart the assaults of reality. At first, the boy transforms Virginie's earthy body into the mythical garden: "On Virginie's shoulders I stroke the wheels of the wagons, the runaway mules, the fur of the guzzling bears, I stroke the bumps of the bisons and the bears." Although to combat her father's warning against the things of the senses she makes herself more tantalizing and available, she spurns the boy if he has not first worked on the book. For the boy, the book is a means of making words once again contain things. Berger's implementation of the concept of the mythic, and therefore poetic, origins of language suggests that he has absorbed the ideas of Ernst Cassirer, and perhaps of Emerson, who said, "Words are also actions."

In the sexual embrace man seeks and finds mortality at its swiftest. As the boy wonders about Virginie's previous affairs, she encourages his jealousy as being a living emotion, and he is fascinated by the infernal word "jealous," in which nothing dwells. They begin to use foul language while making love, each word a maggot which affirms the intransience of the instant. Unlike mythic words which are immortal, coarse words live only by the grace of bodies, "and when the lovemaking is over, they make hideous corpses." He imagines Virginie gone and the return of his passion for words. One night she encourages him to talk lyrically of "the garden" so that she can reply: "Words, and when you have said them, when you have wallowed in them, on them, when you have made yourself drunk with words, then you open your eyes, they fall on me who am waiting ... a real Virginia, of flesh and blood." He begins to detect the odor of death in their insular room.

Finally demanding to see the book, Virginie reads the first sixty pages of what we have been reading — an interesting, though not original, device. Horrified to find "visions conjured out of nothing," her advice about short sentences wasted, she ridicules him. In all his talk of Virginia, for instance, there is not a single mention of the slaves; there are no objects, no precise descriptions. He describes his book as one in which "there are no people and nothing happens." What his father failed to do, he has achieved: he has put the visions into words. In anger and despair, Virginie, who hoped to rescue him, now rejects him because he will never know anything. For him, she has wasted her time and sacrificed her body in vain. In darkness and slavery, he will become his father; he does not deserve to live. She abandons him. Thus, at their most intense, imagination and action both fail because the boy's response can be only an extreme one.

Berger brings the imagination / action development full circle. Upon his return to the estate, the boy is informed that his father has taken a trip. Half-breeds are invading this region of large estates, as they invaded Virginia about 1842, bringing an "excess of civilization which makes time pass, men wear away." He imagines that his father is looking in the mountains for men "for whom words are pictures, almost things." Doubtlessly, he found only a "people without words." But ironically the boy, now a man, repeats the process. Every night he sits in the garden holding his book (the one he has written? the one we now read?). He hears the voices of Virginie and his father, who "put forward words, raised pictures. . . . I can no longer distinguish my father's voice from Virginie's." But the boy thinks that it is his father who "has the words, the pictures, in the darkness which falls and hides my book from me."

The author's own ambiguous position allows readers of each general inclination (imagination / action) to interpret the novel for themselves. But most men are composites of Don Quixote and Sancho Panza. Writing with equal conviction and perception about the two worlds, Berger suggests that the ambiguity of reality and illusion is perpetual. Between the polarities of time and eternity, he creates a field of tension where the two mingle imperceptibly. This ambiguity saves the novel from being esoteric, for it allows ramifications of interpretation which transcend the preciousness of a purely subjective vision.

Although this novel reminds one of the witty and lyrical comedy of Giraudoux (whether some of the ludicrous moments are intentional is not clear), it is Faulkner who haunts *The Garden*. The style of the first seventy pages, on which Berger spent three of the five years that went into the novel, is somewhat like Faulkner's *Absalom, Absalom!* and the themes of the persistence of the past and of incest suggest Quentin and Caddy Compson and their father, Jason, Sr. But in its own right *The Garden* is the creation of an original, and well-seeded, imagination.

While that is really too much to ask of a first novel, it is unfortunately what a reader expects, for though most young writers need to have a trial run, the reader who reads a first novel *as* a first novel is very rare.

the violent world
of joyce carol oates

The legend is that Joyce Carol Oates's extraordinary stories are produced upon the sweeping flood of an apparently inexhaustible creative energy. Frequently come the nights when she locks herself in an upstairs room, emerging not long afterwards with a finished story. One sees copious evidence everywhere to support this legend. To read an Oates story, it is not necessary to buy her latest collection. Go to any newsstand and pick up copies of *The Atlantic*, *Cosmopolitan*, or *Esquire*; then go to a bookstore that stocks the *Kenyon*, *Southwest*, and *Southern* Reviews, and you will have your own collection before Vanguard can assemble the third. She won the O. Henry Award for 1966; for the past four years, both the O. Henry and the Foley collections have included her stories, and one was even dedicated to her. In 1966, she won a Guggenheim Fellowship, and two of her novels have been nominated for the National Book Award (*A Garden of Earthly Delights*, 1967, and *Expensive People*, 1968, the first two novels in a tetrad). Several years ago, one of her plays was produced off-Broadway. Louisiana State University Press will publish a volume of her poems in 1969. In the library, one may encounter her essays on Melville, Fielding, Beckett, and English and Scottish ballads (with which her own stories compete in star-crossed lovers and bloodshed (in such scholarly journals as *Renascence*, *Texas Studies in Literature and Language*, and *The Bucknell Review*; her special critical intelligence is revealed also in a brilliant essay on James M. Cain in *Tough Guy Writers of the Thirties*. She teaches, in no danger of perishing, at the University of Windsor. Miss Oates's already superior talent will probably mature slowly — a prospect of limitless expectation when one learns that she is only twenty-eight.

Steadfastly refusing to listen to critics, she goes right on producing stories of an excellence approached by no one. She "turns out" (to use a phrase normally reserved for commercial hacks) stories that appear upon a literary scene ready to receive and praise yet another one-dimensional "pop art" novel, social problem novel, antihero novel, anti-novel novel, with all the fervor of a fashion-mongering galaxy of coteries. But there is nothing new, nothing avant-garde, camp, pop, absurdist about Miss Oates's stories; reading them is like reading deeply between the hieroglyphic lines of fossils found on lonely landscapes. Her stories offer no isolatable, exploitable elements on which fashion might thrive; nor is the author's personality an exploitable by-product of her work. She is one of the few writers today who has the vision to disturb my sleep, to frighten me when, in banal moments, I involuntarily recall a mood from one of her stories. After reading Miss Oates, one's casual moments are not one's own.

It is difficult, if not foolhardy, to discuss her stories and novels as literary fabrications. If they have form, it is so submerged in "experience" as to defy analysis. Out of such visible lack of formal assertion comes most of the bad writing of non-talented people — and, once in a generation, a writer of Miss Oates's stunning potential. In a time when many writers master form before they imagine anything that can live in it, Miss Oates's shotgun approach to her targets is magnificent, if not aesthetically sublime. Because of their lack of shape and focus, some of the stories linger on as though they were real events one wants to forget.

In 1963, prospects for the future of the short story were brightened by Vanguard's willingness, perhaps eagerness, to introduce Joyce Carol Oates with fourteen short stories, *By the North Gate*. Despite the success of Philip Roth's *Goodbye, Columbus*, such collections, particularly by new writers, promise only a meagre return. But few recent first novels manifest a talent as forceful, controlled, and promising as Miss Oates's. Only four of the stories had appeared previously; "The Fine White Mist of Winter" was included among both the *O. Henry* and the *Best American* short stories of 1963. Since many of the new stories are superior to some of the earlier ones, it is clear that Vanguard did not put together a collection on slim pretenses. One encouragement may have been the pattern of relatedness in character, theme, technique, locale, raw material detail, mood, and atmosphere which unifies the collection.

Although an aura of the late thirties and of the forties suffuses the events — that was the period of Miss Oates's childhood — a talent for objectivity sustains a distance between the author and her painfully observed raw material. In a time when many young writers greet their contemporaries on the me-rack of subjectivity, this writer utilizes the third person, central intelligence and, on occasion, the omniscient-point-of-view technique. And although most of the stories are set in rural upstate New York near Lake Erie in fictional Eden County and a powerful sense of place is evoked, these are not regional stories. In this collection, an ability to conceptualize is in control, and a vision begins to take shape. But the farm and small town social context, and the family unit, though conceived in terms of generations coeval, are not depicted through the kind of historical continuity that is characteristic of Southern fiction. There is no history beyond the immediate family. The universal family and society of man is projected with an almost pure radiance in the violent light of a dismal rural landscape, devoid of the pastoral, observed in extremes of summer heat, autumnal decay, and winter snow.

The organization of the collection is expressive, opening and closing with stories about old men who refuse to believe at the end of life that irrational violence and hatred are dominant forces in human nature, until each is disillusioned by a direct encounter. Expressing the attitude of many Oates characters, the grandfather's son in "Swamps" whines that he is "sick of this life." But the old man tells his grandson, "You pay him no mind. This-here is a damn good world, a *god*-damned good world, it's all you got an' you better pay attention to it." In his refusal to allow a pregnant woman to commit suicide, the grandfather celebrates birth. But when the mother slays her baby and wounds the grandfather, he spends his last days whining, "They robbed me." In "By the North Gate," old Revere's affirmation of life is betrayed by unprovoked violence, also.

In each story some form of sudden, irrevocable, senseless violence focuses a crucial moment in the lives of the characters. Usually, a knife is the ritualistic, ceremonial instrument of violence. In her depiction of complex motivations toward violence, Miss Oates often subjects her main character to the revelation that men are brutal but pitiable. However, her compassion does not dim the harsh glare she casts upon the violence in human nature.

Most devastatingly affected are the sensitive female characters, possibly various masks for the author. In a world of violence and evil, these girls live on the verge of self-annihilation. Best of these stories is "Pastoral Blood." Deliberately exposing her beautiful body to violence, Grace forces male complicity in her attempted suicide. Dressed with intentional cheapness, she picks up a man, who becomes desperately concerned for her, and lures other men, creating a situation of drunken violence in which men fight over her like animals. In a resolution of ironic grace, she is returned to the family and fiancé whose blandness had defined her desire to cease "being." A convincing impression of the interior paralysis induced by the suicidal impulse is conveyed.

Using expressionistic, lyrical, and realistic techniques in three other, less successful, stories — "Images," "Sweet Love Remembered," "The Legacy" — Miss Oates discovers theme through a penetrating examination of character. The recurrent character, realizing that it is her capacity for vision rather than violence that estranges her from her family and others, sees her own responsibility and claims a disproportionate and unbearable guilt. Haunted by this vision of human separateness, she suffers the impossibility of identifying deeply with others and of achieving a reciprocal love. Although the point-of-view character, Leo, a young English instructor, is a male, "The Expense of Spirit" belongs to this group. It is as though the girl were drawn out of Eden into the intellectual reality of the university (which Miss Oates knows well), a society even more desperately devoid of love. The smug witticisms, the nauseating fun and games in which the guests at a party indulge are dehumanizing, as an innocent freshman co-ed, whose beauty attracts the violent attentions of a white man and a black man, discovers.

The violent male, sometimes a brother to the female figure, also recurs. Probably Miss Oates's most successful story is "The Fine White Mist of Winter." Driving to the sheriff's office with a captive Negro, Deputy Rafe Murray waits out a violent snowstorm in a lonely filling station. There he encounters two Negroes who talk in sly riddles about him and his captive. Convinced that the Negroes intend to free the prisoner, and sensitive of his image as a young, self-confident deputy, Rafe experiences a fear possibly greater than that which the fugitive feels. But at the height of the tension, the two Negroes reveal that it has all been a joke to win the sheriff's favor. As though it were inconceivable that Negroes would conspire to free one of their own, they had assumed that Rafe caught on to the mockery immediately. Ironically, they insist that this proud Negro be made to endure the same humiliations and torture that they, literally, have suffered. Isolated from the world, and from the others, in the fine white mist of winter, Rafe witnesses the spectacle of degraded men divesting themselves of their humanity, and he is profoundly changed. Few characters in a short story have had their very beings so thoroughly shocked by a single, double-edged, experience.

"In the Old World," a somewhat similar story, is stunningly ironic and perhaps more complex, though not quite as fascinating. Swan, a rural white boy, has cut a Negro boy's eye out with a knife. An innate sense of decency compels him to seek an explanation and a punishment for his crime. His father having failed him, he goes

to the jail in town where he encounters an even grayer
vagueness. The development is handled with remarkable
restraint and an expressive ambiguity.

Three stories of imminent death, "Boys at a Picnic,"
"An Encounter with the Blind," and "The Edge of the
World" project male violence. In the best of these, "The
Edge of the World," Shell, a young motorcyclist, cere-
moniously and fearfully enters a test of courage, to which
Jan, an elderly ex-racer, has challenged him. Ignorant of
the nature of the test as the story ends, Shell does feel
clearly a sudden isolation from his comrades and a rigid
reluctance to die. The superbly observed details of the
junkyard create an atmosphere in which the reader feels
an unbearable sense of impending ritualistic death.

In a Kafka-esque manner, "The Census Taker"
provides another haunting impression of the isolation that
exists among the people of Eden County. "Ceremonies,"
one of the best stories, emphasizes the function of ritual,
convention, and ceremony in Miss Oates's stories. A
funeral ceremony occasions a communal "we" point of
view in the recounting of a local legend. The wildly
beautiful and willful Elizabeth is one of the author's
several memorable characters.

In *By the North Gate*, she showed that she has a remarkable facility for embodying in her characters and
developing in their predicaments her ironic themes. Most
striking was her ability to convey a sense of the very
substance of the reality she perceives. But because she
had not yet achieved a style as commanding as her
themes and raw material, I was perplexed by her sometimes serious immaturity. While she usually avoided
rhetorical excess and strove for precision and accuracy,
passages erupted that were contrived, awkward, and overblown.

Miss Oates has taken as her province one of the most
important phenomena of our time: violence. Refusing
merely to mirror it, she works from within the human
nature of violence outward to its moral and spiritual

manifestations. The young writer who has a vision is rare; rarer still is one who succeeds in a first novel in projecting a haunting sense of that vision. At twenty-six, Joyce Carol Oates in *With Shuddering Fall* was focusing a vision, glimpses of which she had offered in *By the North Gate*. While *With Shuddering Fall* was hardly the novel many predicted, it was much too early to expect mature genius from one who had so recently shown signs of it.

Miss Oates sees life as a racetrack where men take chances, chance being in the very nature of things. Because she depicts everything at the point of extremity, she has been compared with Faulkner. But violence is not just a literary reality; it is a fact we live with. And the author succeeds, finally, in persuading us that the compulsion to violence is a universal so familiar she need not always trace motives. Melodrama is the risk she runs.

Karen, the central character, a sixteen-year-old small-town girl, is obsessed with a guilt that defines her long before she commits traceable acts of her own. Amid catastrophe and death, Karen's family and neighbors find sustenance in the conventions, rituals, and ceremonies of the Catholic Church and in their rural way of life. But Karen has always been a stranger among them. Another stranger, but one who has no sense of guilt, is Shar Rule, a thirty-year-old auto racer who returns to his dying father's bedside only to set him and the house afire.

When Shar attempts to seduce her, Karen is compelled by guilt and shame to jerk the steering wheel so that the car goes off the road, Shar tells her that it will be her fault if he is forced to kill her father. During a fight between Shar and Herz, Karen feels first a rapport with, then an estrangement from her father. "For the moment her shame and guilt might be transformed into pain, concentrated into physical pain; that way she could bear it. Seeking pain as atonement, she has wrecked the car, and later, she allows Shar to rape her; she endures his manifold cruelties and, finally, lets him beat her until he destroys their child. But she is also fulfilling her father's commandment to kill Shar and not to return until she does. Leaving her father beaten almost to death by Shar, she sets out into the world with Shar, blessed with a temporary damnation. "How right he was to judge her; to find her guilty! She understood his judgment and accepted it." She leaves the father who has understood her and returns to him in the end defiled, and thus becomes one with "the community of murderers."

Violence is both willed and accidental in this novel. If some of it seems gratuitous, it is a constant reminder that no one is safe. But man even helps these accidents along. Shar's life is a series of accidents; he is the target of some, the agent of others. His own will and blind contingency conspire. The riot at Cherry River began, in a sense, with his "accidental" birth — perhaps before. Numerous incidents in the novel do not relate directly to the main action; but accidents express a submerged community will: "And, as if in answer to the crowd's secret desire, the car spun suddenly out of control." A continually shifting circular design emerges. Out of the violent encounter between Herz and Shar, Karen, the lamb of innocence, is born as a creature of experience.

The novel depicts the dynamic thrust of a complex dialectic. There are those who act and those who repress; those who race, those who don't; sometimes one is a participant, sometimes a deeply affected witness, sometimes a mere spectator. The central metaphor, the controlling poetic image for the interaction of these opposing relationships, is the circular automobile racetrack. Lives collide as they race in a circle; both reckless spectators and daring drivers move closest to death along the rail, on the curves. Karen, a witness, and Shar, a participant, collide at that outer circle. Shar "had always been on the periphery" of Karen's family, and she draws him closer to the rim, where he finally crashes. In this race, Shar and Herz collide; paradox and irony lie in the fact that Karen's nature as witness causes Shar to be drawn to her and thus her father to encounter Shar. So Karen's very passive innocence sets in motion a series of human encounters which end in the massive explosion of the Fourth of July racial riots at Cherry River.

The car race is "a mock communion" in which spectators are cheated because, though they become the driver, the violence cannot touch them. Shar strives for "speed poised on the invisible point at which control turned into chaos," and the race is a ritual in which the center seems to hold for a moment as the threat of death that terrifies us all is brought careening to the brink, then "mere anarchy is loosed upon the world" once more. Shar wins, kills, dies for us all. Our rejoicing over the victory of the winner is mingled with regret that he has not consummated the inevitable, has not put an end to anxiety, for his triumph reminds us that other races lie ahead. Ultimately the mock Christ pays the extreme price for his walks on the water. It is this spectacle — of spectators and racers in mock communion — that makes witnesses like Karen suffer. The chaotic landscape, with its little circle of controlled violence, is an outward manifestation of Karen's shattered inscape.

Miss Oates conducts us through the labyrinth of blood kinship and of accidental spiritual and psychological kinships; around dark corners we glimpse our ghostly kin as they elude us, collide with us, but seldom accompany us. Though each character may only vaguely sense his community with certain other characters, the reader knows he is kin to others he knows not of, for the author constantly implies various kinds of kinship. And the racetrack image helps to control, to enhance, elucidate the significance of this web of relationship. Most of the minor characters exemplify various facets of the major figures and are variations or extensions of the three basic types: witness, spectator, racer.

Next to Karen and Shar, Max is the most significant character. Max is Shar's manager — "a bloated, insatiable spectator, a product of a refined civilization," who can love only those who ritualistically risk death, so that only

death makes love possible. "Just as Karen realized she
had no existence without the greater presence of someone
to acknowledge her (her father; God), so did Max realize
that his existence depended upon the life of others." And
he loves Karen because she makes all Shar's qualities more
vivid with her fears. Max is "the center of their lives!
He drew them in to him, sucked them in, his appetite was
insatiable."

Shar sums up his own function in life: "I drive a car."
For the other drivers "it's money and for me, waiting to
die." He has been "so many times around a circle" that
he is "sick to death of it; how do you get out of a circle
but carried out in parts?" He conceives of a good way to
die — to feel his body and his car as one soul, then to
plow into the spectators. "When I'm out there, there's no
bastard that owns me." He forces "cars or people or
myself, all the way out, to the limit." His affinity is with
machines, but none is as "finely geared and meshed as he,"
who knows his car better than his own body. Happy only
when in control of *things*, as when he drives, "he came
from nowhere and went nowhere. He seemed also to notice
nothing." Max says of him, "There was only Shar's will,
the deadly whimsical range of his desire," and "the whole
world is shrunk down to fit him — he carries it around in his
head." Neither good nor evil, sinless, he is a child. Max
sees both Shar and Karen as targets and instruments of
accidents. But while Shar operates from the stomach and
can respond to love only with rage, Karen operates from
the heart.

This novel attends, with sometimes too tenacious a
scrutiny, to the development of one of the strangest love
stories in recent fiction. To carry out her father's command, Karen must plunge into an entanglement with
Shar, but since she is incapable of physical violence, she
commits the slow psychological violence that the victim
uses to destroy the tormentor: she makes sex a means of
slowly stripping away Shar's various defenses. Rage is
one of them, but it only defines her purpose, helps her to

hate him more lucidly, reminding her of what he did to her father. Karen becomes accustomed to "a life that began nowhere and headed nowhere, geographically or morally." Though she screams, "Shar is filled with death!" she discovers soon after that he has filled her with life, with a child; he kills and he regenerates, both accidentally. But Shar becomes father-brother-lover for Karen. She achieves both Shar's birth as a loving human being and the death she has willed for him as murderer.

A few times Shar works Karen up to a sexual pitch; and several times he just misses communion with her. But slowly, through his relationship with her, especially the effects of it during their separation, Shar becomes aware of realities outside himself. When Karen finds him at Cherry River, his longing turns instantly to violence upon her, for he wishes to destroy the girl who makes him feel and suffer, and who destroys his control. He does not know that she wants him dead, nor has she told him she is pregnant. "Anger at himself expressed itself in anger at Karen," and he unwittingly aborts the child. Though she now wants the child, she lets him kill it to give him further cause to kill himself. And though her discovery that Shar has learned to love her moves her to love him, she uses his love as a final weapon. "She saw him with wonder. Her heart went out to him, she felt shame for her emotion. I can't help it if I have fallen in love, she thought defensively." But what she says to him is, "You make me sick," and he turns the car off the track as she once turned his car off the road.

"A hell of a world," Shar said suddenly and self-consciously, "but at least it's my own fault." Thus he is still in control. Full of love for Karen, Shar extends affection to others. "Wish me luck," he says to Mitch, and hugs him. "Had he wasted his life? All life before he had fallen in love was empty, a mockery, a half-world; he could not really remember it as his own." As he races, he thinks of taking the young Negro driver with him in a crash, but love excludes the old spite, and Shar, who has always felt that he would never live to be thirty, crashes into the wall. Full of love for Karen, he is convinced, ironically, she can never love him, murderer of her child and of her father (he believes that he killed Herz). Max now sees that Karen has set an elaborate, insane trap for Shar; he points at her body as though it were a weapon and accuses her of murder.

This private psychological and physical violence is enacted on a public scale in Cherry River, an hour after Shar's death, which the spectators blame on the Negro driver. Ironically, another Negro, Mitch, the pure-hearted, sacrificial scapegoat and Shar's good friend, becomes the mob's target instead.

Karen moves barefoot among the rioters, blood from her miscarriage streaming down her legs. As she begs God to forgive her for killing Shar, she turns on some rioters and includes them in the communion of guilt, the community of sinners. One of them, in an anguish of pity, guilt, and helplessness, kicks her. The riot, sparked by Shar's death, is also her fault. The fact that she is not directly guilty has no psychological relevance for her; all are guilty of being human, of becoming murderers, and the sentence is life. But after long suffering, grace, of sorts, is possible.

There is in this novel an undeclared but overpowering sense of sin, salvation, and religion. Karen almost fainted with happiness after her first Communion. Through experience she comes to see the soul's struggle as a reconciliation of paradoxes: "It was as if God were struggling to appear to her, not in sunlight but in darkness." To rise with Christ, one must first lie down with Judas. The fires of Miss Oates's vision are fueled with the paradoxes of Blake and Kierkegaard.

By virtue of such will power as she worked upon Shar, Karen emerges cured after a stay in an asylum. Having fulfilled her father's command so well, she returns. But home seems unreal. "Was it a betrayal? No ground is holy, no land divine, but that we make it so by an exhausting, a deadly straining of our hearts." Bereft of

Shar, she is afraid her father will disown her, even though he, like Shar, is a killer (like the mob at Cherry River, he once killed a Negro). Witnessing Shar's and Herz's violence, Karen had realized that she "could absorb their wrath, drown shuddering in their fury." She has emerged contaminated. During Mass in the hometown church she realizes that everybody has "initiated me into the communion of killers." She knows she can blame her father for what she did, and still deny her guilt, but she takes full responsibility, for as the agent of psychological incitements of violence, she is just as guilty as the person who acts. She senses also that her neighbors love her for suffering, to "prove to them the justice of their universe . . . the vague beliefs they mouthed and heard mouthed to them in the ceremony of the Mass." Thus, their relation to her parallels the spectators' relation to Shar.

Karen and her father finally forgive and vow love for each other. But brief, almost begrudged declarations are purchased at an exorbitant price; Shar experienced an hour of human love before his death; Karen, no longer innocent, but no longer a stranger, still has a lifetime before her.

It may be neither possible nor desirable to separate Miss Oates's faults from the ultimate excellence of her effects. Could a better crafted novel have worked its spell as strikingly? Perhaps she belongs with Dostoevski and D. H. Lawrence, among those prophetic novelists who achieve an artless, but shattering, vision. If art becalms, vision both damns and saves.

The faults, however, ought to be cited. Too many false moves in technique and structure and false notes in style provide the reader with countless opportunities for directing his gaze elsewhere. She indulges in an exceeding amount of generalization; page follows page of description of psychological states over vague periods of time through an undefined series of episodic situations. Brilliant passages have the charm of accidents.

We need to believe every moment that the world really

is as bleak, mean, foul, joyless, and violent as the author, with her total lack of humor, insists. When we see the world as Karen sees it and encounter men like her demon lover through her responses, we are convinced. But there appears to be no method in the author's point-of-view technique. While most of the novel is appropriately told through the third person central intelligence of either Karen or Shar, the author rather arbitrarily shifts to minor characters without justification. The resulting diffusion of focus is a serious flaw.

With Shuddering Fall could have been a terrifying novel, and for brief moments it is. Miss Oates has it in her power to frighten us much more profoundly than certain recent books that arrogantly insist upon shock. Had she succeeded in achieving complete credibility in every aspect of her fable, the result might have been artistically exciting, but perhaps humanly unbearable. Finally, I feel that *With Shuddering Fall* is an attenuated short story that soars on wax wings. This novel revealed the struggles of a major talent who may possibly rise to the level of Eudora Welty, Carson McCullers, Katherine Anne Porter, and Flannery O'Connor. It made me hope that she would find the time to devote greater attention to style, technique, and structure without diluting the intensity of her vision or scaling down the magnificent terror of her themes.

Upon the Sweeping Flood is Miss Oates's second collection of stories. In many of these, she sets up a situation, a character relationship, a state of mind that is conventional, circumscribed, made predictable by a rigid ceremonial frame — then chance violently intrudes. Some aspect of the family context usually serves as a frame. In "Stigmata" and "In the Seminary" the family exists within a larger, religious context (Catholic). In "Stigmata," the family gathers at Easter around a patriarchal father whose palms bled for a few hours the previous Easter, and who has become famous. He is now on the threshold of sainthood. His son Walt is the unpredictable intrusion. It is to Walt, alienated from society and family, that the old man confesses: "I hurt." The look in his father's eyes moves Walt to cry out that God is punishing his father for taking the love of his children without reciprocating. In "In the Seminary," the focus is on brother and sister. Sally, with her parents, visits her brother Peter at the seminary where he is undergoing a "spiritual crisis." Wearing sunglasses and a sneer, carrying her martini, Sally follows the priest and her family on a tour of the seminary. The priest proudly shows the cold, antiseptic new buildings, ending in the chapel, where a white, immaculate Christ hangs. The element of chance that intrudes upon this dehumanizing atmosphere and that replaces Sally's superficial contempt of it with purposeful awe is her own menstrual blood, which suddenly begins to flow. To shock them, Sally stomps about behind the priest and her family until the blood seeps into her shoes and marks the clean marble floor, and provokes her brother out of his pale, bloodless, smothering rituals of withdrawal; he had fled his domineering mother, his timid father, his masculine sister. But the shock of blood forces him to share this secular equivalent of a vision; so boldly smitten by womanishness, he takes it (Sally) by the throat. Sally's blood is nature's cry of outrage against the artifices of man that substitute for vital human and spiritual events. Sally's responses to chance provide her and the others with an opportunity for seeing their lives in relief, within the family and religious context. Miss Oates suggests that they all but miss this moment, as man has all but missed the exemplary moment on Calvary.

In "The Death of Mrs. Sheer," Miss Oates parodies her own preoccupation — shared with many twentieth-century writers — with the search for a father and with the significant consequences of chance. This is a grotesque, rural, Faulknerian black comedy, a story of absurd surfaces, shuffled about with gusto, like a mover in a dream throwing tacky furniture about in a loft.

Focusing on father-son, sister-brother, mother-son, mother-daughter relationships, Miss Oates constructs the entire web of blood-ties, and examines the hatred, spite, strife, conflicts, traps, anguish, and guilt in family love. In "The Survival of Childhood," Carl has escaped the ugly backwoods life, "the curse of his family." His younger brother Gene "had always evoked in his parents and brothers and sisters fierce conflicts of love and hate. Suddenly, enigmatically, Gene appears in Carl's life, strangely in need of some kind of help. Carl returns to his family to "endure them," to free himself of them. All Miss Oates's stories do violence to the reader somehow, and the final ten pages of this one are virtual agony. Carl sees that Gene's wild life was a reaction against his avoidance of death the day Carl almost shot him, accidentally. In "Norman and the Killer," Miss Oates examines a similar brother-brother relationship. In their childhood, Norman and his brother were suddenly attacked by a gang of boys, and the brother was killed. Years later, Norman, by chance, recognizes his brother's killer. He feels compelled to exact justice even though he did not particularly like his brother: "they were doomed to be brothers forever and could do nothing about it." He resents the responsibility, and feels guilty because his own life has not justified his survival. For violence and suffering, within the family and outward into the family of man, each man blames another. Though one person appears to be responsible, his act is simply the hub, and Miss Oates traces all the spokes that make the wheel turn toward a precipice; and thus all men are seen to be, to some degree, both guilty and innocent.

What is it in human nature that produces, needs, thrives on violence, personal and vicarious? What control has morality and convention over it? How, indeed, does morality contribute to it? How is it aggravated by the violent impingements of chance? In exploring these questions, Miss Oates runs the risk of melodrama. But in a decade that has witnessed the acts of Whitman in Texas, of Starkweather in Nebraska, of the man who killed the Chicago nurses, and of the assassins of John and Robert

Kennedy and Martin Luther King, that is a relevant risk to run. In her depiction of motiveless violence, an extreme form of behavior, she suggests that much human behavior is apparently motiveless at bottom. "The Man That Turned into a Statue" is about a thirteen-year-old runaway girl and a forty-year-old drifter, whose life is full of bad luck. When his plea for help is rejected, he plunges a knife into a man's throat. The incredible irony of this situation is that while the killer has a very deep sense of compassion for the girl, he can easily butcher a father, his wife, and child, then sit down with the girl to gobble up the meal his knife interrupted. "You know how it is," he tells the girl. After reading Miss Oates, the reader certainly does.

A typical Oates beginning is "Just around the turn, the road was alive." "First Views of the Enemy" is the story of a superficially secure, undemonstrative young woman's realization of the savage in her domesticated little boy, provoked by a chance encounter with some boisterous Mexicans who block the progress of her Cadillac. Another highway encounter with the vicious poor occurs in "Upon the Sweeping Flood." One of Miss Oates's favorite situations is that in which a man who thinks of himself as routinized and gentle encounters violent, unfeeling, crude people and ends up taking on their characteristics. The process is provoked in this story by a rainstorm and flood, which also aggravate the worst in the girl and her simple-minded brother — who, along with similar characters in other stories, is a human representation of the mindless, valueless forces in nature that work on men trying to live within some rigid context. The good Samaritan is so transformed by natural and psychological disruptions that he is moved to try to kill the boy and the girl he has risked his life (and neglected his family) to save; thus a man's impulsive altruism is converted by natural and human violence into hatred and homicide. He cries to the rescue boat, "Save me!" — from himself and the forces he has experienced.

Miss Oates examines the operation of love and chance in the lover relationship also. In "Archways," she depicts ways in which seemingly unrelated events somehow juxtapose in the mind so that they trigger changes and action, and she shows how one moves through the archways of other lives onto one's own steady course. "What possibility of happiness without some random incidental death?" In "Dying," one of several stories in which people are physically, emotionally, or spiritually ill and wasting away, Miss Oates depicts a relationship in which a girl maintains her own health by prolonging a degrading friendship with a man who once loved her, and who is now dying, very slowly. In all relationships, one lives, to some extent, upon the dying of another. "What Love With Death Should Have to Do" begins: "At last, she said, 'I'm bleeding.'" The image of a young couple in a motorcycle race, the girl bleeding, the boy not hearing his wife's cries is excruciatingly appropriate for Miss Oates's world. "But what has this to do with Love, May thought dizzily, what has blood to do with love and why did they go together?" In these stories, blood marks the spot where love and violence contend.

While Miss Oates has certainly enlivened, if not transformed the genre, these stories show that she has yet to achieve a style as commanding as her raw material, themes, and creative voice. That a style so often clumsy distracts no more than it does is amazing. Like Dreiser, she has no ear at all for the cadences of good prose. (*Too* fine a style, granted, would distract also.) The following examples come from one of her best stories, "Stigmata": "Walt was met inside by a young nun"; "Walt's blood throbbed foolishly"; "there were a large number of cars parked there"; "welcomes were general"; "the well-fed voice"; "a dull red flush overtook her cheeks." Too frequently "this" is used vaguely, without an object; "everyone murmured over this, perhaps agreeing, perhaps disagreeing." One senses an innate control, but conscious control is also needed to augment the sheer, overwhelming power of her talent. A frenzied, reluctant, upstate-New York Cassandra, Miss Oates seems compelled to get it said, to hack a path through dense thicket to some place of desecration.

Miss Oates projects a stark authorial authority. She never uses the first person, and in six of the present eleven stories the main character is a man. One feels along one's spine and scalp the heat of creative energy as she violently renders the involvement of her characters in their miserable predicaments, yet her cold objectivity expends no warmth upon the characters. Though she apparently writes in a burst, gives birth to her stories (to resurrect the original vitality of the cliché), she is a genuine prophetess, for her utterances belong to the mysterious force that produces them, and there is no subjective indulgence in the act — the creature born, the cord cut, it lives its own life.

If in bold outline Miss Oates's latest novel, *A Garden of Earthly Delights* (1967), seems melodramatic, in the reading that term becomes irrelevant. It is the story of Clara Walpole, daughter of a Kentucky migrant worker. The three parts of this long novel are named for the three most important men in her life: Carleton, her father; Lowry, her lover; and Swan, her son by Lowry. Her mother, Pearl, dies when Clara is a child, and a tough young girl moves with Clara's father and his other children from town to town. When she is fifteen, Clara meets Lowry and runs away from her father to a small town. Though she never sees him again, his presence never leaves her; before the Depression his father had owned a fairly prosperous farm, and Carleton's strange conviction that something special about him sets him apart from other low-class people survives in Clara. She rents a room in Tintern, works in the five-and-dime store, and waits for Lowry's irregular visits. For several years, he treats her like a child, doesn't make love to her; when he finally does and she becomes pregnant, he runs away to Mexico. Desperate, Clara turns to Curt Revere, a middle-aged, prosperous farmer, who sets her up in a pleasant farmhouse; he thinks Swan is his own son. Clara waits for Revere's invalid wife to die. When Swan is about five, Lowry returns, certain that Clara will go away with him. But his leaving her was a decisive moment in her life, for it was then that she took control of her own life and willed out of it, as much as possible, accidental encounters and impulsive actions. She wants money, property, and respectability for Swan, first of all, and for herself. Lowry has great power over her, but less than material security. Before he leaves, he tells Swan, "I can see in your face . . . all the things you're going to kill and step on and walk over." Clara never sees Lowry again. But just as the dominant force in Carleton's spirit survived, twisted a different way in Clara, so Lowry's dangerous fear and hatred of himself and of people comes out in Swan. He must also strive to earn the love of Revere, who he thinks is his real father, though the accidental encounter with Lowry haunts him. When Revere's wife finally dies, Clara and Swan move into the Revere mansion. Clara takes control of her new life as legal wife to Revere and mother of his three sons. But Swan is a brilliant though extremely sensitive child who is constantly hurt by his stepbrothers. One day he accidentally causes Robert, who dislikes him the least, to shoot himself with his hunting gun. Clara accumulates more and more material possessions, grows to love Revere and to feel affection for his sons, insinuates herself into the lives of Revere's other relatives, and has a few casual affairs, while Swan grows up totally alienated from the environment she has struggled so hard and long to provide for him. Then the American Dream becomes a Nightmare. Just as he is about to inherit the Revere empire, Swan decides to shoot himself and his mother, but he accidentally shoots Revere instead, and then kills himself. Though not yet forty and still beautiful, Clara goes away to a nursing home. That's Miss Oates's story, and knowing it beforehand will not prevent any reader from living it.

Having written essay reviews of her first two volumes of stories and her first novel, I see no value in my saying anything more in the future about Joyce Carol Oates's work. Even though all her technical faults remain untouched, *A Garden of Earthly Delights* not only fulfills her early promise, it makes her, for me, the second finest writer in America. Wright Morris is a better writer because I think aesthetic values are of more lasting importance. I am unable to explain in aesthetic terms the mystery of Miss Oates's genius for sustaining the intensity of her vision and for creating such totally alive characters and situations. I know of no other young novelist who succeeds in creating life with an apparent absence of art. She seems to make criticism irrelevant; it elucidates her work very little beyond offering an introduction. (The opposite is true of Wright Morris.) Joyce Carol Oates is a phenomenon, an original, a natural — not a mentor, as Joyce, Morris, Hemingway, and sometimes Fitzgerald and Faulkner are. She must be experienced, not analyzed — this is simply a brute observation, not praise. The young writer who cites Miss Oates's writing as justification for his own faults disguised as virtues can only suffer, and may not survive.

form and life in the novel:

toward a freer approach to an elastic genre

An interesting characteristic of many theories and definitions of art is their own proximity to aesthetic perfection. Stephen's formulations in *A Portrait of the Artist as a Young Man* themselves provide a sense of wholeness, harmony, and radiance; they have an almost sculptural serenity.

The feelings excited by improper art are kinetic. . . . The esthetic emotion . . . is . . . static. The mind is arrested and raised above desire and loathing. . . . Beauty expressed by the artist . . . induces . . . an esthetic stasis, an ideal pity or an ideal terror, a stasis called forth, prolonged and at last dissolved by what I call the rhythm of beauty. . . . Rhythm . . . is the first formal esthetic relation of part to part in any esthetic whole. . . . Art . . . is the human disposition of sensible or intelligible matter for an esthetic end. . . . Truth is beheld by the intellect which is appeased by the most satisfying relations of the intelligible; beauty is beheld by the intellect which is appeased by the most satisfying relations of the sensible. . . . The most satisfying relations of the sensible must therefore correspond to the necessary phases of artistic apprehension. . . . *Three things are needed for beauty, wholeness, harmony and radiance.* . . . When you have apprehended that basket as one thing and have then analyzed it according to its form and apprehended it as a thing you make the only synthesis which is logically and esthetically permissible. You see that it is that thing which it is and no other thing. The radiance . . . is . . . the *whatness* of a thing. . . . The instant wherein that supreme quality of beauty, the clear radiance of the esthetic image, is apprehended luminously by the mind which has been arrested by its wholeness and fascinated by its harmony is the luminous silent stasis of esthetic pleasure. . . . Art necessarily divides itself into three forms progressing from one to the next . . . the lyrical form, the form wherein the artist presents his image in immediate relation to himself; the epical form, the form wherein he presents his image in mediate relation to himself and to others; the dramatic form, the form wherein he presents his image in immediate relation to others. . . . The artist, like the God of the creation, remains within or behind or beyond or above his handiwork, invisible, refined out of existence, indifferent, paring his fingernails.

"Trying to refine them also out of existence," observes Lynch, the young friend to whom Stephen has delivered his lecture on aesthetics. When abstracted from the flow of life with which it is mingled, Stephen's theory is austerely beautiful. But what makes the entire ten-page passage novelistically exciting are life's interruptions, intruding as ironic counterpoint: "A crude grey light, mirrored in the sluggish water, and a smell of wet branches over their heads seemed to war against the course of Stephen's thought." "A long dray laden with old iron came around the corner of Sir Patrick Dun's hospital covering the end of Stephen's speech with the harsh roar of jangled and rattling metal." Stephen's single-minded vision and the world's irreverent chaos express Joyce's divided attitude. Like nonartistic Lynch, Joyce fears that the processes of art may refine life out of existence. But this novel comes closer than most to exemplifying the very qualities Stephen attributes to a work of art. (To contrast *Portrait*, a triumph of compression, with the diffuse *Stephen Hero* demonstrates the point.) Joyce sought a balance between the raw materials of life with its ironies and ambiguities on the one hand, and the artistic means of control on the other. This novel sustains a tension between the tyranny of life and the dictates of art; but only momentarily, in the epiphanies, are these elements fully arrested.

But no work of art, least of all a novel, not even that novel in which they are presented, could adequately demonstrate Stephen's definitions (he offers no example himself). The nature of the novel, as it has been or might conceivably be written, prevents it from ultimately realizing such ideal conditions as "wholeness, harmony and radiance" or from fitting such classifications as "lyrical, epic and dramatic." While the ideal is clearly inaccessible, it is also obvious that this inaccessibility is not scrutinized seriously enough in discussions of the aesthetics of fiction. It is easy to place too much stress upon form, because that is what critics feel competent to discuss. Perhaps that is one reason why art critics revel in nonobjective painting, and why, in this age of prose, criticism has focused on poetry. There is too little scrutiny of that perilous region between practical rules and ideal definition, both of which (especially the latter) are general in nature, and both of which fail to account fully enough form any fine novels that are full of life, but that fail Stephen's test: *Don Quixote*, *Moll Flanders*, *Vanity Fair*, the novels of Sir Walter Scott, *Père Goriot*, *Moby Dick*, *Crime and Punishment*, *Great Expectations*, *Huckleberry Finn*, *Sons and Lovers*, *Look Homeward, Angel*, *The Adventures of Augie March*. In most novels, the impulse to mimesis triumphs over the dictates of formal rhythm. While beautiful theories give us a way of seeing the beautiful formal aspects of novels, they may put other elements out of focus. Do we describe a more valid condition when we call *Crime and Punishment* a masterpiece of the novel or when we call it a flawed work of art?

In no medium has an artistic creation more than approximately arrived at that state of perfection which most definitions of art predicate. Because most theories of art are conceived ideally, they disregard or fail to account fully enough for the realities of the creative process and the unavoidable degree of crudity that must be an aspect of every artistic creation, keeping the realization of theory magnetically in the future.

While excellent literary criticism about the novel has been written, Austin Warren is correct in saying that "Literary theory and criticisms concerned with the novel are much inferior in both quantity and quality to theory and criticism of poetry." The aesthetic theories, conceptions, methods, criteria of such poetry critics as Coleridge, Poe, Swinburne, Pater, Hulme, Richards, Ransom, Tate, Brooks, Robert Penn Warren, Empson, Blackmur have been smuggled into criticism of fiction and drama; this criticism has been practiced in universities and developed in the works of such fiction critics as Lubbock, Frye, Muir, Schorer, Crane, Tate, and of such novelists as James.

Many good critics have written on the nature and form of the novel, but each demonstrates once again the dubious status of the novel as an art medium. The title and contents of one of the few anthologies of criticism devoted strictly to the novel, *Approaches to the Novel: Materials for a Poetics*, edited by Robert Scholes, testify to the novel's defiance of attempts at aesthetic codification. To his phrase "antagonism between sensory experience and meaning" (in *Mimesis*), Erich Auerbach might have added the antagonism between those two elements and form. In "Novels of Action and Character" (from *The Structure of the Novel*), Edwin Muir declares that "The only thing which can tell us about the novel is the novel." Thus, he accepts as the forms of the novel those forms found in novels that have actually been written, and concludes that the novel of character is one of the most important divisions, and that flat characters serve such a novel best. In *The Rise of the Novel*, Ian Watt stresses something called "formal realism."

E. M. Forster, in *Aspects of the Novel*, differentiates between story ("narrative of events arranged in their time-sequence") and plot ("narrative of events, the emphasis falling on causality"); plot must have mystery, making demands on the reader's intelligence and memory. In "The Nature and Modes of Narrative Fiction" (from *Theory of Literature* with René Wellek), Austin Warren calls the novel one of the two great art forms (drama is the other). Having pointed out that "the two chief modes of narrative fiction have, in English, been called the romance and the novel," Warren simply surveys, discharging a freight of insight along the way, traditional aspects of the novel, and leaves us as remote as ever from an aesthetic. Irving Howe takes us even further away when he emphasizes the novel's social ties in "Mass Society and Post-Modern Fiction." Percy Lubbock's attempt in *The Craft of Fiction* to order Henry James's reflections on the nature and techniques of fiction, found scattered among his prefaces and essays, results in an emphasis on "picture, drama and point of view." Norman Friedman in "Point of View in Fiction" traces the development of this critical conception and offers an even more sophisticated breakdown of point-of-view possibilities than Lubbock provides. One of the finest essays arguing the supremacy of art over raw life in the novel is Mark Schorer's "Technique as Discovery." "When we speak of technique, then, we speak of nearly everything. For technique is the means by which the writer's experience, which is his subject matter, compels him to attend to it; technique is the only means he has of discovering, exploring, developing his subject, of conveying its meaning, and, finally, of evaluating it." David Daiches, in "The Criticism of Fiction: Some Second Thoughts" (an essay not included in Scholes's anthology), suggests a criterion that would reinstate all the writers Schorer's criteria expel: "*Interestingness* is a criterion no serious critic has dared to apply to art, but I can see no reason why it should not be applied." While "interestingness" is certainly a quality of every novel that succeeds in any sense, it is questionable whether it describes any major aspect of what happens when we experience the authentically aesthetic aspects of a work of art. R. S. Crane in "The Concept of the Plot of *Tom Jones*" pleads for "the more specific kind of criticism of a work that takes the form of the plot as its starting point and then inquires how far and in what way its peculiar power is maximized by the writer's invention and development of episodes, his step-by-step rendering of the character of his people, his use and elaboration of thought, his handling of diction and imagery, and his decisions as to the order, method, scale and point of view of his representation."

To conclude this grossly oversimplified but I hope suggestive survey of familiar literary criticism on form in the novel, let us look at Northrop Frye's plea for synthesis: "There is surely no reason why criticism, as a systematic and organized study, should not be, at least partly, a science." ("The Archetypes of Criticism" from *Anatomy of Criticism*, reprinted in another valuable anthology,

Myth and Method: Modern Theories of Fiction, edited by James E. Miller, Jr.) "Certainly criticism as we find it in learned journals and scholarly monographs has every characteristic of a science." A scientific literary discipline would be based on "the assumption of total coherence" or "total form" in literature. "Our first step, therefore, is to recognize and get rid of meaningless criticism; that is, talking about literature in a way that cannot help to build up a systematic structure of knowledge." (The next step, I assume, is to get rid of novels which fail to provide raw material for such refining analysis.) In another section of his book (reprinted in *Approaches to the Novel*), Frye lists "myth," "romance," "high and low mimetic," and "ironic" as fictional modes; the "four chief strands binding" the form of fiction together are "novel, confession, anatomy, and romance." Using two concepts emphasized also by Forster, Frye says, "We may call the rhythm of literature the narrative, and the pattern, the simultaneous mental grasp of the verbal structure, the meaning or significance." The rigidity of Frye's approach, as of any attempt at absolute theory, is seen in the inadequacy of his archetype concept. As partial perspectives on what happens in novels, all the theories alluded to above are valuable. But the nature of the novel vigorously resists any attempt to resolve the ambiguities of life, as depicted in the novel, into the clarity of a system.

I speak of aesthetic form, in respect to the novel specifically, as an ideal state of creation embodying such absolute characteristics as those described by Stephen. Since each novel, no matter how discursive it is, no matter how hysterically it strives to break out of time into spatial dimensions, has its own form, I use *aesthetic form* in its strictest sense, as derived from discussions of painting and sculpture (Lessing), of epic, comedy, and tragedy (Aristotle), and of poetry (Coleridge, Poe, the New Critics). In "The Problem of Esthetic Form" (from *The Analysis of Art*) Dewitt H. Parker lists six principles of aesthetic form: 1] **organic unity**, unity in variety, wholeness; 2] **theme**,

dominant elements; 3] **thematic variation**, elaboration
and texture; 4] **balance**, disposition of elements; 5]
hierarchy, disposition of elements in an ascending scale;
6] **evolution**, progression. The first principle is the most
important and contains all the others. All art is beset by
the problem of the conflict between content (life) and form
— particularly all literary art, but even more particularly
the novel genre. David Daiches concerns himself with this
problem in "The Criticism of Fiction: Some Second
Thoughts." From an earlier work he quotes his sober
definition of form in the novel: "Fiction as an art form is the
narration of a series of situations that are so related to
each other that a significant unity of meaning is achieved;
the situations are presented in language such that at each
point in the progress of the narrative the kind of relation
between retrospect and anticipation is set up that continually and cumulatively reinforces the desired implications of the plot, so that plot becomes symbolic as well
as literal in its meaning." Daiches himself now sees the
failure of any such ideal definition of form to account for
the mystery of creation with which the sense of life invests
most novels.

How does literary form differ from form in other
media? My point is that the novel is so incomparable with
other media that only confusion has arisen from the effort
to discuss novels in terms of aesthetic form, terms often
appropriated from a critical language developed for other
media or genres. In criticism of the novel there is, of
course, as much discussion of the multifarious life aspects
as of the formal aspects; in David Daiches we see a
struggle for balance between the poles; in James both
approaches are found in the critical writing, if not in his
novels. But in all discussions, whether "the sense of felt
life" or formal expressiveness is asserted as the central
focus, there is an unspoken sense of inferiority about the
novel for its failure to qualify as art. (Serious criticism of
the cinema as an art is in a similar position today.) The
open-ended possibilities for formal qualities in the novel

genre account for both the desperate attempts of some
critics to urge pure theories of aesthetic form and for the
facile attempts of other critics to urge anarchy in our
approach to novel criticism. Each kind of critic writes in
direct or indirect reaction against the other; the points
of controversy still are less clear between opposing critics
of the novel than between critics of poetry.

Though the numerous theories of aesthetic form often
conflict, we talk with relative ease about form, but what is
"life" in the novel (not as opposed to, but as, in a sense,
distinguished from, form)? The life of a living organism (to
which "artistic" novels have often been likened) is
inseparable, naturally, from its form. Life has form. Form
has life: even the form of a rock has, like Stephen's
basket, a symbolic life in the rhythmic and tensional relations among its lines. In some kind of form, the entelechy
of all life is expressed. The life of a novel is (to develop a
variation of Aquinas' concepts) its animated radiance, its
multi-whatness within the form the writer has given it.
Although it has many other formal aspects, *Tom Jones* is,
according to Stephen's definition, epic in form; its life
consists of such aspects as its sense of change, movement,
tension, comedy, action, suspense, curiosity, of its resplen-
dence of "human" qualities that attract and hold
interest, that generate a reader's emotional responses.
The life of a novel intrigues, excites, delights from moment
to moment, while form, once the entire novel is apprehended, primarily satisfies the intellect.

Is it not in the nature of the novelistic genre of
artistic expression that the life elements should pre-
dominate? In sculpture, we may accept such complete
nonobjectivity and delight in such pure form as is impossible in the novel. Although form may both restrain
and enhance the elements it controls, to the extent that
pure form is vigorously insisted upon, it smothers the life
of a novel; this sense of life is practically unlimited. In
Gide's *The Immoralist* and in some novels by Flaubert
and James, one is inclined to discuss form because there is

relatively little raw life; the life is mostly aesthetic, as in the form of a rock. The mysteries of imaginative creation are just as importantly at work in the life aspects of a novel as they are in formal aspects; but life aspects are more difficult to discern and to discuss in aesthetic parlance. Stephen was wrong; sculpture is one of the most perfect media of art, as his discussion of the basket suggests. In sculpture, even in a short poem, the sense of life derives more from form than it does in the novel. The simultaneity which true art achieves is, in the novel, sustained imperfectly by memory. Rarely does a novel achieve an acute balance between the sense of life and the apprehension of form. When a novel does, we may intuitively perceive balance at that still point where it makes its momentary stand.

Implicit in this discussion has been the question, Is the novel an art form? Because of its inherent incapacity for approaching to an adequate degree the realization of ideal standards, it is only with major qualifications that a novel can be called a work of art. All art (except music) imitates life, but most art — painting, sculpture, poetry, drama, the dance — must select and arrest at some still point a very limited aspect of life. Like the cinema, the novel, however, generally imitates a large area of life and is involved in its movement and variety. This condition thrives upon life elements; the result is relative formlessness; simultaneously, when it does tend toward art, the novel demands a careful concern with form, which is certainly inseparable from the novel, but the total work is seldom, if ever, an aesthetically achieved whole.

A craftsman in the fine arts, whether a novelist or a sculptor, should not be called an artist until he has made a novel or a piece of sculpture which conforms to some system of aesthetics. The concept *art* demands a systematic definition. There are good and bad works of art, some contend. But is not the term most useful if applied to works within the range of *good*? Otherwise, almost anything made within the class of fine arts can be called a work of art, bad though it may be. Further confusion arises when the product of a craft (a cabinet) is called a work of art; or when literary critics loosely employ the term tragedy.

Directly or indirectly, aestheticians have discussed, or influenced literary critics in the discussion of, the form of the novel. But they go little further than literary critics in arriving at a coherent aesthetic. Cassirer, Langer, Fry, Collingwood, Bell have been helpful, but their thinking applies with much greater confidence and meaning to such a medium as painting. Croce's descriptive metaphor of the novel as "a tissue of images" that leaves one with a single image is brilliant, leading me to look in a well-formed novel for what I call its poetic image: the green light in *The Great Gatsby*, for instance. But unless the novel is re-examined with the intention of developing a system of aesthetics peculiar to it, discussions of the novel as aesthetic form will only perpetuate confusion and relativism in aesthetics.

Work of art is used as a value and/or as a descriptive term. The descriptive use of the term fails to distinguish good from bad. If the novel is not an art, must it therefore be inferior to art? Though one novel may come closer than another to fulfilling certain criteria of art, to call a novel good or bad art according to the degree to which it approaches the conditions of art is to disregard the nature of the genre. Need we ask, Can the novel be an art? If so, how? One might better ask, Why should it be? To say that the novel is not an art form is not, logically, to use the term either descriptively or eulogistically; it is simply to say that total concepts of aesthetics do not apply to the novel. To deny the novel the label *art* is to deny it nothing that it every rightfully possessed. Just because a work of art is a thing of value, we do not assign value to the novel simply by calling it art. It has other values, peculiar to itself; it has inherent capacities for doing much more, and in an artistic way, than other media. Who would ever think of attempting to expand the value horizons of music or painting by saying of a symphony, for instance, that it is like a novel? And yet to say that a certain novel is like a poem or a fugue or a painting is to suggest its aesthetic achievement.

If, of all the modes of creation, the novel is the most difficult in which to approach an aesthetic ideal, it is also the freest, and has, by direct consequence, its own special richness. Because of the symbolic range of words, and of their connotations and denotations, and the dynamic interplay between levels of meaning, the novel can appropriate for its own uses the dominant characteristics and devices of art media, though it may never itself be art. There are those arts which come under the category *plastic*. The novel might well be classified as the *elastic* medium.

Man strives, collectively, to achieve in society a provisional order based on practical considerations, but individuals dream up utopias where everything is in order, all makes sense. The absolute is in all things a state we aspire to. It is in the process of becoming the absolute that we know the finest emotions. But could we once know, possess, the absolute we would be referred to other imperfections. Men venerate the quest, Browning reiterated in poem after poem, far more than the find. Thus, utopias would fail because man's nature demands ambiguity, uncertainty, and stress, even as it aspires, sometimes viciously, to clarity, certainty, and stasis. For instance, love, unmixed with the ambiguities of hate, is static. The ideal, like God, is greatly to be desired, but in art as in life it is more efficacious to work on the assumption that the ideal will never be achieved, as though in the midst of a flood someone were to say, Let us all pray to God to stop the rain, and someone else were to insist, That is to be desired, but only after we have placed sandbags against the flood.

Man aspires to the sublimity of perfection. The approximation of perfection is most possible in art. It is desirable that most artists strive to reach an ideal state.

Ideal aesthetic formulations provide an image for this
aspired-to condition. But being in no way perfect in his
nature, man also needs vicariously to experience imperfection, a certain lack or seeming lack of form and order,
if art is to have verisimilitude while it has form. In
pursuing the aspiration to order and to art, finer, more
sensitive imperfections are created (most especially in the
novel). Just as perfection appeals mainly to the intellect,
imperfections appeal mainly to the emotions. But all art
is imperfect. And imperfections, the nearer a work
approaches an ideal artistic condition, are transformed into
sources of pleasurable tension. If this were not true, a
perfect circle would be the highest artistic achievement;
but a good circle in the process of becoming a perfect one
is more interesting. Perfect art would be maddening. It is,
however, impossible, just as the apprehension of a perfect
circle is impossible. Prolonged contemplation of a perfect
circle would eventually impair that perfection, because the
circle would, because of optical imperfections, tend
backward in the direction of the formlessness out of which
it was created.

Outside the forms of tragedy, pity and fear are
destructive forces in the aesthetic sense. But high tragedy
in demanding the life experience of pity and fear, enables
us to experience a high form of disorder, of imperfection.

One function of ideal theories can be to force us to
reflect, with beneficial results, upon ever-existent imperfections. The beneficial possibilities of the inaccessibility of the ideal have not been, as I believe they may and
should be, sufficiently explored. While full realization of
the remoteness of the ideal may inspire freedom, that
freedom must be qualified by the very ideal in relation to
which it stands. Thus, I am not making a plea for anarchy
in the novel. Even in the absence of evidence that the
ideal can ever be realized, the artist must continue always
to move toward it (though its attainment would only
create another ideal). But the avenues of approach are
myriad. We must, therefore, account for every novel that

fails in certain respects, while succeeding in others, to achieve a close approximation to ideal concepts of art. Stephen's ideal precepts may be applied with relative ease to such rare short works as Camus' *The Stranger* and Fitzgerald's *The Great Gatsby*. Because, in formal terms, they are so nearly perfect, to discuss their structure is not difficult. *Gatsby* achieves as nearly as possible everything it intends; its form needs no elucidation. The demands *The Stranger* makes on its readers are not in its form, but in the philosophical implications of the character and behavior of Meursault. Discussion of form becomes more and more superfluous the more fully an artistic creation embodies definitions of form. Of course, no novel can be totally amorphous. Close analysis shows that Benjy's section in *The Sound and the Fury*, which seems chaotic, or at least impressionistic, is the most ordered, consciously formed part of the book. Even if it were not, the patterned repetitions would suggest a tendency toward form, a tendency of the parts to cohere, to relate and produce rhythm. Céline's journey narrative, sprawling over life, seems to lack form, yet a sort of form emerges. (Still it is not truly relevant to discuss form in *Journey to the End of the Night* because Céline does not always conform even to simple chronological sequence or to the concept of character development; that the narrator remains essentially the same person is partly because of the somewhat picaresque mode of the novel.) We need to ask such questions as, Is it possible for a good novel to have wholeness without harmony, or radiance without either of the other two? Is it possible for a novel (a medium in time) to have any of these to the extent that the spatial arts possess them?

In the novel, the imperfect as subject and substance is the reader's major concern. Moving in the direction of formlessness, we move toward chaos and delirium, artistic floundering, which, if regarded as an achievement (as in Burroughs, for instance) is escape from the rigorous responsibilities of art. But artificial form, created out of an attempt to impose order in a manner not organic with the subject, is escape from the risks of life. To the extent that form in the novel approaches the realization of ideal definitions of art it will become artificial, unless it has life in close proportion. *The Immoralist* fails to achieve balance because form overcontrols life.

But that artistic creation which lacks conscious form will fail to endure. The individual works of the dadaists are not memorable; because the life element in a dada painting insists by its nature upon a momentary emotional response, a momentary delight in the bizarre, the same bizarre object loses its attraction the more familiar it becomes. A high degree of form is inseparable from many of the best novels (which are also full of life): *Wuthering Heights, The Ambassadors, Fathers and Sons, Portrait of the Artist, The Great Gatsby, To the Lighthouse, The Sun Also Rises, Ulysses, Pilgrim Hawk, The Sound and the Fury, All the King's Men, The Stranger*. Also, such recent work as *The Garden* by Yves Berger, a young French writer, and *The Field of Vision* by Wright Morris; even so-called popular works like James M. Cain's *The Postman Always Rings Twice* and Horace McCoy's *They Shoot Horses, Don't They?*; and such short stories as those of Chekhov, Katherine Anne Porter, and Katherine Mansfield, stand up quite well under severe aesthetic scrutiny.

Historically, the "purest" works of art have been highly but simply symbolic and formal, typical or archetypal in significance. Art endures longer the nearer it is pure symbol: the Greek female statue, most religious symbols, the universal circle as sun, as cycle. Such purity is, Flaubert insisted, possible in the novel. That is how Flaubert could entertain the possibility of writing a novel without a single character. But that possibility tends in the direction of form for form's sake, and in fiction implies a mind which, obsessed with form, lacks the kind of imagination that not only transforms life into form but into such new energetic expressions as only the novel can utter. Primitive art probably did not come out of conscious contemplation of form; form naturally evolved out of the spontaneous expression of simple emotions or ideas. And to a simple, living feeling, form comes naturally. Even a cry of pain has its natural form, which fiction imitates. But because numerous novels (Faulkner's, for instance) are full of many cries of pain, the novel becomes complex, and form, the more it is insisted upon, becomes artificial; and thus, form debilitates the life of the novel. The novel moves in the direction of complexity; it explores facets of imperfection; the possibilities of the novel go in many directions away from form, embrace more, quantitatively, of life than the strictures of art can control.

A number of forces operate against form in the novel. One of these originates in the reader: taste. How may we transcend taste in judging literature? One way is to erect formal theories (often sources of conformity) and avoid or abuse the life of a work. It is largely because of taste and the times that certain forms, certain themes and subjects undergo change and variations. I find that my adverse criticism of a novel is nearly always derived from taste, while my favorable criticism is based (even with a novel that I do not particularly like) on a consideration of the book's own form and life. I am not making a defense of taste (nor of my own in particular). Taste for the majority can become a general predilection for Frank Yerby. And it is impossible, fortunately, to make of taste a criterion. But we must examine taste more closely as a formidable, active agent even in the most discriminating readers. Most past theories are curiosities of literary history. All rules or theories of form have been broken, giving rise to new ones. In the formulation of these, the tastes of powerful and articulate critics and writers have been a forceful determinant. We need always to remember this process when looking at the novel.

A second force operating against form has more to do with the nature of the novel itself: time. While certain aspects of a novel may sustain an artistic feel, because of the problem of distraction other elements will fail to.

Some plays are easier to remember because of the picture frame of the stage, the added enhancement of having more palpable images to see, sounds to hear (more passivity, that is), and because of the short duration of the experiience; this ease is facilitated if there is a unity of time and place. Art is more possible in the drama (though not necessarily any more desirable) and in the short novel; thus, in that sense, *The Stranger* is much more a work of art than *War and Peace*. But the cinema, drama, and the novel are always art in process; one can never behold a novel whole. A novel is always moving, never arrested, even after one reaches the end. It is kinetic, though not in the pejorative sense Stephen meant. Generally, to the extent that a novel tries to arrest life (in the sense Stephen described), it is doomed. In a novel, the comprehension of the whole dissipates quickly into a breakup again because of the time factor. The present moment is not intelligible except in relation to what preceded it and to the probabilities set up of what may come. As we read a novel, the details of what went before get hazier at the same time that the general idea gets clearer. The longer a novel, the less chance of its being artistic. Although as a whole it is pervaded with life, *Ulysses* is made up of artistic sections. But in a Wolfe novel, there is little art, and the effect of the whole is not an aesthetic sense of life; rather, his mammoth works are made up of segments of life; this fragmentariness is caused mostly, in the absence of certain formal qualities, by the range of years or months separating the many episodes.

The picture in *Tom Jones* is not complete until we reach the end, but it is never quite complete, because the end refers us to the beginning, which insists upon clarifying other portions. On the way to the end, disorder, seeming formlessness, holds our attention. A work of art may send us outside itself, but, unlike the didactic novel, for instance, it demands that we return to it; a work of art is the beginning and the end, while for its inner tensions it depends partly upon reference to the outside. However, if we do not return to a bad novel (even though theme and characters may be universal and form be adequate), it is because the life of the work does not reside fully enough in it. The novel, for its complete effect, refers to things outside itself. A circle does not. An idiot, more than an intelligent person, can delight in a circle. But a novel is too suggestive to be self-contained. As we read, or afterwards, we keep asking such questions as: Why did Quentin in *The Sound and the Fury* have to drown himself? Why could he not . . . ? In the novel as in life, sheer harmony is deadening, as continual happiness would be awful, prolonged ecstasy suicide.

All art media exist by virtue of the same elements, but in each medium certain elements by necessity dominate despite the experimental artist's attempt to transcend them to achieve certain kinds of depth or expansion. Next to words, the major mode of the novel is time. But few novelists really seize upon and master this given element and integrate it into the very life of the work, making it the formal essence. Faulkner's very interesting and nearly successful attempt in *The Sound and the Fury* only indicates the degree to which this basic element (time) fails to become a conscious part of the essence of form. Time is operative in, and must to a degree inform, every printed work, whether or not the writer incorporates it with artistic intent. But it is a difficult problem to ground the form firmly in time, the medium in which it has its being. The problematic complexity of form in the novel is further increased by the fact that, symbolically, space is also involved, even in the simple description of a room. Some writers (Robbe-Grillet, Beckett, Burroughs) dispense with chronology and other elements to give the sense of space more than symbolic force. But in space the reader's imagination will tend to wander away from form if it can.

The novelist in trying to master certain formal elements may end enslaved to them, the irony being that, by virtue of his intention, those very elements often should not have prominence. The mastery of time would not be as effective in many novels as it is in *The Sound and the Fury*. Had Gide concerned himself with time as a major element in *The Immoralist*, what he did achieve would probably have been minimized. *Tom Jones* has a wholeness and a harmony that is apparent, but it would be difficult to locate or describe or even feel its radiance, its whatness, to a degree as nearly approximate to the ideal as the other two qualities. To the extent that radiance is not as fully realized there is, therefore, disharmony and incompleteness in *Tom Jones*. But could Fielding, or need he, have achieved it any more nearly than he did? In Samuel Beckett's *Molloy*, we feel the radiance of character because it is so incompletely disclosed, and for the same reason we feel harmony in the character of Molloy. The introduction of new or other parts for the sake of completeness would probably disrupt the wholeness already achieved. Such considerations as these indicate how unconducive the novel is to the conditions of art which Stephen and others describe.

In the drama, preconceived notions of form degenerated from Sophocles to Sardou. In varying degree and ways this process often occurs. In a novel with too much life — by Dickens or Wolfe — form suffers, it seems. Over a novel too much concerned with form, *The Immoralist*, for instance, the pall of lifelessness hovers. Faulkner demonstrates in *The Sound and the Fury* that a novel can excel in both form and life. Thus, categories are as misleading as they are helpful. Stephen's "forms" — "lyrical, epic, and dramatic" — are good and useful, partly to the extent that they suggest others, or variations within themselves. But though we may say that *The Immoralist* and *Wuthering Heights* are "lyrical novels," what categories can indicate the essential distinction between these two? For *Wuthering Heights*, in many important respects, is just as close to *The Sound and the Fury* as it is to Gide's novel. Is it by formal considerations that the distinction can be made? Each good novel creates its own special or peculiar formal personality even as it conforms to, or is informed by, other existing concepts of form. Thus, comparison of one book to another, of Wolfe to Gide, in terms of form, results in easy but not really discriminating distinctions in the realm of life. The essential differences are more difficult to discuss, and perhaps the finest differences are only intuitively perceivable.

To say, as Stephen does, that one form is superior to another (dramatic to lyrical, for instance) is to negate possibilities, from which real richness comes. We need to consider those kinds of differences which a comparison of radically different kinds of criticism suggests. External criticism asks: Why is (or why is not) this work of art what is should be? But internal criticism asks: What makes it what it is? The interesting thing is not the absolute principle that all living organisms are composed on the same fundamental cell structure, but that it makes possible so many variations of organisms: apes, kangaroos, ocelots, walruses, giraffes, insects, toads, cobras, zebras, men and women of myriad inclinations. The differences between Stephen and Quentin (who are in some ways similar) do not result so much from form as from other factors — life factors; and the similarities and often the differences among most authors on either formal or life levels are only superficial (Hemingway and Camus are stylistically similar but tremendously different in more important respects). It is on the life level that most of the differences, the difficulties, and the delights are.

So long as form is overstressed in a novel, a negative conflict between form and life will exist. But in a positive sense this conflict arises from the novel's special nature; this paradoxical tension between form and life creates a middle condition which would seem to be the true province more of the novel than of any other medium because of the range and complexity of experience that is possible. The multiplicity of forms and of life aspects possible within a single novel produces tensions that are sequentially resolved and reiterated on every page. This process occurs in drama and cinema but to such a lesser degree that it remains a distinguishing characteristic of the novel.

As long as we simply talk about a given novel (or compare it with others) much illumination can be achieved, but when we force it into the realm of art theory we will ultimately face the frustrations of relativity. What one rule of form can we insist upon among all novels? What does it mean to say that Tom Jones or Quentin is deficient in radiance, in whatness, or one of them more or less deficient than the other? For instance, is it possible to dispense almost entirely with such a novelistic fundamental as narrative? In *Malone Dies*, the element of narrative exists only as a joke, a diversion for the dying Malone.

In the scholar's study and in the writer's workshop considerations of form can be used as a bag into which to stuff the life of a work. Classicism, romanticism, realism, naturalism, surrealism, symbolism, the historical, psychological, philological, philosophical, moral, Marxian, sociological, traditional, biographical, Freudian, categorical, mythological, traditional approach — any specialized theory is exasperating, based, it often seems, on an intrinsic dislike of art, upon the conceit of uncreative minds. The study of literature should not be based on either / or propositions (although these may be adequate for other art media), but rather upon both / and propositions.

Perhaps the best way to evaluate literature is to come to it relatively free of formal preconceptions, but as fully aware as possible of all the formal possibilities for expressing "life."

the fallacy of
the subject-dominated novel

When the artist or the hack is so bemused by the timeliness, the controversy, the strangeness, the importance of his raw material that he neglects the mysterious dictates of art, he is involved in the act of writing a subject-dominated novel. For instance, no novel was ever more dominated than *Uncle Tom's Cabin* by its subject: the condition of the Negro under slavery. That's an extreme example. But in *Invisible Man*, Ralph Ellison tried to utter more than the Negro's cry of anguish and protest. In an interview he said of Malraux's *Man's Fate*, "The book lives not because of a political position embraced at the time, but because of its larger concern with the tragic struggle of humanity. Most of the social realists are concerned less with tragedy than with injustice. I wasn't, and am not, *primarily* concerned with injustice, but with art." *Invisible Man*, I suspect, was so highly praised, because here at last was a Negro writer who had achieved both protest and art; but the critics' praise was also motivated by white guilt and a desire to help the Negro. The test of this novel's survival as art alone will come when the conditions for protest have passed. It is not, however, Ralph Ellison, the artistic Negro, but James Baldwin who is the Negro's spokesman among fiction writers. For Baldwin, one of the decade's most superb essayists, is less interested in art than in issues such as the race problems and the homosexual dilemma.

In discussing the subject-dominated novel, I may sound a little evangelistic, for as a sort of type, it has been tolerated long enough, and my purpose is to attack it. In historical perspective, it includes, of course, books no lover of literature would willingly do without. But recently this sort of novel has begun to attract more attention than it deserves and, what is worse, to be confused with art, often because of the public reputations of its authors. It appeals to readers who pamper what they like to call their tastes. It does not make it difficult for the reader to willingly suspend his disbelief; the close and faithful depiction of reality in Steinbeck, for instance, is not likely to tax anyone's willingness to believe. It often communicates ideas and feelings properly conveyed by nonfictive means, and arouses emotions and attitudes external to the aesthetic experience. The novel becomes merely a box, enclosing an idea or a likely assortment of raw material fragments. While art unifies the particular and the general, the subject-dominated novel immolates itself in the particular. Primarily concerned with externals, it encourages us to look outside itself. The author of such a novel is likely to commit what I call the notion fallacy: the writer's fascination with his subject leads him to embrace as a genuine conception what is in reality a mere notion. Most students of literature differentiate between theme and subject. Theme is the central idea or thesis the writer strives to express about his subject. But in my definition of the subject-dominated novel, theme or thesis can often become a kind of subject matter, as in, for instance, the philosophical novel. (My remarks apply as well to drama and poetry.)

The problem of the subject-dominated novel accompanied the birth of the genre. Many of the best early novels were somewhat picaresque, vehicles for social satire; as an old and entertaining form with a venerable tradition, the picaresque type has encouraged the proliferation of the artless subject-dominated novel, for the picaresque is very episodic, held together mainly by a central character and a thesis. The fathers of the English novel illustrate this split between subject and art. Richardson was interested almost solely in sensibility, having Clarissa speak her mind in letters. But Daniel Defoe was a journalist and an idea man, who, fired with purpose and filled with his subject, wrote *Journal of the Plague Year*. In the best novels, these two conflicting tendencies are reconciled in artistic triumphs of unity, for in a work of art, subject and form are inseparable. But in subject-dominated novels aspects of art are forced to serve the dictates of subject matter. In *The Art of Fiction*, Henry James said, "We must grant the artist his subject, his idea, his donnée; our criticism is applied only to what he makes of it." Too many novelists seem to write on the assumption that to grant the artist his donnée is to accept the absence of almost everything else.

In a time when nonfiction threatens to make fiction obsolete, it is dangerous for fiction to focus on subjects which are more proper to nonfiction, especially if all that is added are the devices and the semblance of fiction. Subject-dominated works encourage the trend and prepare readers for the transition, if it comes, from imaginative literature to the near absolute prevalence of a hybrid nonfiction, which at its worst produces what we call nonbooks and at its best produces books like Spengler's *The Decline of the West*, which is as much visionary poetry as it is history. Nonobjective art has gone, at least until recently, to the other extreme and totally banished subject matter; refusing to photograph, as a mere matter of record, the events of our time, it is obsessed rather with the projection of the spirit of our age in artistic forms that are timeless and universal, though inspired by the transient shapes of a shifting culture. The movies exhibit both extremes: *Last Year at Marienbad*, about a love affair that may or may not have happened, is a pure aesthetic experience; *The Cool World*, about a Negro dope-addict hoodlum, exploits subject matter. The writer should not be a slave to passing events. A novel, self-perpetuating and permanent, should be an event in itself. As Ezra Pound says, "Literature is news that stays news."

What are the general conditions that have produced an acceleration of this trend toward focus on subject matter? One might as well blame this, as well as everything else, on the age, for as Flaubert said, novels are the mirrors of their age. In *Fiction of the Forties* Chester Eisinger presents the thesis that the novels of the forties and fifties (of this Atomic Age, Age of Survival, Age of Anxiety) show an interest in social issues; but many turn away from these issues to find their real center in moral-ethical problems, or in what concerns the inward, private being. The sixties are a little different. More writers today zero in directly on problems and issues. Still, writers today cannot find or accept a set of common assumptions. Our culture, marked by incoherence and uncertainty, offers the writer neither an ideology nor a faith that might sustain him. The writer must examine the possibilities for literature in a universe of fragmented beliefs where a multiplicity of values or none at all have long ago replaced a unified world view. He has to ask himself: Can I, under the circumstances, find a way to communicate with others, or should I give up and keep silent? Many have become apolitical and disengaged from the surrealistic disorder of history. But though alienated, the writer has refused to choose silence. He has, in fact, thrived on the tensions and violence produced by the radical disjunctions of his culture.

In almost full possession of the facts, we live in an age that is seeking more desperately than ever the answers. Working against real and phantom deadlines, the artist and his readers attempt to seize the tools with which to re-mobilize the malfunctioning cultural machinery of our Era of Technology. Give us the facts, not fantasy, is the universal cry! In an era that has produced changes like TV and the space breakthrough, and horrors like the extermination of the Jews which overwhelm the imagination, we are benumbed. Sensation and controversy barely stir us. "The artist," says novelist Wright Morris in his critical book *The Territory Ahead*, "has a disquieting and numbing apprehension that such future as man has may dispense with art. It is the nature of the future, not its extinction by the bomb, that produces in the artist such foreboding, a chill of heart at the prospect of a world without consciousness."

In *The Territory Ahead*, Wright Morris examines the raw material fallacy as it has always plagued even America's best writers. What I call subject, Morris calls raw material. "Raw material," he says, "the great variety and rawness of it, has been the central ornament of American writing since Thoreau." When Henry James

advised writers to "try to be one of the people on whom
nothing is lost!" he was speaking more of meaning than
of material. On certain occasions in American literature
craft has broken through "this devotion to raw material,
but the resulting masterpiece had about it the air of an
accident." *Walden, Leaves of Grass, Moby Dick,* and *The
Adventures of Huckleberry Finn* are "moments of grace"
for their authors that were achieved under "the pressure
of the raw material." The classic American writer felt
"the need to domesticate a continent." Melville observed
that "It is not so much paucity as super-abundance of
material that seems to incapacitate modern authors." Still,
writers of great vitality like Wolfe have tried to capture
the continent, and we have praised their magnificent
failures as though they were successes. Whitman's
"barbaric yawp" reappears in "the gargantuan bellow of
Wolfe," whose books offer us the spectacle of "the artist
as cannibal." But what was once raw about American life
has now been processed so many times that the material
we begin with is itself a fiction, one created by Twain,
Hemingway, or Fitzgerald. "*From Here to Eternity* reminds us that young men are still fighting Hemingway's
war. After all, it is the one they know best: it was made
real and coherent by his imagination." So the only raw
material regions left are those the artist must imagine.

Morris admits that an excess of raw material has been
the "dominant factor" in his own career as a novelist.
"The realization that I had to create coherence, conjure
up my synthesis, rather than find it, came to me, as it
does to most Americans, disturbingly late. Having sawed
out the pieces of the jigsaw puzzle, I was faced with a
problem of fitting them together." An almost perfect
example of a novel which triumphs over this raw material
curse, and blessing, is *The Great Gatsby*. "In Fitzgerald's
The Great Gatsby," says Morris, "and I think only in
Gatsby, the mythic vastness of this continent, the huge raw
material banquet that Wolfe bolted, received its baptismal
blessing and its imaginative processing." We may go to

Fitzgerald's early books, such as *This Side of Paradise*, for the raw material details of the Jazz Age for which he was the spokesman, but *The Great Gatsby* is not freighted with such details. Rather it reflects the spirit of an age in aesthetic universals that remain relevant after that age has passed.

What is the writer's alternative to immersion, and ultimate immolation, in his raw material? Wright Morris again has the gospel: "The history of fiction is a series of imaginative triumphs made possible by technique. . . . The creative act lives on only in those minds with the audacity to transform it. . . . Art survives in and through an endless series of transformations. . . . Technique and raw material are dramatized at the moment that the shaping imagination is aware of itself." In this act of awareness "the transitory, illusive facts are shaped into a fiction of permanence. . . . It seems to be the nature of man to transform — himself, if possible, and then the world around him. . . . Imagination, both talent and imagination, are of little value without conception. . . . In the novel, it is conceptual power, not style or sensibility, [or subject matter] that indicates genius." Morris cautions, though, that "there is no substitute for the material itself — the *life* in literature. . . . If devotion to his craft deprives a man of living, it will end in depriving him of art." In *Finnegans Wake*, for instance, "raw material has literally dissolved into technique." The artist must become a paradox — "both a visionary and a realist." I have quoted Morris at such great length because he speaks with special authority, as a novelist who not only states the raw material dilemma and the aesthetic alternative so well, but whose sixteen novels are fascinating illustrations of the problem and of triumph over it.

These observations on the subject-dominated novel ask, by implication, What is a novel? While it is one of the beauties of the form that it accommodates a great variety of styles, subjects, and techniques, this accommodation also creates confusion and encourages mediocrity and sham to parade under the banner of art. There are more types of novels than there are critical biases, and those swarm like wasps. Perhaps one will have to conclude that almost anything that calls itself a novel is legitimately a novel. I hope not.

What effect has the flourishing of this raw material or subject matter trend had upon the writer? It has created an army of careerists, of writers who perform more for the public than for the muse. Allen Ginsberg and most of the beats are glaring examples of careerism. Robert Frost, Carl Sandburg, Faulkner, and Hemingway didn't become public figures until after they had produced their best work. "Who killed Dylan Thomas?" asks Kenneth Rexroth. "You did, you S.O.B." is Rexroth's answer — including, I would hope, himself. Faulkner knew for a long time and Salinger apparently knows very well that careerism is a threat to the artist. The subject-dominated novel will tend to thrust the artist, at first unwillingly perhaps, into the public arena, and make him wish he had stayed in the garret. B. Traven, a sadly neglected American writer, finally flushed out of hiding by a young Mexico City reporter after thirty years of willed obscurity, had feared the effect of public recognition upon his art. He was right. We now know where B. Traven, the man, lives; he will even sell you a beer in his tavern; it is the artist, now, who has gone into hiding. Several years ago, the young Russian poet Yevtushenko looked at us from the cover of *Time* and *The Saturday Evening Post* because he had written some outspoken poems and recited them in public (five years after Ginsberg and Ferlinghetti had read aloud to the accompaniment of jazz in America). The poems are bad, but the poet was hot copy. Another pawn of international tensions, which are irrelevant to art, was Boris Pasternak. *Doctor Zhivago* may be a book of considerable achievement, but that it was critical of Soviet society and that it had earned Khrushchev's disfavor had more than a little to do with the intemperate praise it received in this country.

Certain types of novels encourage the subject-dominated novel more than others. Some types have been created by this natural interest in subject matter. When one enters most large paperback stores, he encounters a manifestation on a popular level of this subject preference. At present, the shelves marked DOCTOR AND NURSE novels occupy almost a fifth of the floor space. WAR is another division, along with the more expected WESTERNS, MYSTERIES, and HISTORICALS. With the play *Men in White* in the thirties, Sidney Kingsley, whose purpose was social criticism, started the Dr. Kildare-Ben Casey-Nurses craze that recently thrived on TV. The subject appeal is one of professional glamor; here are men and women we all know, since we all get sick, but who possess secret skills. Best sellers such as *Not As A Stranger* lend sophistication — and sex — to this basic appeal. Leon Uris' *Battle Cry* is a war novel that exploits our ready-made interest in a universal experience second in craving and intensity only to sex. It appeals on a low level, while other war novels do strive for higher meaning and finer form. Westerns unpretentiously exploit a raw material area. But in *The Ox-Bow Incident*, Walter Van Tilburg Clark shows the possibilities of the western for going beyond Luke Short to a work of purpose and art. The mystery or detective novel is another unpretentious subject area. We read Earle Stanley Gardner for one reason only. But the tough school of writers — James M. Cain, Horace McCoy, B. Traven — suggests that even this raw material area may yield works of a special art. And *Gone with the Wind* and Frank Yerby's books don't represent the limits of the historical novel. This has proved to be a rich area for more artistic talents: Robert Penn Warren, Thornton Wilder, David Stacton, and John Barth have proved that history need not merely be the object of plunder by best sellers. Another model departure from mere historical recording, and drab biography as well, is Virginia Woolf's *Orlando*.

The sea novel is a minor subject area today, but it is

interesting to note that one of the greatest artists of the form, Joseph Conrad, was admired in his time for his ostensible subject matter: adventure at sea and in exotic places. His fiction was read with the same eye for subject matter as was Richard Henry Dana's eyewitness exposé, *Two Years Before the Mast*. The appeal of this raw material area is great. I know. I, too, wanted to be the man who was there and to come back and give a report of the matter. As I did, in a sea novel called *The Beautiful Greed*, the epigraph for which came from Conrad's *Lord Jim*: "There is such magnificent vagueness in the expectations that had driven each of us to sea, such a glorious indefiniteness, such a beautiful greed of adventures that are their own and only reward! . . . In no other kind of life is the illusion more wide of reality — in no other is the beginning *all* illusion — the disappointment *more* swift — the subjugation *more* complete." At best, our infatuation with subject matter is a beautiful greed. It led four other novelists that year to write sea novels: Gwyn Griffin, *Master of This Vessel*; Peter Matthiessen, *Raditzer*; Lawrence Sargeant Hall, *Stowaway*; Shepard Rifkin, *What Ship? Where Bound?* All five of these novels suffer to some degree from a "subjugation" to subject matter.

Graham Greene is a serious novelist who recognizes the difference between using subject matter for its obvious, fleeting entertainment value and transforming it into art. Thus, he calls some of his books "entertainments," while others deserve, he feels, the classification "novel." Compare his purely melodramatic treatment of a hired killer named Raven in the entertainment *This Gun For Hire* with the melodramatic but religious treatment of the homicidal punk named Pinky in *Brighton Rock*.

At the opposite pole from the subject-dominated novel is what might be called the pure novel. A concrete subject matter is only a launching pad for the universal in the pure novel. It is not primarily interested in social and political realities. It refers to and depends upon nothing outside itself for its effects. Like nonobjective painting, it is its own subject. It creates experiences for their own sake, but strives to contain and control those experiences through the various means of art. No ideal examples of the pure novel exist, but several writers come close. I have but to mention Flaubert, who once expressed a desire to write a novel without any characters, and to cite not so much *Madame Bovary* as the exotic romances *Salammbô* and *The Temptations of Saint Anthony* to suggest what I mean. We don't read James Joyce's *Ulysses* to gain insight into the plight of the middle-class Jew in Dublin nor to explore the intricacies of Dublin as raw material. Contrast the French movie *Hiroshima, Mon Amour* with John Hersey's *Hiroshima*. The movie stirs one no less than the book with the horrors of the bomb, but the movie is primarily a profound metaphysical experience, not just a raw cry of pain as the book is. The book says: this is what it was like that day; the movie says: this is what it is like eternally. The pure novel offers somewhat pure, aesthetic experiences, with only as much relevance as a work of art needs.

The most obviously subject-dominated types of novels are the thesis or propaganda novel, the proletarian, the exposé or protest, the sociological novel. A great many critics and readers consider the social function of fiction primary. We may observe in such writers as Farrell, Dos Passos, Steinbeck, and John O'Hara that a rich raw material can by its massive pressure result in at least one good novel for each writer obsessed by it. The cry-of-pain novel is a more intense version of the protest type. Concentration-camp novels offer some of the best examples. Fictionalized personal testimonies told with passion and conviction have attracted great attention in the past few decades, and no man of good conscience will turn a deaf ear to these cries of pain. But these novels are too consciously truth and fiction at once to suggest anything more moving than the author's own struggle with his raw material. The only book on concentration camps which I have discovered even haunting the environs of art is Jorge Semprun's recent novel *The Long Voyage*, whose artistic conception salvages his rotting raw material.

Another kind of protest novel which is getting a great deal of awed attention these days is the race novel, which focuses public attention on the Negro's profound suffering in body and spirit. Two recent plays by blacks continue the old and introduce the new trend in Negro subject matter: James Baldwin's *Blues for Mr. Charley* and Le Roi Jones's *The Dutchman*. Both plays satisfy the need of liberal and cultured whites to experience guilt and to activate their consciences over a situation many of them, ironically, have long been trying to correct. (No segregationist is likely to see the plays.) Reminding one of the thesis plays of the thirties, they are rather crude, artless, and preachy, full of violence and sex. In a review, Philip Roth voices my own feeling about such writers: "I am not happy to see Mr. Jones being hailed in the papers and on television for his anger; for it is not an anger of literary value, and he is a writer. Rather it is rage, blind rage, and, may well have made it nearly impossible for him to write an important play."

My argument is not so complex that I need produce more of the many examples of the subject-dominated novel. It is perhaps enough, then, to end by simply citing various types of novels, whose names are descriptive, and each of which has its own special characteristics that dispose it to encourage the subject-dominated impulse: the political, the philosophical, the religious, and the prophetic novel; the initiation or education novel; the psychological or subjective novel (including sexual, homosexual studies; the author as his own subject; the cult of personal experience; and the novel of adolescence); the milieu novel (including the regional novels of the soil, of the South or of New York City, the my-year-in-Rome novel, the exotic setting, the underworld milieu); the academic novel; the war novel; comic and satirical novels; the experimental novel (experimentation itself may become a kind of subject dominance that often prevents the transformation of raw material into art).

I have been identifying and attacking a trend which has become in recent years a threat to the novel as an art. To will the subject-dominated novel off the shelves of our libraries would be almost to empty them. Should the authors of such novels fall silent, we would miss the voices of some of our favorite writers. I am merely asking for a lowering of our tolerance and our acceptance of the novel whose subject matter is its major claim to our attention.

"harlan, kentucky...sunday... things at rest": *a lyrical essay*

In spring, when the floods aren't raging, in summer, when there isn't a drought, and in autumn, when the mountain slopes aren't ablaze, eastern Kentucky is lovely. Toward winter, though, one refrains with difficulty from calling it a nightmare landscape — the natural landscape recedes, the human landscape comes sharply into focus.

Let me tell you what I see in eastern Kentucky.

Look at Harlan, for instance, in early autumn when things are at rest on Sunday morning.

From my bed in the hotel across from the railroad station, I listen to rubber tires on wooden bridges and cars climbing crooked mud-and-cinder streets in first gear.

When the morning mist clears, I look out the window down the river and across the tracks at the motto painted on the side of the tallest building in Harlan: **work, think, buy coal.**

Hazy Sunday morning sunlight gilds the artificial limbs displayed in a window next to the hotel. Up the street, several windows are piled high with boots and shoes beyond repair. In a pawn shop window: little black-muzzled, pearl-handled revolvers lie on fuchsia satin cushions.

Just outside Harlan where the highway curves into the mountains, a wooden bridge with steel cable and beam supports reaches over into one of the coal camps. I pause to watch two women far down the wide, dry riverbed cross to the opposite bank and disappear on the dirt road among Indian cigar trees. They carry, slung over their shoulders, filled tow-sacks, and wear clothes of another decade that come, likely, from far back in Louisville clothes closets — perhaps my wife's.

As I start on across, I see a blonde girl walking toward me on the bridge which sways as we move. A carton of empty Royal Crown bottles in one hand, her little brother's hand in the other, she has a stately stride. Maybe the shift she wears means she's pregnant, but maybe it's just what came to her from the Bluegrass plains. The bridge was mended after the flood, and the new pine smells good, and she feels it through her pink thong sandals. She has a gaze you can't meet and hold long. If she's pregnant, it's to her advantage not to be married; the government will support her in a fashion no husband here could match.

I look over the bridge railing to see if there is at least a trickle of water. There is, but I also see a man in a blue ballcap, a faded orange shirt and torn jeans, squatting in the riverbed, rooting with a mattock in the loose dirt, two large lard buckets by his side, full of small pieces of gray shale coal. Nearby, five barefoot boys dig — one with a lid, another with a piece of wood shaped by raging water, another with a tin sand shovel decorated with puppy dogs that are peeling off the handle. I am about to offer the man my last dollar to buy some coal. But I trust the intuition that makes me suspect my impulse. Instead, I go down.

One of his eyes, he tells me, is buried under tons of coal dust in a mine shaft. Later, when he lifts the buckets, he will limp. As he sifts for grains of coal, I look up and see the two women climb the steps to one of the houses high on the hill, their sacks full. He talks about Detroit, Chicago, Louisville, and President Kennedy. He doesn't want a lot of money, he tells me; he can do without the worries that hound a rich man. True, he has worries of his own, but if he could just get a little work — mining, preferably — he'd be content.

The boys are dirty; their noses and their sores run. One of them reminds me of pictures of children liberated from Dachau, but another, the littlest, is chubby. With a fixed, sullen, fearful gaze, he seems to thread me and, turning the wooden spade in his hand toward his chest, to reel me in.

There are easier methods for mining coal than the one this man uses. If you venture up steep dirt roads cut by bulldozers, you may watch massive auger rigs bore seventy feet into a mountainside. They start at the top and work their way down, boring holes five feet wide, three feet apart. It is partly because of the augers that I meet this miner in the dry bed of a river that flooded Harlan last spring.

I leave the miner and climb up to the road and into the coal camp.

Five boys walk out of a store that looked abandoned; the camp has a ghost-town look. Standing in the dirt road as the noon sun stokes up, I listen to the boys, who tell me that they have no desire to leave the camp. They've tried. Several have quit school and gone to work tobacco in the Bluegrass. They all like Harlan. But the camp is not as it used to be.

"More to do in the old days. See that other camp down along the river? Every Saturday night boys used to come roaring out of there and set fire to deserted houses up here. They set *that* one afire. Then we'd sneak down and tear up one of theirs. Cops down here *all* the time. Beat you up a little and toss you in jail, then let you out in time to make it to school Monday morning.... The teachers? They're okay. It ain't easy on them. I hated school, but I wish I didn't quit."

One of the boys walks on with me, and as we stand on a narrow swinging bridge that reaches over to his house, he tells me why he's going back to high school. Near Hazard, between Hindman and Mousie, in the little village of Pippa Passes, is a two-year college called Alice Lloyd, named after its founder, a Boston lady who came into the region on a mule a few years ahead of the railroad. Tuition is about forty dollars a year, and many of the students' parents are on relief. Each student has some job of work to do around the college, and each pledges to return to the region once he's become a professional, and contribute to building it up. The girls wear white uniforms with red ties and the boys attend classes in ties and coats. Fraternization between boys and girls is discouraged. The campus resembles a converted mountain resort. But most of the buildings were constructed by the students themselves. Divided by a creek and a dirt road, they cling to the steep mountainsides. Unfortunately, if you don't live within a fifty-mile radius, you can't send your children to Alice Lloyd.

The boy goes on over the swinging bridge and I walk along the river. Along a stretch of road by the railroad track across the river, cars brought back from Detroit, Chicago, and Louisville, behind in payments, are parked under willow trees.

Wrecked cars lie in the river where they crash, until spring floods transport them downstream. A woman steps out onto her back porch which overhangs the river bed and dumps her garbage and slop jar. Was she surprised one morning after a flash flood to find the early light winking at her from the spidery cracked windows of the Chevrolet, whose raised hood points at her now, like the beak of some fantastic bird? From the branches of thin brown trees, that in summer congest the banks with green, hang shreds of red cloth like distress signals.

I have not seen many churches here. But I see one now, across the road. A middle-aged man sits on the fender of his green pickup truck. I cross over and talk with him. The congregation, he tells me, consists mostly of old folks, a sprinkling of babies, and some teen-age boys and girls who can't sit still. This man is waiting for church to let out, so he can take his wife home.

I sit on the other fender, and as we lean toward each other over the hood, he tells me a story. There was a girl from around here who went to a faith-healing tent revival. She had no ailments, but while everyone was singing, she got drawn into the excitement. She went down on the ground with the others, mostly women. When the preacher asked her to get up and testify and she opened her mouth, out came a song — "Power in the Blood." But she couldn't speak a word. Soon, the congregation realized she'd been made speechless by a vision. Forsaking father and mother, and still singing, she took the guitar somebody handed her and walked out of the tent and began to climb the highway into the mountains.

For forty days, on into winter, she wandered over eastern Kentucky on foot, singing. Drivers of coal trucks came back telling of seeing or hearing about her in Roxana, Blackey, Neon, Cody, Vicco, Wayland, Quicksand, Dwarf, Cumberland, Marrowbone, Majestic, Lovely, Drift. When the spirit moved her, no matter where she happened to be, she sang. She had been called on a singing ministry for Jesus.

Then one morning, she showed up at the kitchen door, and when she woke up the next day, she was the same girl who had entered the tent forty days before. She can talk fine, but she hardly ever sings.

As if on cue, the people inside the church began to sing, "Just As I Am."

Just outside town, I hit the railroad track again. I come to a break in the shimmering trees that stand between the road and the tracks. Three hundred feet away, two gigantic coal trucks are parked nose to nose in front of a small brown house and a massive willow tree. A woman in her thirties, wearing a flowered housedress, stands beside one of the trucks, talking to the man inside. Through the window above her head, she hands him his supper in a paper sack. Holding onto the door handle with one hand, she smooths back her long brown hair with the other, then lifts her foot up to the high running board and leans in, and the man's arm reaches around her shoulder.

As I drive my car away from the front of the railroad hotel, I see the coal truck coming and let it go ahead. Then I follow it on out of town.

A slag-heap fire smolders on one side of the highway, and on the other, wooden structures resembling scaffoldings, with vivid yellow lights burning, stand black against the red evening sun. The truck driver pulls over and waits. I go on.

Not far outside Harlan, large-leaved kadziu vines cover the entire landscape and transform the trees from which they hang into a frieze of reptiles, rising out of primeval slime along the undulating horizon against the red sky. With the first heat of the morning sun they will emerge out of a blue mist that tastes of coal fumes, mingled in this season of forest fires with the odor of scorched earth and smoldering wood, living and dead. The tree-smothering kadziu vines are the last green to go.

"the singer": *a short story*

Thank you, Reverend Bullard. Your introduction was exaggerated, of course, but I won't say it made me mad. Ladies and gentlemen, I want to say first what splendid work your church has been doing. And I'm speaking now not as a man but as a citizen and a Christian. As the reverend was saying, the church must play a role in the important issues of this changing world of ours. Now don't anybody go away and tell it on me that Pete Simpkins talked here tonight like some radical. Politics is one thing, and the hard facts of social life is another. You can't legislate morality. But now you *can* educate people about the facts of their state government and where it's not doing right by the people. So "Christian Program on Politics" is a good, 100 per cent American name for what you're doing in this election year. Now with the ward your church is in, I don't have to guess how most of you folks have voted for the last half-century, but tonight I just want to *show* you some of the mistruths that the present administration is forsting upon the people, and you can vote accordingly. Because this movie I'm going to show you — which I was in on making — is to show you the truth, instead of what you read in the papers, about how they're wiping out poverty in eastern Kentucky.

You know, in spring, when the floods aren't raging, in summer when they ain't a drought, and in the fall, when the mountain slopes aren't ablaze, eastern Kentucky is beautiful. In the winter, though, I don't hesitate to call it a nightmare landscape: nature hides herself under a mossy rock and you see the human landscape come into focus, especially in *this* winter's record cold and hunger. We took these movies all this summer and fall, off and on, up the narrow valleys, creeks, and hollers of the counties of eastern Kentucky: McCreary, Owsley, Bell, Breathitt, Perry, Pike, Laurel, Lee, Leslie, Letcher, Clay, Harlan, Knott, Floyd, and let's see, Magoffin, Martin, Whitley, and Wolfe.

So let me show you what we saw in eastern Kentucky. Now, you understand, we're in the early stages of working on this movie. We got a lot of work and a heap of fund-raising ahead of us yet, before we can get it in shape to release to the general public on TV and at rallies where it can do the damage. So, Fred, if you're ready to roll....

Wayne, you want to get up here with me, so if there's any questions I can't answer, maybe you can? Come on up. You had more to do with this project than I did. As the reverend told you, ladies and gentlemen, Wayne was our advance man. We sent him ahead to prepare the people for the cameras — set things up. I got my poop sheets laying on the pulpit here, Wayne, else I'd let you see how it feels to stand in the preacher's shoes.

You're doing fine, Pete.

Then let's start, Fred.... Ha! Can you all see through me okay? Those numbers show up awful clear on my shirt. I better scoot off to the side a little. Now, soon's those numbers stop flashing, you'll see what the whole national uproar is about. People better quit claiming credit before it's due, just because they're trying to win an election.

Now these washed-out shoulders you can blame on the Department of Highways and Politics. Coming down the steep mountainsides, you have to swerve to miss holes that look to been made by hand grenades, and then around the curve you try to miss the big trucks. Hard freezes, sudden thaws, and coal-truck traffic too heavy for the roads they travel can tear up a cheap narrow road. But if the administration kept its promises to maintain certain standards of construction....

Folks, that's not an Indian mound, that's a slag heap. Something else that greets you around every curve: slate dumps from shut-down mines and sawdust piles from abandoned woodpecker mills, smoldering, thousands of them, smoldering for ten years or more. The fumes from these dumps'll peel the paint off your house. A haze always hangs over the towns and the taste of coal is in the air you breathe. That smell goes away with you in your clothes.

Good shot of one of those gas stations from the thirties. Remember those tall, skinny, old-timey orange pumps with the glass domes? This station was lived in for about twenty-five years before it was abandoned. They don't demolish anything around there. Plenty of room to build somewhere else. Look at that place. You know, traveling in eastern Kentucky makes you feel you're back in the thirties. Ah! Now this is a little ghost town called Blackey.

I think this is Decoy, Pete.

Decoy. And I mean, there's not a soul lives there. But plenty of evidence a lot of them once did. You get there up fifteen miles of dirt road. Millions of dollars were mined out of there. That's the company store, there's the hospital, post office, jail, schoolhouse — turned coal camp gray, and may as well be on the dark side of the moon. See the old mattress draped over the tree limb, and all the floors — see that — covered with a foot of wavy mud that's hardened over the summer. That crust around the walls close to the ceiling marks the level of the flood that bankrupted what was left of the company. Ripped couches in the yard there, stink weeds all around, rusty stovepipes, comic books, romance magazines, one shoe in the kitchen sink, the other somewhere out in the yard under the ropes where they've hacked the swing down. Rooms full of mud daubers building nests, dead flies on the sills and half-eaten spiderwebs. And over the crusts of mud in the houses and in the yards is strowed about a bushel of old letters from boys that joined the services out of desperation or hoping for adventure, and photographs the people left behind when they fled to God knows where. So it's just out there in the middle of the wilderness, doing nothing. Decoy.

Here we are in a typical eastern Kentucky town. Harlan, wudn't it, Wayne?

Hazard.

Hard to tell them apart. Well, next time we show this thing, God willing, it'll have one of the biggest TV announcers in Louisville narrating.

See the way the slopes of the mountains kindly make a bowl around Harlan? Houses cover the hillsides — just sort of flung up there. No streets or even dirt roads leads up to some of them. Swaying staircases and crooked paths go up to those porches that hover above the road there. Go along the highway, and see washing machines and re- frigerators parked on the front porches. See high up, just below the clouds, that brown house with the long porch — just clinging to the cliffside? Houses like that all over, deserted, some of them just charred shells, the roofs caved in under tons of snow, the junk spewed out the front door.

Now *this* you see everywhere you go: old folks sitting on the front porch in half-deserted coal camps. On relief, on the dole, *been* on the dole since the war. That old man isn't near as old as he looks. Worked in the mines before they laid him off and idleness went to work on him like erosion. Wife got no teeth, no money to get fitted. Dipped snuff and swigged RC's to kill the pain of a mouth full of cavities till the welfare jerked them all out for her. And there comes the little baby — right through the ripped screen door — grandchild the daughter left behind when she went to Chicago or Cincinnati or *De*troit or Baltimore, which is where they all go. Didn't they say this baby's momma had it, Wayne, just had it, so they could collect on it?

	Yeah.

And another girl, under twenty-one, had four babies and drew on *all* of them. Why, the government takes an interest in her that no husband could hope to match. Look at that baby's little tummy, swollen out there like a — Fred, you shoulda held on that one.

And this is a general view of how high the mountains are. *Way* up high.... (What *was* the point of that, Wayne?)

	(I don't know.)

See that stream? Watch.... See that big splash of garbage? Fred, did you get a good shot of that woman? *There* you go ! She just waltzed out in her bare feet and tossed that lard bucket of slop over the back banister without batting an eye.

Even the industries dump ——

Well.... And that stream — Big Sandy, I think. See how low it runs? Well, every spring it climbs those banks and pours down that woman's chimney and washes out every home along that valley. See the strips of red cloth left hanging on the branches of the trees? Like flagging a lot of freight trains. And rags and paper and plastic bleach jugs dangle from the bushes and from the driftwood that juts up out of the riverbed mud. In the summer those banks swarm with green, but don't let it fool you. See how wavy that mud is? And that little bright trickle of poisoned water. Fish *die* in that stuff, so leave your pole at home. And stay away from the wells. Lot of them polluted.

This is a trash dump on a slope high above Harlan where whole families go to root for "valuables." Look like bats clinging to a slanting wall, don't they? But if you go in among them, why, seems like it's just a Sunday family outing.

Most of the graveyards are up on a hill like this one, to escape the floods, I guess. But living on the mountains, maybe the natural way of thinking is up. Look close under that inscription : it's a photograph, sealed in glass, showing the deceased sitting in the front-porch swing with his wife, morning-glories climbing the trellis.

With that red sky behind them, those kadziu vines crawling all over the hillsides, dripping from the trees, look like big lizards rising up out of the mud. Come around a bend on a steep mountain highway and they've crept to the edge. Those kadziu vines are the last green to go.

Here we are up in the mountains again. (Who said to shoot the scenic overlooks, Wayne ?)

(Nobody. Fred loved to shoot the view, I suppose.)

(That'd be fine if this was called "Vacation in Eastern Kentucky.") Now, this part, Wayne, I don't remember at all.

> This is Cumberland. You were still asleep and Fred and I went out for coffee and passed this big crowd — Wait a minute....

Actually, folks, this is the first time I've had a chance to see the stuff. I told Fred just to throw it together for tonight. The real editing comes later.

Just a bunch of miners standing on a street corner. You might take notes on some of this stuff, Fred, stuff to cut out, and, ladies and gentlemen, I hope *you* will suggest what ——

> Good Lord, Fred!

(Watch your language, Wayne. I saw it.) Fred, I think you got some black-and-white footage accidentally mixed in. Folks, please excuse this little technical snafu, but as I say, we wanted to get this *on* the screen for you, get your reactions, and I think Fred here — Well, he's worked pretty hard and late hours, these past three weeks especially, and we only got back to Louisville a few days ago.... Ha! Ha. Fred, how much of this? ... As some of you folks may know, Fred is mute.

> Now this, ladies and gentlemen, is the girl some of you have been reading about in the *Courier*. And the other girl, the one leaning against the front of that empty pool hall, is ——

Wayne, I don't think — I'm sure these fine people aren't interested in hearing any more about *that* little incident. Listen, Fred, that machine has a speed-up on it, as I recall.

> I think he brought the old Keystone, Pete.

Oh. Well, folks, I don't know how long this part lasts, and I apologize for Fred, but we'll just have to wait till it runs out.

In the meantime, what I could do is share with you some facts I've collected from eyewitnesses and that my research staff has dug out for me. Barely see my notes in this dim light. The Cumberland Mountains are a serrated upland region that was once as pretty as the setting of that old *Trail of the Lonesome Pine* movie. It has a half-million inhabitants. But there's been about a 28 per cent decline in population of people between the ages of twenty and twenty-four, and an *increase* of about 85 per cent old people. In some counties about half the population is on relief and it's predicted that some day about 80 per cent of the whole region will be drawing commodities. There's about 25 per cent illiteracy for all practical purposes, and those that *do* get educated leave. And something that surprises me is that there's only about fifteen per cent church affiliation. All in all, I'd say the poverty is worse than Calcutta, India, and the fertility rate is about as high, seems like to me. In other words, the people are helpless and the situation is hopeless. The trouble with this administration is that they *think* a whole lot *can* be done, and then they claim credit even before they do it, to make *us* look bad. We don't make no such promises. Because we see that the facts ——

> I think a lady in the audience has her hand up, Pete.

Ma'am ... I'm sorry, that old moving-picture machine makes such a racket, you'll have to speak louder.

> Pete, I think what she asked was, "Did any of us get to talk with her?"

With who? Oh. Ma'am, that really isn't what this movie is about. We went in there with the best color film money can buy to shoot poverty, and where Fred got this cheap black and white newsreel stock ——

I think it was from that New York movie crew.

Now, Wayne, this is not the place to drag all *that* business in. We came here tonight to show what it's like to live in the welfare state where all a body's got is promises instead of bread to put on the table. *I* know. I *come* from those people. Now there *are* some legitimate cripples, caused by explosions, fires, roof-falls and methane gas poisoning in the mines, and some have been electrocuted and blinded and afflicted with miner's asthma. But a majority that's on relief are welfare malingerers who look forward to getting "sick enough to draw," and whose main ambition is to qualify for total and permanent disability. For those people, all these aids, gifts, grants, and loans are the magic key to the future, but I see it as what's undermining public morals and morale. That's the story I was hired to get, and as I remember that's the story we *got*, on those thousands of feet of expensive color film. And if ——

Well, now we're back at the heart of the matter. Here we are on Saturday in Hazard.

> Pete.

What?

> I think that's Harlan.

Wayne, I was *born* in Harlan.

> Well, Pete, there's that twelve-foot pillar of coal in the middle of the intersection, which you told us to shoot because it belonged to your childhood.

Fred's got the whole thing so fouled up, he's probably spliced Hazard and Harlan together.

> Okay....

Now the shot's *gone*. That, as you could see, folks, *was* the breadline. The monthly rations.

I guess Wayne was right, after all. Says WORK, THINK, BUY COAL, painted right across the top of the town's highest building.

Here you see a mother and her four kids standing beside the highway, waiting for her goldbricking husband to row across the river and pick her up and take the rations and the donated clothes over to the old log cabin — caulked with mud, see that, and ambushed by briars and weeds. That's their swinging bridge, dangling in the water from the flood last spring that he's too lazy to —

Now this is *really* the kind of thing we went in there to get. That's not a desert, that's a dry riverbed those two women are crossing. What they're lugging on their backs is tow-sacks full of little pieces of shale coal that — Now see that steep ridge? You can just barely make them out on the path now. See that? See that man under the bridge? A little too dark.... Get down under there, Fred. *There* we go! Squatting on the bottom of that dry riverbed with his five kids, actually rooting in the dirt for pieces of coal no bigger than a button that the floods washed down from the mountains. Whole family grubbing for coal, looking toward winter. Sunday. Bright fall morning. Church bells ringing in Harlan while we were shooting. Kids dirty. Noses and sores running. Don't that one remind you of pictures of children liberated from Auschwitz? Look at the way he stares at you. I offered to *buy* the man a truckload of coal. What he said, I won't repeat. Who's he talking to now, Wayne?

Fred.

Sure got a good close-up of him, Fred. Now, the eye that belongs in that empty socket is under tons of coal dust in some choked-up mine shaft, and when he lifts those buckets and starts to follow the women, he'll limp.

Black and white again, Fred! Now where did this suff *come* from? Who's paying for this waste?

That other movie crew, Pete, when they went back to New York, they practically gave it to Fred in exchange for a tank of gas.

(Wayne, I wouldn't be surprised if Fred put up as much as he made on the whole expedition.)

(Frankly, I think he did.)

Fred, shut off the dang picture and let the thing wind ahead by itself.

This is the old machine, Pete.

(I don't understand how he could make such a mistake. Anybody can see when they've got color and when ——)

Pete, young man in the back has his hand up.

Yes? ... Listen, son, I don't know one thing about that girl. In fact, I'd be happy to forget what little I *do* know. All three of them, in fact, and the motorsickle and the whole mess.... I'm sorry, you'll have to talk louder.... (Wayne, you should have *pre*viewed this movie!) Now, son, I don't have a thing to say about that girl.

(Well, somebody better say *some*thing, Pete. It's only human for them to be interested.)

(Then *you* tell them. You're as bad as Fred was — *is*.)

To answer your question, young man. No one has yet located the parents of the two girls.

These shots show them walking along the highway between Whitesburg and Millstone. The smoke you see is coming from one of those slag heaps Pete was telling about. It's the first light of morning before the coal trucks begin to roll. Later, on down the road, one of those trucks, going around a hairpin curve, turned over and slung coal almost two hundred feet. That's The Singer, as she was called, the one with the guitar slung over her shoulder, and there's the friend, who always walked a few steps behind, like a servant. These black and white shots were taken by the crew from New York. I don't think *they* were mentioned in the newspaper stories, though. But they crossed paths with the girls in Wheelright, Lovely, Upper Thousand Sticks, Dalna, Coal Run, Highsplint, and other towns along the way. Yes, Reverend Bullard?

What did he say?

He said no smoking on church premises, Pete.

Oh. Sorry, Reverend. Nervous habit, I guess.

Somewhere in here is a shot of the preacher who started it all. Soon after people started talking about The Singer, he described himself as God's transformer. Claimed God's electricity flowed through *him* into *her*. The day they found the girls, he put it a different way — said he was only God's impure vessel.

Ladies and gentlemen, I would like to focus your attention on a really fine shot of a rampaging brush fire that ——

Hey, Fred, I didn't know you got those girls in color!

Okay, Fred, okay, okay! Just throw the switch! Lights, somebody! Lights!

Fred, Pete said to cut the projector off!

Folks, I apologize for Fred, but I had no way of knowing. Fred, this is what I call a double cross, a real live double cross, Fred! You promised that if I'd hire you back, you'd stay away from that New York outfit and those two girls.

(Pete, aren't you doing more harm than good by just cutting the thing off?)

(This stuff don't belong in the picture.)

(Just look at their faces. They want to know all about it, they want to *see* every inch of film on that reel.)

(This ain't what I come to show.)

(She couldn't be in *all* of it. We didn't run into her that often, and neither did that New York bunch.)

(It's distracting as hell.)

(The poverty footage is *on* the reel, too, you know.)

(You *want* to tell them, don't you? *He* wants to *show* them and *you* want to tell all about it. Admit it.)

(Look, Pete, it's only natural ——)

(Yeah, like looking for a job when you're out of one. Go ahead. Tell them. If Fred wasn't a mute, he'd furnish the sound track in person.)

Folks, this is just our little joke tonight. We thought we'd experiment. You know, give you a double feature, both on the same reel.

Here, Fred got a shot of the revival tent in Blue Diamond where she first showed up about five weeks ago, early in September. That's a blown-up photograph of Reverend Daniel in front of the tent. Sun kind of bleached it out, but the one in the paper was clear.

That's the old company store at Blue Diamond and the photographs you see on the bulletin board there are of miners killed in the war. Maybe one of them was The Singer's brother.

The tent again....

The way people tell it, Reverend Daniel was preaching pretty hard, lashing out at sinners, when he suddenly walked straight to the back, pointing at a girl that he said he knew wanted to be saved because she had committed a terrible sin that lay heavy on her heart. And standing where the tent flap was pulled back, dripping rain, was this girl. Thin and blond, with the biggest eyes you ever saw.

Good footage on that wrecked car in the creek, Fred. You know, the young men go to *De*troit to work awhile, get homesick and drive some broken-down Cadillac or Buick back home and leave it where it crashed in the river or broken down in the front yard, and the floods ship it on to the next town. Hundreds of roadside scrap yards like this one where cars look like cannibals have been at them. Good panoramic shot. Fred's pictures are worth a thousand words when he's got his mind on his work.

And here's Fred shooting the mountains again. Couldn't get enough of those look-offs.

So there she stood, a little wet from walking to the tent in the rain, and Reverend Daniel led her up front, and pretty soon he began to heal the afflicted. They say he was great that night. Had them all down on the ground. He laid hands on them, and there was speaking in tongues, and those who weren't on the ground were singing or doing a sort of dance-like walk they do. And when it was all over, he went among them with his portable microphone and asked them to testify.

Then he came to *her*. And instead of talking, she began to sing. A man that lived nearby was sitting on his porch, and he said he thought it was the angels, coming ahead of Gabriel.

She sang "Power in the Blood" for an hour, and when she stopped, Reverend Bullard — excuse me — Reverend *Daniel* asked her what she suffered from. And when she didn't speak, he said he bet it was rheumatic fever, and when she still didn't speak ——

Moving on now, we see a typical country schoolhouse. In the middle of the wilderness, a deserted schoolhouse is not just an eyesore, it's part of the country. When people live on the front porch, relics of the past are always in view, reminding them of times that's gone: the era of the feuds, of the timber industry, of the coming of the railroad, of the moonshine wars, and of the boom and bust days of coal.

Ha! Fooled you, didn't I? Thought it was deserted. Ha. There's the teacher in her overcoat, and the kids all bundled up in what little clothes they have. See that one girl with rags wrapped around her legs in place of boots? That's the reason: gaps between the boards a foot wide. And believe me, it gets cold in those mountains. Now what's the administration going to say to the voters about *that* when they go to the polls in November? They claim they're *improving* conditions.

From the highway, you don't often see the scars in the earth from strip mines and the black holes where the augers have bored. I suppose those New York boys are trying here to give you an impression of the landscape The Singer wandered over. On the highways, you may pass a truck hauling big augers, but to watch the auger rig boring, you have to climb steep dirt roads. That's where The Singer and her friend seem to be going now — not on purpose, I don't think. Just aimlessly wandering, those New York boys following close behind with their black and white. Now, who's *that* girl? Oh, yeah, the one that starred

in *their* movie. What was her name? Deirdre....
Back to The Singer again. Going on up the
winding road, and those black eyes staring at you
out of that far hillside — auger holes seven feet
in diameter. The dust those trucks stir up barreling
down the mountain is from spoil banks that get
powder-dry in the summer and it sifts down, along
with coal grit, onto the little corn and alfalfa and
clover that still grows in the worn-out land. With
its trees cut down by the stripping operation, its
insides ripped out by the augers, this mountain is
like some mangy carcass, spewing out fumes that
poison the air and the streams.

Where these augers and the strip mining have
been, snows, rains, floods, freezes, and thaws
cause sheet erosion, and rocks big as tanks shoot
down on people's cabins. This used to be rich
bottomland. Now it's weeds, broomsedge, and
thickets. Don't look for an old bull-tongue plow
on *those* hillsides. And the big trees are gone.

Of course, the blight got the chestnuts, but what
do you call *this*?

Wayne, let's keep in mind the money that helped make this
movie possible.

Well, this, friends, was once called Eden. Some
people have reason to call it dark and bloody
ground. There's places that look like the petrified
forest, places like the painted desert, but it's a
wasteland, whatever you call it, and the descend-
ants of the mountaineers are trespassers on
company property that their fathers sold for a jug,
ignorant as a common Indian of its long-term
value. And they can't look to the unions any more.
The UMWA has all but abandoned them, some
say, while the bulldozers that made that road and
which drag that auger apparatus into place for

another boring every hour continue what some people call the rape of the Appalachians.... I'm sorry, I didn't hear the question?

Young lady wants to know what happened next.

Next? Oh. You mean about The Singer? Oh, yes. Well, the story, which we got piece by piece, has it that when the girl didn't speak, Reverend Daniel got a little scared and looked around for someone that knew her.

In the entrance to the tent, where The Singer had stood, was another girl: black-haired, sort of stocky, just a little cross-eyed, if you remember the picture, but pretty enough to attract more men than was good for her. She didn't know The Singer but was staring at her in a strange way, and several boys in leather jackets were trying to get her to come away from the tent and go off with them.

Now this is a shot of the girls drinking from a spring that gushes out of the mountain with enough force to knock a man down. Her friend sees the cameraman and steps behind The Singer to block her from the camera. Those New York boys would barge right in without blinking an eye.

Well, Reverend Daniel did find someone who knew her and who said there was absolutely nothing wrong with her, physically or mentally, that when she saw her the day before The Singer was just fine. That made everybody look at Reverend Daniel a little worried, and he turned pale, but an old, old woman began to do that dance and speak in tongues and when she calmed down she said *she* knew what had come over the girl. Said she had what they call ——

Now here we see the Negro section of Harlan. Notice ——

> Just a second, Pete.

> The old lady said that the girl had got a *calling*, to sing for Jesus. And The Singer began to sing again, and the girl that travels with Reverend Daniel *gave* The Singer her guitar, said, "Take it, keep it, use it to sing for Jesus." Then *she* took up the tambourine, the whole tent began to shake with singing, The Singer's voice soaring above it all, and listen, ladies and gentlemen, before that night nobody in that area knew a thing about her singing.

You pass this condemned swimming pool and that grave-yard of school buses and go over a concrete-railing bridge that humps in the middle and there you are in the Negro slums. The cement street turns into a dirt road a country block long, and the houses are identical, and the ones that haven't turned brown are still company green. See, the street is just a narrow strip between that hill and the river that floods the houses every year. At each end, wild bushes reach up to the tree line. At the back steps, a steep hill starts up. There's no blackness like midnight dark in the Cumberland Mountains, but the white man can walk this street safely. No one wants to discourage him from buying the white lightnin' and the black women. And here we are inside the dance hall where the Negroes are having a stomping Saturday night good time. Awful dim, but if you strain a little....

> Want to let me finish, Pete?

> Then The Singer walked out of the tent and they followed her up the highway, but she kept walking, higher and higher into the mountains, and the people kept falling back, until only one person walked behind her — that black-haired girl with the slightly crossed eyes.

You through?

Sure, go ahead.

(They just *missed* the greatest shot in the whole movie.)

(They saw it, Pete.)

(The hell. They were listening to *you*, 'stead of looking at the *move*-ee. For an Ohio Yankee you sure act like you know it all. Now when *my* part is on, *you* shut up.)

(Fair enough, Pete.)

More of the black and white.... Shots of The Singer at a coal tipple near Paintsville. Truck mine. No railroad up this branch, so they just pop-shoot it with dynamite and truck it out.

Anyway, what would happen was that The Singer and the other girl would walk along and whenever and *wherever* the spirit moved her, The Singer would sing. Just sing, though. She couldn't, wouldn't, anyway *didn't* speak a word. Only sing. And while she sang, she never sat down or leaned against anything. Hardly any expression on her face. Sometimes she seemed to be in a trance, sometimes a look on her face like she was trying to hide pain, sometimes a flicker of a smile, but what got you in a funny way was that the song hardly ever called for the little things she did, except the happy songs, "I Love to Tell the Story," or "Just As I Am," you know — those she'd plunge into with a smile at first, until she would be laughing almost hysterically in a way that made you want to hug her, but, of course, nobody, not even the kind of women that'll take hold of a sweating girl full of the Holy Ghost and drench her with tears, really dared to. No, not The Singer. She wasn't touched, that I know of, though people sort of reached for her as she passed. But then sometimes you'd feel that distance between you and her and next thing you knew she'd be so close in among people you could smell her breath, like cinnamon. She had ways of knocking you off balance, but so you only fell deeper into her song. Like she'd be staring into your eyes, and her lids would drop on a note that was going right through you. Or coming out of a pause between verses, she'd suddenly take three steps toward you.

They walked, they never rode. They walked thousands of miles through those hills, aimlessly: through Sharondale, Vicco, Kingdom Come, Cumberland Gap, Cody, along Hell-for-Certain Creek, and up through Pine Mountain.

And here we are in a jailhouse in Manchester. Handle a lot of coal around there. And these boys you see looking through the bars are teenagers the sheriff rounded up the night before. Out roving the highways in these old cars, shooting up road signs. They loved having their picture taken — a mob of little Jesse Jameses.

Now, I ask you: can the administration just *give* these youngsters jobs?

Winding road ... coiled up like a rattlesnake. See where those boys — watch for fallen rock. Just shot it all to pieces. Most of them will end up in the penitentiary *making* road signs.

Now in this shot — in Hellier, I think — The Singer has wandered into a church and they've followed her. And off to the side there, among the parked cars and pickup trucks, you can see the other girl, leaning against the door of a car, talking to some men and boys. Can't see them for the car. There. See them? Talking to her? Well, that's the way it was, after awhile.

A boy told one of the young men on the New York crew that he was outside the tent at Blue Diamond that first night, and that the black-haired girl was going from car to car where the men were waiting for their wives to come out of the revival tent and the young boys were waiting for the girls to come out. But *this* girl never made it *in*. They always waited for her outside, and she went with all of them. And then — I don't know who or where I got it — the girl heard the singing and left the cab of a coal truck and went to the entrance of the tent, and then when The Singer went out to the highway, she followed her. Then after about a week —

Oh. Go ahead, Pete.

Folks, here we are, back on the track, with a shot we were afraid wouldn't come out. Good job, Fred. A carload of pickets waiting to join a caravan. Eight young men in that car, all of them armed. You can hear them at night, prowling up and down the highways in long caravans, waking you up, and if you look between the sill and the shade by your bed, you can see lights flashing against Black Mountain under the cold sky, full of stars.

And here we are swinging down the mountainside.... Some of the early September shots before this record cold drove people indoors. We just suddenly, in the bright morning sunlight, came upon this train, derailed in the night by dynamite. Don't it look like an exhibit out in that big open space, all those crowded porches huddled around on the bare hillside?

Going along the highway, you can expect to find anything in the yards, even in front of inhabited houses. See that car? Pulled up by a block and tackle tossed over a tree limb — looks like an old-time lynching. This man's taken the junk that the floods leave on his porch — sometimes on his roof — and arranged a *dis*play of it all in his yard.

You look up and see those long porches, hanging over the road, seems like, clinging to the steep slopes, and what it reminds *me* of is little villages in Europe when I was in the army. Whole family sitting out there, on the railing, on car seats jerked out of wrecks on the highway, on cane-bottom chairs salvaged from their cabin home places far in the mountains, talking and swirling RC's and watching the road. For *what*?

Well, for *her*, wouldn't you say, Pete? Word of her singing ran ahead of her, and since nobody knew where she'd turn up next.... One time she even walked right into a congregation of snake handlers and started singing. But not even that brazen New York crew got any shots of *that*. And sometimes she'd walk right out of the wildest woods, the other girl a little behind, both of them covered with briars and streaked with mud.

Here — somewhere along the Poor Fork of the Cumberland River — Fred seems to be trying to give an impression of the road, the winding high-way The Singer walked. Pretty fall leaves stripped from the branches now. Abandoned coal tipples, bins, chutes, ramps, sheds, clinging to the bare hillsides like wild animals flayed and nailed to an old door. Those stagnant yellow ponds where the rain collects breed mosquitoes and flies the way the abandoned towns and the garbage on the hillsides breed rats. You may leave this region, but the pictures of it stick in your mind like cave drawings.

Here you see The Singer and her friend walking along one of those mountain roads again. Too bad those New York boys couldn't afford color. A light morning rain has melted most of the snow that fell the night before. This is along Trouble-some Creek and they've already been through Cutshin, Diablock, Meta, Quicksand, Jeff, and Carbon Glow, Lynch, and Mayking. By the way, the reason the girls are dressed that way — style of the thirties — is because they're wearing donated clothes. Remember the appeal that came over television and filled the fire stations with clothes after last spring's flood?

These artificial legs were displayed in a window near our *ho*tel next to the railroad depot in Harlan. Nice, hazy Sunday morning sunlight, but *that*, and this shot of a pawn-shop window — little black pearl-handled revolvers on pretty little satin cushions — reminds you of what kind of life these people have in the welfare state. And those windows piled high with boots and shoes beyond repair are something else you see at rest on Sunday in Harlan.

There they are in front of a movie theater — What's that showing? Oh, yeah, an old Durango Kid movie. Fred and I saw that in another town — Prestonsburg, I think. Never forget the time she walked into a movie theater and started to sing right in the middle of a showdown in some cowboy shoot-out, and one big lummox started throwing popcorn at her till the singing reached him and he just left his hand stuffed in the bag like it was a bear trap.

Anyway, as I was telling before, the other girl, after about a week, took to luring the men away from The Singer because they began to follow her and bother her and try to start something with her, so the friend had to distract them from her, and ended up doing the very thing she had tried to stop herself from doing by going with The Singer. They say The Singer never seemed to know what was going on. She'd walk on up the highway or on out of town and the other girl would catch up.

See how they just nail their political posters to the nearest tree? Sun sure bleached that man out, didn't it?

Here, Fred got a shot of the New York movie crew getting out of their station wagon. Three young men and a girl. Looks like somebody scraped the bottom of a barrel full of Beatniks, doesn't it? The local boys and men kept teasing them about their beards and they tried to laugh along, but finally they would get into fights, and we'd come into a town just after they had gone, with the police trying to get people out of the street, or the highway patrol escorting the crew into the next county. They came down to shoot what they called an art movie. They told Fred the story once and I listened in, but I can't remember a thing about it, except that this girl named Deirdre was going to be in it. She *was* in it. Yeah, this is one of the scenes! Shot her *in front of* a lot of things, and she would kind of sway and dip around among some local people — just like that — and everybody — Yeah, see the big grins on their faces? And the director kept begging them to look serious, look serious.

That one's *yours*, Pete.

Shots of old men in front of the courthouse.... Young boys, too.... No work. Bullet holes around the door from the thirties. Bad time, bad time.

What those guys did, Wayne, was make everybody mad, so that when *we* came rolling into town, they were ready to shoot anybody that even *looked* like he wanted to pull out a camera.

Yeah. Always pointing those loaded cameras at things and running around half-cocked, shoot, shoot, shooting.

Then they ran into The Singer and her friend, and — Yeah, this is the one, this is actually the *first* shot they took of The Singer. First, this is a close-up of *their* girl — Deirdre — you're looking at, long stringy hair, soulful eyes. One time they even put something *in* her eyes to make the tears run. And in just a second they'll swing to catch The Singer. That's it! See the camera jerk? The script writer saw The Singer on the opposite corner and jerked the cameraman around. Here you can see The Singer's friend standing off to the side, on the lookout for trouble-makers — front of a little café in Frenchberg. Cameraman got her in the picture by accident, but later when the director caught on to what she was *doing* with The Singer, he hounded her to death. Made her very angry a couple of times. Deirdre in *his* movie though —

Pete....

What's you want?

Your part's on.

Well ... that's as you can see — the garbage in the streams there — kids with rickets — brush fire in the mountains....

I was about to say about the folk singer from Greenwich Village — Deirdre — she got very angry too, over the way the movie boys took after The Singer, so she threatened to get a bus back to New York. But after they had listened to people tell about The Singer in the towns they came into, not long after she had gone on, and after they had tracked her down a few times, and after Deirdre had heard her sing, she got so she tried to *follow* The Singer. Deirdre ran away from the movie boys once, and when they caught up with her the black-haired girl was trying to fight off some local boys who thought Deirdre was like *her*. But she wasn't. Not after The Singer got to her, anyway. I don't know *what* Deirdre was like in New York, but in the Cumberland Mountains she heard one song too many. I never saw her after she changed, either. Finally, the New York boys had to lock her in a room at the Phoenix Hotel in Salyersville and one stayed behind to watch over her. Wish we had a shot of that hotel. White, a century old, or more, three stories in front, four in back, little creek running behind it. Three porches along the front. Sit in a broken chair and watch the people go by below. If you're foolish, you sit on the rail. If you leave the windows open in the room at the back, you wake up covered with dew and everything you touch is damp.

Pete.

Shots of another abandoned shack....

Go ahead, Pete.

They can see it okay. Same old thing....

Oh. Now *that's* Reverend Daniel, the one that ministered to The Singer in Blue Diamond. He'd moved his tent to Pikeville and that's where we saw him, and got these shots of his meeting. Promised him a stained-glass window for his tent if he'd let us, didn't we, Wayne? Ha! Anyway, next time we saw him was a week ago, just before the accident, and he told me how he had offered to make The Singer rich if she would sing here in Louisville. Told her people all over Kentucky would read about the wandering singer for Jesus, and that he could make her famous all over the world, and they could build the biggest church in the country, and stuff like that. She just looked at him and walked on. He pestered her awhile, but finally gave up after about six miles of walking. Wayne, you saw him after it happened, didn't you?

Yeah. He blames himself. Thinks he should have looked after her. As though God meant him to be not just a transformer but a guardian angel, too. He'll never put up another tent as long as he lives.

And that girl — Deirdre — that come down from New York, she could be dead, for all we know. The boy that was guarding her ——

> Said he shouldn't have told her about what happened on the highway.

Slipped out of the Phoenix *Ho*tel somehow and vanished.

> She *may* turn up in New York.

And she might turn up alongside some highway in the mountains, too.

> This is one of Fred's few shots of the girls. He hated to disturb them. Actually, The Singer never paid any attention to us or to the other crew, did she, Pete? Mostly, Fred listened to her sing, standing in the crowds in Royalton, Hardburley, Coalville, Chevrolet, Lothair, his camera in his case, snapped shut. Right, Fred? But here, while they sat on a swinging bridge, eating — well, the friend eating, because nobody every saw The Singer put a bite of food in her mouth, just drink at the mountain springs — Fred got them with his telephoto lens from up on one of those look-offs beside the road.

Kind of grainy and the color's a little blurred, but it looks like it's from a long way off through a fine blue mist at about twilight. Nice shot, Fred.

There's those numbers again. What about that? Fred, you want to catch that thing — film flapping that way gets on my nerves.

> Personally, I'm glad nobody's got the *end* on film.

Know what you mean, Wayne.

> What the papers didn't tell was ——

That the boy on the motorsickle ...?

> Wasn't *looking* for the girls.

And he wasn't a member of some wild California gang crossing the country, either.

> Go ahead and tell them, Pete.

That's okay. You tell it, Wayne.

> The way Fred got the story — Fred, this is one time when I really wish you could speak for *yourself*. Fred was the one who kept his arms around the boy till he stopped crying.

Tell them where it happened, Wayne.

> Outside Dwarf on Highway 82. The girls were walking along in the middle of the highway at about three o'clock in the morning and a thin sheet of ice was forming, and this motorcycle came down the curve, and if he hadn't slammed on his brakes ——

More or less as a reflex ——

> It wouldn't have swerved and hit them.

You see, Fred had set out to catch up with them. Me and Wayne'd left him to come on back to Louisville alone, because he said he was going to stop off a day or two to visit his cousin in Dwarf, and when he pulled in for coffee at Hindman and some truck driver told him he *thought* he had seen the girls walking, out in the middle of nowhere, Fred got worried, it being so cold, and ——

> So he tried to catch up with them.

> The girls and the boy were lying in the road.

Kid come all the way from Halifax, Nova Scotia.

> Yeah, that's where they got the facts wrong in
> the paper. Saying he was some local hoodlum,
> then switching to the claim that he was with a
> gang from California. The fact is that the boy had
> quit school and bought a brand-new black
> Honda, and he had set out to see the United
> States.

Wait a second, Wayne. Fred's trying to hand you a note.

> Thanks, Fred. Oh. Ladies and gentlemen, Fred
> says here that it wasn't *Halifax*, Nova Scotia. He
> says, "It was *Glasgow*, Nova Scotia. Not that it
> matters a damn."

the virgin spring:

anatomy of a mythic image

Ingmar Bergman took a medieval ballad narrating a legend and transformed it into a film expressing a myth. Ulla Isaksson's script is faithful to the thirty-four stanzas of the ballad, retaining its cruelty, beauty, and simple Christian message, but overreaches the limits of legend into the realm of myth. Perhaps the motive for making *The Virgin Spring* was religious in some sense, but the effect is a supreme aesthetic metaphor in the mythic mode. Isaksson and Bergman have not simply reconceived intellectually the raw materials of the folk song. Their unifying vision has created an organic whole whose mythic anatomy I wish to feel out as though it were Braille.

To the early Greeks *mythos* meant "the thing spoken," usually during a religious ceremony; the speaker's words described an event which was simultaneously being enacted; thus, the word and its image were a single experience. A myth contains mythic characters, moments, objects, and symbols; is composed of a chronological series of interdependent activities, which have a unitary character, marked by a lucidly perceived beginning, middle, and end; a clearly defined time span, spatial scope, and social compass; a single formula or thema (a series of thematic patterns), which is more interesting if complex. "The forces that are responsible for the course of mythic events are always psychic forces, and the representation is always concrete and sensible (not conceptual). The thema that a myth exemplifies, however, is abstract (a virtual universal); it is a condensation, a compression of particulars" (Henry A. Murry, *Myth and Mythmaking*).

But images and narrative events in films have a reality that cannot be subordinated successfully to an attempt at abstraction. Karin's white horse may be one of several symbols of her virginity, but the nature of film forces us to experience horseness in a context of reality first. While Bergman never departs from this basic realism of films, he achieves transcendence in the creation of mythic image-gestures whose cumulative force, generated by conceptual and sensory energies, transmits the total mythic image.

The proliferation of realistic particulars rigidly conforms to the mythic thrust; Bergman makes these images repeat again and again, in a complex pattern, the basic simplicities of the mythic image. If Resnais, in *Hiroshima, Mon Amour*, creates myth by an intricate technique that fragments the conventional narrative frame while unifying the essence of the experience, Bergman's technique creates myth within the conventional frame. We may contemplate this mythic anatomy in terms of its most forceful gestures.

Three focal narrative-thematic gestures, each of which is of approximately the same duration, express the Virgin Spring myth: i] **The Offering.** ii] **The Violation.** iii] **Vengeance** and **Reconciliation.** Literally, Karin, the Virgin, sets out to church with an offering of Maria candles; three herdsmen violate her; Karin's father slays the herdsmen; then, as penance for vengeance, he promises God he will build a church in the clearing where Karin was slain; as a sign of His acceptance of this offering, God makes a spring well up where Karin's head fell. Symbolically, Karin is the offering; man is violated; vengeance expresses man's outrage, and reconciliation is God's grace. Many offerings are made; many violations occur; but there is only one act of vengeance and reconciliation, toward which the first two gestures extend. Each of the film's images is a direct or indirect equivalent of one or more of the three basic narrative-thematic gestures, and their components, which reveal the myth. Here is an iconical representation of the major gestures and their components, with their focal image-gestures:

I. OFFERING

1 FIRE Ingeri, the dark sister, prays to Odin
2 PRAYER Tore and Mareta, the Virgin's father and mother, pray to Christ | Mareta mortifies her flesh
3 FOOD They eat the morning meal | Ingeri curses Karin's bread

4 DRESS RITUAL   Karin wakes, rises, dresses for the journey | Her relations with mother and father are shown

5 OFFERING-KARIN   Fair and Dark Sisters set out on horses to church with candles | They encounter Simon

II. VIOLATION

1 SEX-ANIMAL   At the bridge, between the farms and the forest, the sisters part | Ingeri encounters the old pagan

2 EVIL   The three herdsmen see Karin, entice her into the clearing

3 VIOLATION   After fun and games comes the breaking of the cursed bread

4 VISION   Ingeri beholds the rape, robbery, and slaying of the Virgin by the three herdsmen | Snow falls

III. VENGEANCE-RECONCILIATION

1 KARIN'S PRESENCE   The three herdsmen appear at the manor gate | Food and shelter are offered, accepted | The beggar terrifies the boy

2 KARIN'S PRESENCE   The Virgin's mother and father argue in their bedroom | The boy screams | The thin slayer offers to sell the Virgin's garments to the mother

3 VENGEANCE PREPARATION   The mother shows the Virgin's dress to the father | The father prepares himself for vengeance | He uproots the birch tree

4 PURIFICATION-VENGEANCE   The father performs a purification ritual in the bathhouse, assisted by Ingeri | The father slays the herdsmen

5 WATER-CHURCH   Father, mother, Ingeri, and farm folk journey to the scene of the violation | Father prays for forgiveness, makes vow | The Virgin Spring appears

As we watch these elements being developed almost simultaneously, we experience the transformation of habit into ritual, flesh into word, reality into myth.

I-1 FIRE: This Friday in May begins, between four and five, with the sound of Ingeri's breath, blowing the embers on the manor hall hearth into flame, and we see her "evil" face, lit by the flames. Having opened the vent and breathed life into the fire, she prays to Odin, the old Viking god, that her stepsister's (Karin's) breath will become extinguished. Bergman develops fire as an image-equivalent of Karin's life breath.

In I-3, seventeen-year-old, pregnant Ingeri is sent to the provision shed to prepare a food sack for Karin; in a pan, she carries embers from the hearth; as she is about to extinguish her torch, she almost sticks it into a toad; she grinds it out "triumphantly" on the floor.

In II-1, knowing that Karin will encounter evil in the forest, Ingeri, as a gesture of keeping Karin alive, blows on the embers in the old pagan's shack by the bridge. The open vent there reminds her of her morning prayer to Odin. The old man's closing of the vent foreshadows the smothering of Karin's life which begins in the next sequence.

From a clearing scorched by fire, the three herdsmen look down on Karin; in this clearing they will slay her. Karin had awakened that morning with a fever, an anticipation of her body's burning in the rape; this "fire" is beaten out with a stick.

When her slayers enter the large manor hall for warmth, the twelve-year-old herdsman is in a fever, about to faint; thus, Bergman keeps this "fire" image constant. The vent is still open, but the fire is dying. As Tore leaves the hall, he says to the herdsmen, "You can keep the fire burning tonight, it will be bitterly cold." Then the beggar whispers to the boy, "Do you see how the smoke trembles up there in the vent? As if it were moaning and frightened?"

Symbolically, he reconstructs Karin's crossing of the narrow bridge into the hell the herdsmen made for her: a chasm "vomits fire like an oven" that swallows murderers and violators. Then, sensing the boy's basic innocence, reminiscent of Karin's, the beggar soothes him.

The fire in the bathhouse, where Tore purifies himself before slaying the murderers, emits smoke suggestive of Karin's breath. Tore and the thin killer struggle in the fire, where Tore knocks out his life (repeating the action that slew Karin). Thus, the fire that Ingeri blew alive that morning burns her sister's murderer.

I-2 PRAYER: I-1 ends with Ingeri invoking Odin over the sacrificial fire: "Odin, come. I ask your service." (Not until 3 do we suspect that she has cursed Karin.) I-2 begins with Mareta's and Tore's morning prayers to Christ. Bergman contrasts Karin's parents in their manner of praying as they kneel side by side: Tore's body is relaxed, and he yawns; Mareta's is tight, sharp, tense, and she severely makes the sign of the cross. She often bullies her husband with her suffering-Christ attitude; prayer and pain for her are inseparable; she drops hot candle wax on her arm; thus she is still almost as pagan as her step-daughter, Ingeri. By openly treating Ingeri like a "thorn" and Karin like a "rose," Mareta partially provokes Ingeri into cursing Karin. Mareta dreamed last night of evil; at the bridge, Ingeri has a premonition of Karin's death. In Ingeri, Mareta's dark fantasies accompany Karin on her journey. Mareta even utters a mild analog to Ingeri's curse when she tells Karin that if she always gets her own way, the devil will be annoyed and give her boils and toothaches. Tore reinforces this mock curse when, just as Karin is leaving her room, he says playfully that he will "ride up to the mountain" with her, declare that he doesn't want to have such a naughty daughter, and have her imprisoned in the mountain for seven years.

In his morning prayer, Tore asks God to guard him and his family from harm this day. As Karin sets out.

Tore says, "The Lord Christ bless your young life." (He ignores his dark daughter, Ingeri.) The beggar sings a kind of hymn-prayer about a maiden moving into the loveliness of nature; Karin repeats the song as she rides along. The beggar's utterances are all prophetic in some way, especially when the herdsmen appear at the manor; he predicts that such a beautiful day will end in misery, speaks symbolically of Karin ("the May Queen"), and refers to the fact that goats were stolen from a farm nearby. Frida, the housekeeper, scolds him: "You haven't done anything else but harp on death and misery since you came back."

Playing fussy housewife in the clearing, Karin gaily arranges the food on a white cloth, and invites the herdsmen to sit around her. (*II*-3) As she says grace over the bread Ingeri has cursed, the tongueless herdsman points at her expensive clothes: "You (Christ) make me worthy to receive this bodily bread,/You save my soul from the eternal dead." As her slayers sit opposite him at the place of honor, Karin's usual seat, her father says the same prayer — and it frightens the killers. (*III*-1) As the herdsmen sit down, Mareta, psychically shocked, makes an unintentional movement of rejection with her hand.

Later, Frida urges the boy killer to pray; he clenches his hands as Mareta has just done; but Frida doesn't understand his fear of prayer, and when she says "the Lord is merciful," he thinks she is referring to his crime. Like her father, Karin recites her prayers ritualistically. His casual prayers during the day contrast with his passionate prayer over his dead child: "You saw it, God. You saw it!" Then he asks for forgiveness and vows to build a church as penance. In the end, Tore and Ingeri pray to the same Christian god. The tension between paganism and medieval Christianity in Sweden is dramatized in the prayers uttered throughout the film.

I-3 FOOD: Breakfast is very prolonged, with much

handling and eating of beer, milk, cheese, butter, and spiced rye bread, while the piglets suckle in the lower part of the hall. Ingeri doesn't eat; Karin is still asleep. Mareta makes a sign of the cross over her bread and eats very tiny bits. She orders Ingeri to prepare a food sack for Karin. The shed is stuffed with food. In a kind of black mass, a cannibalistic eucharist in which she defiles and eats her sister's body, Ingeri devours meat off a bone; she spits on Karin's bread; when she decides to wrap the toad inside the bun, she eats the slices of meat and the insides of the bun. When Mareta offers Karin hot beer, Karin wants Ingeri to have it; Ingeri refuses. Later, as she parts with Ingeri, Karin offers her and the old pagan her food sack; out of fear, rather than spite now, Ingeri rejects the offer. When the boy sees the food sack, he wants it immediately. The herdsmen will accept Karin's food only if she will partake of it with them. Karin is aware of the mouths eating and drinking; ironically, their ravenous hunger makes her eat voraciously. Eating her food, they eat her body.

She offers the bun to the boy out of fear; terrified, she drops it and the toad jumps out on the virginal white cloth. As Karin is slain, the boy devours the pudding Frida had sent to the priest in exchange for prayers. The boy vomits, an action anticipated in his convulsions of excitement at the obscene sounds the tongueless killer's mouth made in response to Karin's body. Later, at Tore's manor hall, the boy, watching the others drink beer and eat, is so terrified he can't eat. Mareta offers him bread and meat. He eats, vomits, screams. Innocence rejecting evil deeds, he is like Ingeri who rejected Karin's food sack at the bridge and thus her own wish for the death of Karin's body. The boy's vomit on Tore's table is Karin's devoured body. With one stroke of his arm, the thin killer sweeps this evidence of murder off the table, away from the eyes of men. The image of Karin as dead meat comes at the end when flies leave the open wounds on her back where she had been repeatedly hacked with a stick.

I-4 DRESS RITUAL: There are two major dress rituals. Karin wakes, rises, and dresses in her finest Sunday clothes (in **III-3**, after Mareta shows him Karin's blood-spotted dress, Tore puts on his Sunday clothes). Karin dresses very slowly and gracefully; the killers will disrobe her, as though flaying an animal, very quickly and efficiently; Tore, too, dresses slowly, before slaying the killers quite deliberately and skillfully. Karin carries flowers to them; Tore carries a sword.

Fifteen maidens made Karin's yellow silk shift. Her clothes help to awaken her to her body as a source of sensual delight. She preens herself eagerly in the silk shift, the blue cloak with pearl embroidery, the white stockings and blue shoes, decorated with roses. Her desire for sensuous clothes and her pleasure in gazing at and stroking her own body anticipate the herdsmen's desire and lust for both dress and body.

In **III-1**, when Tore, coming in from the cold, peels off his coat in front of the herdsmen, we are reminded of their peeling off Karin's shift. Later, as Tore lies in bed, Mareta sits on a chest, sewing a clasp on one of Karin's gowns — Bergman's brilliant way of keeping in focus the image of Karin in her dress. Then Mareta, until now dressed severely in tight clothes, goes in a loose gown to the manor hall to comfort the screaming boy. Like Karin (and Ingeri) earlier, she senses something is wrong, but when she sees the thin man rise from a crouch with a shift across his arms, she doesn't for a moment focus the image. To us, he rises as though from the body of Karin just after she stopped screaming. He says the silk shift is all that is left of his sister, the loveliest thing she owned, surely the work of nine maidens; she died last Candlemas (the day of the purification of the Virgin Mary when candles are blessed). Mareta receives the shift into her arms, suppressing her horror. To free her arms, she slings it around her neck, and bars the door, quietly. Then, she lays it across Tore's chest, as though it is her daughter's body. Tore, naked as Karin was when she woke that morning, dresses, first in his usual clothes, then in his best, which are tight. He enters the manor: on his dining table, slightly rounded as though Karin's body still filled them, are spread her clothes, as on a store counter, to lure the women to buy in the morning. This image stresses the image of eating Karin's body. Tore attacks the tongueless killer first. The climax of the dress image comes when the tongueless killer throws Karin's cloak into Tore's face.

I-5 OFFERING — KARIN: Karin sets out to take the offering of Maria candles to church; she herself becomes the offering to a *new* church. In the rape, she burns physically; the spring from her head is a spiritual manifestation of the revelatory light God offers for man's redemption and reconciliation. Bergman makes this concept visible in many images of the candles, but also extends and elaborates this offering gesture in other ways.

Mareta carries the candles into the hall and wraps them in pure white cloths to prevent their breaking. (In making hot wax from votive candles drip on her arm earlier, she offers her own body to Christ.) She orders Frida to deliver the candles to the church. Frida, knowing that the priest knows she has sinned, is frightened. Tore releases her from the mission by insisting that Karin go, for a virgin must deliver them. Along with the lovely, slender candles (Karin), Frida herself sends to Father Erik a few thick ones (herself). As in a pagan religious ceremony, Karin, the human sacrifice, is served by all (as is a Christian priest making a symbolic sacrifice): mother; father; beggar (holds her horse); Frida (packs candles in saddlebag); Ingeri (packs food); Simon (helps her onto her horse); even the old pagan (leads her horse over the narrow plank bridge). Karin is certain her errand will protect her; she tells Simon and the old pagan, and tries to impress her assailants, to whom she confesses that she overslept the Mass, and hangs her head in shame. The candles become phallic (as in pagan festivals) when the tongueless man, who was the first to rape her, stomps on them; they, like her body now, aren't worth much.

Hospitality is a form of the offering gesture. Mareta gives bread to the beggar at breakfast, ritualistically — to score another merit on God's ledger; at supper, in the presence of her daughter's killers, she repeats this gesture. Listening to the sad tale of the thin herdsman, as the tongueless man makes faces behind her back, Karin, out of pity, offers the men her food sack. Later, it is her own father who takes care of them by offering food, warmth, shelter, even work. When they set Mareta's mind at ease by assuring her that nothing seemed wrong as they passed through the forest, Frida offers the herdsmen beer: "Thank you for looking lightly on the world."

Carrying the candles, Karin moves from the light of common day into the light of the divine spirit and becomes a luminous source of revelation, particularly to Ingeri, Tore, and Mareta. That we are to regard Karin as a human offering is suggested in the scene in the old pagan's shack (temple), just after Karin has gone into the dark forest alone. Even Ingeri is horrified, especially now as she senses danger to Karin, when the old pagan offers her several dead human parts (perhaps his own) to sacrifice to Odin to gain power over man and nature.

Who is this Karin who is offered, then violated, then "sainted"? Bergman ran his greatest risk in his depiction of Karin; in his use of images that project her innocence while showing that she is not perfect, he triumphed. Karin is sometimes childish, silly, petulant, peevish, sulky, pouty. Pretending to be sick, as she does this morning, she often oversleeps the Mass. While Ingeri, ordered to wait on Karin, can't finish her breakfast, Karin wants hers in bed. Ingeri equates Karin's fever with sexual burning at the dance last night; Frida declares she is still a child who dances with and smiles at everyone. Mareta worries about Karin's dancing, for last night she dreamed of evil; but Karin, innocent of her meaning, says, "I wish I had dreams too — about great, wonderful things." If she must

ride to church with the candle offering, she insists on
riding with dignity, in her silk shift; this prideful indulgence is fatal. Tore reproaches Mareta for being tender
only with Karin; we see her try to be strict with Karin
but she cannot; nor, finally, can Tore. Karin often talks
cruelly to her mother; when Karin ignores her, Mareta,
feeling unworthy of love, scratches her arm until blood
flows. She requests a farewell kiss, but Karin only waves,
then kisses Tore.

Karin blows into her father's ear to beguile him into
letting Ingeri accompany her so she can get away from the
farm for a while; she happily tells Ingeri she may go with
her. (One may suspect that, subconsciously, she only wants
the contrast to set off her own beauty: Ingeri, pregnant,
dress unbuttoned, long hair uncombed, dirty, ragged, is
Karin's exact opposite. Rocking heavily in the saddle, a
scornful smile on her lips, Ingeri follows Karin like a dark
parody of the virgin.) The beggar follows them a short
way, singing joyfully. (His voice and Karin's and the
jew's-harp music, evoke in the film a quality of the folk
song that inspired it.) When Ingeri accuses Karin of
making love to Simon last night, Karin, panting with
anger, slaps her. But Karin worries that Ingeri may
have pregnancy pains, and when Ingeri is trying to
persuade Karin to return home, Karin is afraid she'll
cry so hard she will hurt the baby; she asks the old man to
let Ingeri rest in his shack.

Everything she encounters this beautiful May
morning delights Karin's innocent, open spirit: sun, air,
wind, birdsong, flowers, fields, trees, woods, paths,
streams. Like a child, she waves to the farmers, and they
stop working to enjoy the sight of her. Bergman creates a
rich sense of life going on in pastoral work and in nature
(both corollaries to purity of spirit) as though nothing
were happening or has happened: manure is spread from
loaded sleds, men are plowing, cattle grazing, goats roving,
their bells tinkling; the farmers sow as the virgin is cut
down. There is a sense of wood (in nature and in buildings)

throughout the film, an aura of food, milk, beer, fermentation, gestation. There is an intricate pattern of background sounds: birds, water, work noises. A sense of rebirth with pain pervades the film. Ironically, the new human life in the spring will be the dark sister's baby; this image of pregnancy prepares for the birth of the spring from Karin's head and the spiritual rebirth of the people affected by this miracle.

Karin is responding sensually to the sun as she comes round a curve in the forest path and encounters the herdsmen. Her indiscriminate ecstasy impels her to reach for the jew's-harp which the thin herdsman is playing. The deceptive gaiety of the three herdsmen, as they bow, dance, make music, beguiles her; she responds to appearances (evil sees its opportunities in the blindness of goodness). They are happy, but out of sinister expectations. She relaxes completely when they say they are brothers and pretend to be bereft of a sister. (They probably aren't brothers, but in another sense they are, and they kill their "sister.") Her innocence is further manifested in her fanciful pretenses: that she is a princess and that they are enchanted princes (she seems to be carrying on her father's earlier pretenses about imprisoning her in the mountain). Though she senses something wrong in their stares, she flirts more and more in response to their cues, as when the thin man tells her that his tongueless brother says she has a lovely throat, a nice, narrow waist, and delicate hands. As she responds provocatively with her body and her voice, we recall her narcissistic preening that morning and see how she must have flirted at the dance last night, and Karin herself slowly perceives the looming consequences of aggressive "innocence" in a world of vigilant "experience" (to use Blake's terms). Karin's charming of her scolding mother and her angry father into obedience to her whims becomes an incitement to murderous lust.

II-1 SEX-ANIMAL: The image of animal sexuality is

focused in the scene in which the old hunchbacked pagan
bridge-keeper attempts to seduce Ingeri (already pregnant
by Simon, the farmer). Worship of Odin, sex, and human
sacrifice are all concentrated in this scene. Ingeri is the
product of sexual looseness: "bastards beget bastards,"
she tells Frida, who is also sexually loose. As Simon
approaches, Ingeri rides on up the road. We need at this
point to see Karin talking normally with a man, before her
very different encounter. Simon suggests her sexuality,
mildly, when he says it would be better that she brighten
the road than languish in church. When he says she is
dressed like a bride for a groom, she impulsively puts a
flower in his shirt. He thanks her, suggestively, for last night.
(Bergman seems to want here at least a temporary ambiguity: did she go beyond flirting last night?) He strokes
her ankle. Karin strongly pushes him away. (This will not
work later with the herdsmen.) When Ingeri says she saw
Karin with Simon in the barn last night, Karin protests
that she only wanted to persuade him to take care of
Ingeri and the baby.

Bergman creates an aura of human and animal
sexuality, but most of the people in the film are animalistic
because he also wants a context of general animality to
emphasize the conflict between the animal body and the
divine spirit. Karin transcends the flesh into spirit, and in
the end Ingeri, Tore, and Mareta (in contrast to the three
herdsmen) aspire toward the spiritual. In the manor hall
itself, we see a sow with its sucklings before we see human
beings (other than Ingeri). Frida says that Ingeri is like an
animal, in her looks, habits (sleeping out all night), and
her sexual conduct. Later, trying to reach Karin, to undo
the evil she has wished upon her, Ingeri moves through the
dark forest on all fours. The grace of the virgin is constantly
contrasted with the clumsiness of the dark sister; but
just before Karin becomes all spirit, the sisters become
one as Karin, like a goat, crawls on all fours, surrounded
by the herdsmen, who are like wolves.

The animal perspective on the human situation is

suggested when Frida plays God to the innocent chicks. Later, when the herdsmen enter, the watchdog growls, and the chickens panic. The menace emanating from the herdsmen makes Karin's horse Svarten skittish. The herdsmen are wild and animal; their faces show it. They have stolen goats (as they will steal Karin's innocence); we first see the tongueless man with a kid under his head. Her declaration that she knows they stole the goats from Simon confirms them in their intention to attack her. Danger to herself makes her extend it to other, like-creatures, so that she reaches instinctively for one of the goats.

II-2 EVIL: As the three herdsmen come into view, we come directly into the presence of evil. Numerous images evoking evil have prepared the context. Ingeri so radiates evil just after her worship of Odin that Frida makes a sign of the cross. The toad, a traditional symbol of death and the devil, is the palpable image of her evil wish. Fretful Mareta warns Karin that the devil is a seducer of the innocent; he always attempts to destroy everything at its start (we see this happening to the boy). Mareta turns to Christ only in fear of the devil, and thus she conjures him up — and her evil thoughts and dreams are visited upon Karin (who asked her that morning why she thought so often of the devil). The old man at the bridge — hunched, one-eyed, with stumps for fingers — is an objectification of the toad. He says he has no name; nor do the herdsmen; nor does illegitimate Ingeri. While Karin's innocent eyes are blind to the herdsmen's look of secret camaraderie in evil (which we see immediately), the heathen old man says to Ingeri: "I recognized you immediately when I saw you on the road" — by her eyes, mouth, hands. The old man urges Ingeri to share the seat of honor with him. Her hands on the armrests touch carvings of Odin's and Thor's heads; heathen runes and animals are carved on the chair; bear and wolf skins lie around. He carries a bundle of human parts to the fire as a priest carries the Host to the altar. (As he sacrifices the three killers later, Tore, too, is a kind of priest.) When Ingeri says, "You have made a human sacrifice to Odin," she sees that she has, too: Karin. The old man says he hears hoofs on the bridge, above the roar of the river and the waterfall. Three dead men, he says, just rode north. (This audio image antici- pates the three herdsmen we are about to meet.) The toad, jumping out of the bun (the host, Karin's body) onto the pure white linen triggers the act of violation. Immediately it appears, we cut to Ingeri's face and see the scene from the distance of evil. Ingeri holds a stone, but drops it, taking wild pleasure in the scene of violation (as, perhaps, the movie-viewer, consequently, does also). She, they, we become toads. The old man's question, "Do you have labor pains?" and Ingeri's answer, "It's worse than that," suggest that her wish gives birth to the deed which is about to occur; the imminence of the birth trauma anticipates the boy's convulsions and vomiting just after the murder; and the toad sitting on the dead virgin's stomach is born from the mind of her pregnant sister.

II-3 VIOLATION: Anticipatory equivalents of the gesture of violation are presented in many forms. Self-violation is the first we see: Mareta mortifying her own flesh. When Tore protests, she says, "It is Friday, the day of the suffering of our Lord Christ." It is as though her self-abuse declared: "Jesus, I will suffer so that you will heed my prayer that Karin escape suffering." This ritualistic mortification is contrasted with Tore's whipping his body with branches later, for an extreme occasion: "I will suffer," he seems to say, "so I will deserve the right to punish those who made Karin suffer."

Ingeri wishes on Karin the violation *she* experienced (Karin is shocked to learn that Simon raped Ingeri). The effect of rape on Ingeri (it makes her sullen and scornful) is a prepared contrast for the effect of rape on Karin. And Simon's behavior toward Ingeri is a contrast to his con- duct toward Karin. On the road, with the mention of

Ingeri and Simon, rape is evoked. It is nearly rehearsed in Ingeri's encounter with the old man; he leers at Ingeri as she lies on the ground, a foreshadowing image of Karin soon after. Someone violated the old man, too — his hunched back (though, possibly, he cut his own fingers off to sacrifice to Odin).

Each herdsman violates Karin for different principal reasons: the thin man for sex, the tongueless man for her valuable clothes, and the boy for food. Karin's fear acts as a further stimulus to the tongueless man; then his lust and desire to violate stimulate the same passions in the other two. All three fall on her and rape her, as her feet kick at the turf, while goats rush about and Svarten whinnies in panic. Karin is broken by the rape; she looks awful, worse than Ingeri. That morning, Karin's naked foot sticking out from under the quilt made Mareta feel so tender she wanted to kiss it. But the tongueless man, confronted with the sight of such innocent flesh wounded, is outraged, and beats her quickly with a stick. Thus the victim is an accomplice in her own destruction. The tongueless man feels the horror of what he has done because he was himself violated once: his tongue was cut out. Bergman repeatedly shows evil making a momentary gesture of kindness, as when the thin man, leaving the boy alone to tend the goats, throws the jew's-harp to him (Karin had wanted it herself). The boy starts to defile Karin's corpse, but flings dirt upon it, as if to cover up his crime (as the thin man later wipes the boy's vomit off Tore's table).

That night, Mareta, praying, digs her nails into her arm; moments later, the boy, terrified at hearing Tore recite the same prayer Karin said in the clearing, is subdued by the other herdsmen — they dig their nails into his arm: a composite image of self-violation and external-violation. Tore's killing of the three men is a kind of violation, too.

The film's silences are impressively appropriate to a ritual, ceremonial progression. The tongueless man's tonguelessness is a metaphor for the film's use of silence. To convey awe of the violation, Bergman follows it with a long, palpable silence.

II-4 VISION: We see the virgin's eyes as she receives the first blow on the head. The tongueless man pushes up her eyelid — her eye has burst. The stick strikes Karin — we cut to Ingeri's face as it expresses horror. This vision image is carefully developed from the first shot; Bergman's choreography of lights, darks, and shadows creates rhythmic responses in the viewer that enhance the gestures of good and evil, offering and violation, vengeance and reconciliation.

Ingeri makes light by blowing on the embers. As Karin admires her body in a barrel of water, she tells her mother, "You're in my light!" — a carnal expression of the ultimate spiritual significance of her death, which is to bring light. Bergman makes the darkest act of all, the violation, happen in full sunlight; snow, frost, black darkness follow. He creates distance from the violation by showing us part of the same scene twice, then close-up from Ingeri's concealed point of view. Evil as they are, she sees the herdsmen's hidden glances, and feels a conflict of anger toward them and scorn of Karin. It is as though, focused in one field of vision (Ingeri's), we see the violation from the slayer's point of view. Having invoked Odin in the hall, Ingeri senses the consequences at the waterfall with an inner eye; at the clearing, she sees with external vision the realization of her prayer. Later, the boy sees things as Ingeri does here: his eyes look with a vision infused with terror upon the manor hall scene. When Tore stands over the three with a knife, it is the boy's eyes that open first. (We recall Mareta standing over Karin, putting her hand on Karin's head, causing her eyes to open.) The vision image is given audial expression in Tore's anguished cry to God: "You saw it!" In minor ways, the "you saw" or "I saw" motif recurs constantly.

III-1 KARIN'S PRESENCE: Just before Tore slays Karin's killers, Bergman, in various ways, evokes Karin's living presence in the manor hall, so that we never leave her. The three are frightened as they enter the hall, but the warmth and the look of the people (Frida, the beggar, Mareta, farm hands) calms them, just as their counterfeit image of familial good will calmed Karin. The thin one bows (as he did to Karin); to us, this gesture has the weird aura of a bow of apology for having killed Karin. The jockeying about of the stolen saddlebags containing her clothes asserts Karin's presence: the tongueless man tries to conceal them, Frida moves them so the boy can lie down, and Mareta trips over them as she reaches to comfort the hysterical boy. Mareta's threading of the needle as they enter is a re-enactment of the rape; she begins to spin; that morning, she picked up a spindle that had fallen beside Karen's bed; now the wool on the spindle decreases through her fingers, and then she drops the spindle.

The boy, who was a bridge between Karin and the other herdsmen, is the human equivalent of Karin in these scenes. Like Karin, he is a child, relatively innocent. "Poor boy," she said to him on the road, "who takes care of you?" Later, Mareta, Frida, and Tore, and the beggar do, as they took care of Karin that morning. Karin's slayers threaten the boy when he refuses to tend the goats. Just after the rage of life, he sees everything in a scene that is as silent and inert as Karin's body. The world's body, too, is outraged, dies, turns cold, and the snow is God's gesture of recognition of this death. Immediately, we cut to Tore, towering in his doorway, looking down his cold, dark, sinister yard at the three killers, shrunken forms at the gate, silhouetted against a hostile landscape. Karin's fear in the clearing is sustained now in the boy's absolute terror as he clings to the two slayers. That morning, the beggar inspired Karin's gaiety with songs of a maiden in spring; now, lying head to head with him, the beggar terrifies the boy with visions of hell. Mareta did not hear her own child cry out, but the boy's scream awakens her; for a moment, she thinks it was Karin's, as in a nightmare. She goes to comfort him, ironically responding to a cry from one of Karin's murderers. Karin is evoked when we see, from Tore's point of view, the three murderers sleeping, looking as innocent and helpless against harm as Karin did to Mareta that morning.

III-2, 3, 4 KARIN'S PRESENCE│VENGEANCE PREPARATION│ PURIFICATION-VENGEANCE: Karin's presence, discovery of the killers and purification for vengeance, and the execution itself are the three parts of the gesture that extends over 2, 3, and 4. Tore, as the agent of vengeance, is seen in 1, standing in his doorway like the Old Testament God, the image of great power and authority as he calls to the herdsmen standing at the gate. When the thin killer offers to sell Mareta her own daughter's dress, she says, "I must ask my husband about what reward would be fair for such an expensive garment." Tore feels the evidence lying across his chest (Karin's shift); his movements henceforth are ritualistically deliberate and clear. First, he starts to bar the door, but Mareta already has. The door image was introduced with Ingeri's opening of the vent that morning; Bergman makes all entrances and exits through doors impressive, portentous. At the door, Tore discovers Ingeri, surprised she is alive.

Before the act of vengeance, Tore purifies his mind and body through work, water, and self-inflicted pain. Half-pagan, half-Christian, he feels he must be clean before vengeance, as before a sacrifice. The lone, young, tender birch we glimpsed as Karin began her journey her father now uproots. Since Karin was killed with a branch and fell into the branches of a fallen tree, it is appropriate that Tore expends much of his anger upon this nature-equivalent of Karin (in a sort of divine parody of her ravishment). Tore cleanses himself of wrath by rubbing and flailing himself with switches from the tree. Ingeri, who does routine chores around the farm, now get Tore's steambath ready. She also fetches, at his command. the slaughter knife (Karin used a little domestic knife to cut the cake in four equal parts; the boy threatened her with a knife; as the men appeared in the doorway to the hall, Frida pointed at them with a domestic knife to indicate that they were to enter).

Now, Tore enters the hall: he will do here what they did in the clearing. Bergman develops many parallels between the hall and the clearing; it was here that Ingeri conceived their deed; in a sense, Karin never left; she was sacrificed on that table, as Tore sacrifices the tongue-less man when he drives his knife into the killer's heart. For a moment, Tore stands with the knife (pagan) in one hand and the vent pole (suggestive of Karin-Christianity, for she was killed with a stick, and the crucifix in Tore's room is a rough stick) in the other, looking at his "goats." The thin man tries to climb this vent pole to elude Tore. The father's efficient work on the herdsmen recalls their work on Karin: the virgin's grace is paralleled by her father's deliberateness; the clean precision of the two men's movements, disrobing her, was a mockery of her grace, while the boy's nauseated con-vulsions paralleled Karin's as she was being raped and beaten. No one will take care of the boy now; he runs, screaming, to Mareta, and hugs her waist. Though Tore looks with pity on the boy (sensing his affinity to Karin), Mareta shakes her head and hits the boy's hands with her house keys.

In a film so full of enormous silences, the dialog frequency is effectively patterned. I-1 has only one line; III-4 has only two: "Bring me the slaughter knife!" at the start, and "We must search for Karin," at the end.

The splendor of movement in this brief film, and the feeling that everything we see is a variation, again and again, of the three main gestures — stressing one now, while anticipating the other two — creates an over-whelming sense of simultaneity. From the moment Tore sees Karin's dress to the end seems one clean thrust of vengeance. From early one morning until the next, the

film is one lucid narrative thrust. The various bodies of
humans and animals moving in relation to each other; the
movement of the camera itself, the editing, with its sudden
shifts, as from the snow falling on Karin's body to the
three herdsmen at the gate; and the easy suddenness with
which the thin man offers Mareta the dress — these
elements convey the simple enactment of ritual, and, above
all, the awesome inevitability of Greek tragedy.

III-5 WATER-CHURCH : Water images in many forms anticipate the gushing forth of the spring from under Karin's
broken head. The very title of the film is suggestive: what
springs from the violation of a virgin in the springtime,
etc. (Allusions to the candles for Maria, the Virgin, also
keep this title before us.) Karin looks at herself in a barrel
of water; as she sets out to church, spring air is releasing
snow into water, roofs are dripping, there are puddles in
the yard, tiny streams from rain in the road; the roar of
the stream passing under the old pagan's shack and of the
waterfall nearby are violent anticipations of the spring;
Tore carries water into the bathhouse on his shoulders,
and the steam is Karin's ghostly breath; he pours water
from a barrel over his head, a rehearsal of baptism, as
Ingeri, a kind of "good" priestess now, watches. As they
all go to find Karin, it is another beautiful day (it is, in a
sense, the *same* day), the snow melting as before. When the
water from the virgin spring reaches Ingeri where she
kneels among the broken candles, she violently reaches for
it with her hands, and now, instead of devouring Karin's
body, she baptizes herself in the spring of Christian grace.
The images of blood flowing from Mareta's, then Karin's
wounds, and Mareta's, then the boy's tears and his vomiting,
anticipate the gushing spring. Bergman focuses on Karin's
head, whence the spring flows: Mareta puts her hand on
Karin's sleeping head and her eyes open; later, Tore and
Mareta will lift her inert head, and the spring will start
forth. As she sleeps, her hair flows over the pillow, uncombed; she wants it loose, not bound (thus, she excites

sexual desire in the thin herdsman); the combing of her hair is a prolonged action, which the waterfall later re-iterates. When Mareta goes to comfort the boy, her hair, usually severely confined, hangs loose and flowing.

We are left feeling that the spring from Karin's head will shoot up into a church. The church image, too, has been evoked from the beginning. The manor hall is a pagan church for Ingeri; the old man's shed is a continuation of this image. As Karin is about to set out for church, Frida says: "It is a shame that one has to go so far to church!" The beggar tells her of the women and the churches he has known, and Karin's father later vows to build such a church as the beggar described. There is a kind of mock processional and recessional as the herdsmen drive their goats down from the clearing and the tongueless man leads Karin and her horse back to the clearing (where the church will be built). In the manor hall (one image of the church) Tore kills the tongueless man caught in the seat of honor.

In many ways, Bergman raises the question, who is guilty? The ambiguous way in which he raises it provokes the reverse question, who is innocent? The answer is that all, in varying degrees, are both innocent and guilty. While we are judging on evidence as it is being presented, Bergman is subtly establishing minor guilts, such as Karin's when she slaps Ingeri. The verbal image of forgiveness is presented when Karin asks forgiveness. Because she can so freely admit guilt herself, being more innocent than guilty, she is surprised by Ingeri's response: "Don't ask *me* for forgiveness!" We get a black parody of forgiveness when the boy vomits Karin's body on the manor table and the thin killer says, "Please forgive my poor brother." As Tore is about to slay the herdsmen, Ingeri says, "Kill me first. I am more guilty than they are. I wanted it. Ever since I became pregnant, I've hated her. . . . The same day that I prayed for it, he (Odin) made it." The three herdsmen (possessed of the devil) did it; Ingeri willed it. It is visually apt that Ingeri leads Tore and the others into the forest, where she becomes finally reconciled to Karin and to Christ. Mareta reproaches Tore for having been too good. On the road to the murder scene, she faces her own guilt. "I loved her too much, Tore, more than God himself." She hated Tore because Karin preferred him, and now God is punishing her. Tore replies that only God knows who is guilty. The sight of Karin makes Tore look at his hands and he knows that he is guilty.

Karin is a bridge between paganism and Christianity. The fury of her father's revenge is heathen; he acts without hesitation or doubt, with his wife's instant complicity. His vow to build a church as penance is the end of his paganism. The Christian context is evoked early, when Frida brings newly hatched chicks into the kitchen in the folds of her dress: "So help me God, I nearly stepped on them out there in the darkness. . . . So now you can live out your miserable life as surely as God allows all of us to live." Near the end, the beggar conjures up the darkness of hell for the boy, then concludes, "But at the same moment when you think you are lost, a hand will grasp you . . . and you will be taken far away where evil can no longer harm you." But this is cold comfort; a few hours later, he dies at Tore's hands. Karin's death is the offering of innocence to reconcile men to each other and to Christ. Bergman's theology is a little paradoxical and ambiguous, to say the least. But as Karin crosses the narrow planks over the stream and rides along the narrow path into the forest, she passes from life into myth. That mythic image is lucid. *The Virgin Spring* is a mythic icon, a modern Grecian urn.

wright morris' *in orbit*:

an unbroken series of poetic gestures

Once focused in his field of vision, an element in a Wright Morris novel becomes reusable raw material. For every element in the latest novel, *In Orbit*, some prototype exists in his other books. The method is familiar to readers of Morris' work: many key characters, concepts, images, even phrases from previous novels are reassembled in new combinations in this one. More poetically compressed, the major themes of his other novels are made new in this brief book: the relationship between the hero and his witnesses; the conflict of the phony and the real; the conflict of the habitual and the natural; improvisation; the acting out of the American Nightmare in the context of the American Dream; audacity; the transformation of the cliché; the cross-fertilization of fact and fiction; the impersonality of love; the life of objects; the transforming effects of travel. Yet Morris never repeats himself, and the familiar never looked so new and strange as in this novel.

In Orbit shows the interaction of sexual, psychological, intellectual, mechanical, and natural forces. Their paths crisscross by chance and finally converge in a tornado. The controlling energy is Morris' conceptual power which compresses chaos into a pattern and gives these forces life as well as symbolic value. Morris opens and closes the novel with this catalytic poetic image: "This boy comes riding with his arms high and wide, his head dipped low, his ass light in the saddle, as if about to be shot into orbit from a forked sling. . . . All this can be taken in at a glance, but the important detail might escape you. He is in motion. Now you see him, now you don't. If you pin him down in time, he is lost in space. Between where he is from and where he is going he wheels in an unpredictable orbit. To that extent he is free." To achieve transcendence beyond the "ordinary" lives he is about to shake up, the boy risks chance encounters: "At any moment it might cost him his life." He is doing what comes naturally, and that takes talent. "This he has. The supernatural is his natural way of life." The boy, Jubal, is running for his life away from one of his own kind, LeRoy Cluett, whose motorcycle he has stolen. Morris rehearsed Jubal in the characters of Calvin, Lee Roy Momeyer and Munger in *Ceremony in Lone Tree*, and he has traits that recall the Oswald of *One Day*. Jubal responds to the immediate moment spontaneously with speed, and the spectacle of his response affects the "ordinary" people who encounter him.

The image of the motorcyclist expresses the nature of the contemporary American character and scene; most of our experiences are moments in motion, seeming to have no relevant past. Is part of our nature a desire to go against nature, and is the machine an extension of that desire? Haffner, the foreigner, observes that "as the Huns were once believed to be part of their horses, these riders look . . . like part of their machines. Gas percolates in their veins. Batteries light up their eyes. . . . When this new breed of creature was perfected the one stop at the diner would be a short one. The model would feature interchangeable parts. A bulb taken from the headlamp would screw into the eyes. A glance at the dials would report what was on its mind." As Jubal approaches Haffner's Volkswagen after he has supposedly raped Holly Stohrmeyer, Pickett's feeble-minded old beauty, Haffner asks, "Out of gas?" A profoundly serious question for a young man like Jubal, for whom to be out of gas is to be nothing — a force wandering from its natural modus vivendi. Charlotte, a young beauty living in Pickett, sees Jubal in animal-sexual-natural, rather than mechanical, terms: "the overall impression of the boy on the bike . . . is that of two cats, piggyback: hard at it." The novel is full of machines, various kinds of cars and airplanes — human imitations of forces in nature. Hodler, editor of the *Pickett Courier*, "doesn't know if the sound he hears is thunder or a passing jet. He doesn't know, that is, if it is the will of God or man." Holly, impressed by Jubal's crash helmet, inspires Hodler to visualize this headline: "VISITING SPACEMAN ASSAULTS HOLLY STOHRMEYER." Similarly, a tornado will assault the town.

The natural and the antinatural are the opposing forces Morris depicts. If some things "come natural to knaves, dancers, lovers and twists of the wind," some people are "too clean-cut to bleed." The women incline toward the spontaneous, the natural: "When Hodler thinks of people in their natural state — when he thinks of it as being a good one — he thinks of Pauline Bergdahl," who runs the One-Stop Diner on the outskirts of Pickett. In his novels, Morris often stresses the irony of the American's persistent suppression of the natural desire to expose oneself to risk. When Pickett's historic elm falls in the wind, "small fry stand in a circle anxious to be hit by falling branches." The elm greeted the first settlers, "hardy, stubborn men who worked like slaves to deprive their children of all simple pleasures, and most reasons to live." After decades of suppression the natural pioneer recklessness comes out perversely in the President's accused assassin in Morris' *One Day*; if he could not act creatively, he could protest in an act of impotence.

Early in the novel the motorcycle and the twister as complementary forces are juxtaposed: "Pauline had merely called to say that in her opinion it was twister weather, and while hosing down her cinders she had seen, just in passing, this boy on the swiped motorbike." At the beginning and at the end, Morris says: "Perhaps the most important detail escapes you. Now you see him, now you don't." Jubal is "as free, and as captive, as the wind in his face." Like the wind captive in a twister, Jubal does what comes naturally: he runs. "He is never doing more than what comes naturally, but it is amazing how many things seem to." Just after his third violent run-in with a Pickett resident, "the wind thrusts at his back" as he runs. At the end of the second third of the novel, Hodler "listens to the ominous weather forecast [natural and human]: the barometer is falling. More rain is expected with rising winds. More trouble is expected from the spaceman, still on the loose." Symbolically, the weather is an expansion of the boy and his effect on others: "The windshields of the cars reflected a low, turbulent sky. Would this curtail or expand the goings-on of the man at large?" To Hodler's eyes, Jubal, seen in his fantastic garb just before the twister strikes, appears to be one of the puzzling effects produced by electrical storms.

The motorcyclist and the twister are supernatural and natural forces which happen on Pickett "as luck would have it." The psychological weathers of those among whom the rider moves disturbs his "weather," just as a twister is wind that just happens to undergo the proper atmospheric conditions produced by chance which violently disturb and concentrate it in a core of energy that must move. "Now you see it, now you don't." In *One Day*, Morris sets the scene in fog. "That we are such stuff as fog is made of is hardly a fresh impression, but events have a way of making it new." Are the weathers for our era alternately fog and twister weather? "Is it weather," Haffner asks, "if you can forecast it?" Are people alive and interesting to each other if they're predictable? Weather can be interesting because no matter how accurately we try to predict it, it often enough proves unpredictable. It is this phenomenon in people that intrigues Morris. Aberrant behavior, like aberrant weather, often seems the most natural, and, though violent, the loveliest. "The will of God," Pauline says, "you have to see it." The shambles after a twister is lovely? asks the passive Hodler. "The shambles ain't but it's the will to do it," says Pauline. Even Hodler "is saddened by the thought of the cloud-seeders who will one day take the twist out of the twisters, the fear out of the storm." In this novel we see ways in which the human climate builds up along lines of tension similar to the climate that produces the twister. Hodler sees that twisters are like those people who can't stand being crowded in cities or in strained situations. In the time-span of Morris' works, the twister is a constant factor, a force that always exists in the present alone. And Jubal, child of the present, on his motorbike recalls Lee Roy in his hotrod in *Ceremony*;

both are somewhat deranged hangovers of the Lone Eagle in his *Spirit of St. Louis*.

American culture is always Morris' subject. Editor Hodler has written a book about the Swiss who shaped American culture. "But little consolation it gives him. What, if any, *shape* has it?" Just as weather becomes most visible when it condenses, shapes up into a twister, so we see ourselves, our town, our national character most sharply when a violent catalyst gives shape to various impulses and makes them visible a moment before they disperse again. Three major images are compressed in Hodler's metaphoric summing up of American culture. On his "troubled mind's eye it seems a mindless force, like the dipping, dancing funnel of the twister, the top spread wide to spew into space all that it has sucked up. It is like nothing so much as the dreams of men on the launching pad. Or those boys who come riding, nameless as elemental forces, their arms spread wide and with coiled springs in their asses, ticking off the countdown they hope will blast them out of this world."

More than any other Morris novel *In Orbit* illustrates Croce's concept of a novel as a tissue of images, over which lingers finally a single image. Few American novels come quite as close to poetic immediacy as *In Orbit*. Facets of the opening image interpret moments to come; nuances in the same passage when it is repeated at the very end of the novel poetically summarize and interpret the moments that have passed. Most of the images comment thematically; all others at least seem to say more than they are saying. In his selection and controlled condensation and juxtaposition of images, Morris achieves the dynamism of the dance. Susanne K. Langer's description of what happens in the dance offers one perspective on Morris' magic: "In a world perceived as a realm of mystic Powers, the first created image is the dynamic image; the first objectification of human nature, the first true art, is Dance," which makes the "world of powers" visible by an unbroken fabric of gestures charged with feeling. In this novel, the images are struck on the anvil of the present tense because everything happens in that immediate present in which twisters and motorcycles rampage. "That's the picture: there are those who can take it in at a glance." Poetic simultaneity enables the active reader to do just that.

Morris employs his recurring method: he sets the scene and introduces most of the characters in Chapter 1, alluding to the major public event which will transform, if only momentarily, their private worlds. Familiar Morris characters (often in danger of becoming caricatures) undergo yet another metamorphosis. The long scrutiny in Chapter 2 of Haffner and Charlotte in the car en route to the vet is an example of the sort of static character analysis in Morris which sometimes seems a mere cataloging of quirks.

In Orbit, like most of Morris' novels, examines the human nature of time. This is such an important element in Morris' novels, perhaps the most important, that we ought to trace its evolution. In his early novels (*My Uncle Dudley*, *The Man Who Was There*, *The World in the Attic*, *The Works of Love*) and photo-text experiments (*The Inhabitants*, *The Home Place*) Morris nostalgically sifted the dust in the grave of our rural past, looked at (photographed) things at rest, static situations, attempted to convey a sense of worn artifacts that are metaphysically inhabited and holy (in his most recent book, *God's Country and My People*, Morris returns to this photo-epiphany technique). The author, like the recurring character who is his central intelligence, was captive in the past, observing Nebraskan home folk immolated in clichés. Unconsciously, then consciously, these books were attempts to bury those bearded giants in their self-dug graves. Several transitional novels dealing with the contemporary scene, each reaching more desperately for firmer ground in the shifting sands of the present, were gestures of freedom from enthrallment: *Man and Boy*, *The Deep Sleep*, *The Huge Season*. Then, in *The Field of Vision* he showed how the mind superimposes the home place and the past upon a foreign landscape (Mexico) in the present. *Love Among the Cannibals*, his first major break with the past, dealt solely with contemporary characters in the immediate present on timeless beaches in Hollywood and Mexico. He returned to the Nebraska landscape in *Ceremony in Lone Tree* to make a deliberate break with the past in the midst of its own habitat; that this is the second part of a trilogy whose third part is yet to come suggests that the break is not complete.

A look at the author's last four novels reveals Morris' impressive success in making his characters active in the immediate present. The depiction of neither Horter, the commercial songwriter in *Cannibals*, nor Soby, the professor in *What a Way to Go* (1962), is encumbered by a past; by responding spontaneously to the wisdom of the body, the Greek and Cynthia teach Horter and Soby that sex is one means of living contentedly in the immediate present. On ancient ground (Venice and Greece) wise-cracking Cynthia is the nerve center of the lively present; as she helps him get to the simplicity of the Greeks, Soby brings the dead mythic past alive again in his imaginative field of vision. At its best, travel, new scenes, arouse the impulse to "make it new!" The past is set in stone until one's present emotions give it flesh. In the midst of old-world clichés, Soby observes life imitating art, fact and fiction merging ambiguously. He learns to transform imaginatively his environment and his relationships with the people he meets by chance.

If Soby re-experiences Western culture's past, Warren Howe, middle-aged television script-writer in *Cause for Wonder* (1963) deliberately re-experiences his own past. This book, the realization finally of a novel Morris had tried to write when he was very young and had embellished with zany drawings, demonstrates the simultaneity of past and present in skull time-and-space; past and present in both America and Europe are the ambience of self-discovery. Even forgotten moments of the past sometimes overwhelm the immediacy of the present. Time-past and place-distant are preserved in the creative memory that reconstructs as it resurrects. Howe contemplates as he experiences it the human nature of time-and-space, which are coexistent dimensions of each other. "If you live in the present," he discovers, "you can't help but be ahead of your time." The usable past is "the here and now." Morris shows how the moment of individual creative vision synthesizes memory and immediate perception, time and space.

In *One Day* (1965) Morris makes public and private events impinge significantly upon each other in the immediate present on the American scene; he parallels the trivial events of every day with a single, enormous, historical event (the assassination of President Kennedy) of a single day. Each character is so stimulated by a frightening present to immerse, if not immolate himself, in memories of a haunting, distant past, that the events of the day, even the assassination, pale. Veterinarian Cowie, the Morris voice, wonders: "Who could say when this day had begun, or would ever end?" Morris suggests an answer in the way he restructures time and space in his characters' various fields of vision.

In his latest collection of essays, *A Bill of Rites, A Bill of Wrongs, A Bill of Goods*, Morris writes about fads, fashions, foibles, and follies in our civilization that may make us die laughing. Why is it that when one gets "lost in thought" about the future, one often ends up stupefied by the immediate present? Why does nostalgia for the past so often turn into a timeless nausea? Morris suggests an answer: "What's new makes its debut, and receives our blessings, in the theatre of advertising. The newest thing in our lives of importance is prime time. . . . Who makes it prime? You and me. *Prime* is what is made in our image." Morris arrives on target more by intuitive punning, by image and epigram than by sustained logic. These image fragments pose the question: What ever happened to the American Dream? In the suburbs of Eden, it came true —

revealing itself as a nightmare. From the Nebraska Plains
(the navel of the world) to The Golden Gate, in sixteen
novels, Morris has contemplated American landscapes,
inscapes, escapes, and outscapes in Space. Written in
California, where the past went that-a-way, this is Morris'
intellectual autobiography, his Summing Up; it is in the
artifacts and pseudofacts of just a moment ago that his
past is mirrored.

In Orbit is set in Indiana, similar to the Nebraska
scene; here Morris contemplates volatile images of the
present as they presage the future. Instead of describing
artifacts that are imbued metaphysically with the past,
Morris sets in orbit objects that exist only for the present.
As in most of his novels, the time span is one day, but here
Morris intermingles everyday events with a natural and a
public human event that affects only one representative
American small-town cosmos. The task of imaginative
synthesis is mainly the reader's.

The structure of *In Orbit* visibly expresses the theme.
Each chapter, except the last, opens with a brief scene in
which Jubal encounters one of the other characters; the
novel closes, effectively, with the image that opened it,
repeated almost verbatim, with a few key variations. The
point of view in most of the Jubal sections is shared with
Jubal's so-called victims: Holly, Haffner, Charlotte, and
Kashperl, the proprietor of an Army and Navy Surplus
store. Sometimes the links between one event or consciousness and another seem merely rhetorical: "Like William
Holden he is on his own now, and out of gas." A break,
then: "In matters of gas Charlotte Hatfield knows that
her husband, Alan, runs out of it." But generally the
multiple-point-of-view technique operates more subtly
here than in most of his novels. The montage of points of
view is meaningful, as when Jubal's and Holly's combined
vision is followed by Hodler's. Morris shuttles back and
forth, interpretively, from one vision to another: having
just knifed Kashperl, Jubal is about to encounter Charlotte
when we go back to Haffner, whose run-in with Jubal was

similar to Kashperl's. Jubal's tornado-like encounters with the townspeople are complemented by the way one character's psychological weather impinges upon another's.

We experience this method in the first chapter: the action of the boy passing on the motorcycle affects Pauline, the passive observer, who stimulates Hodler to contemplate elaborately what she reports; then Sanford Avery, the farmer who keeps an eye on Holly, calls Hodler to report the effect of what Pauline saw: the apparent rape of Holly. Holly is sitting on her porch, her hair drying, wearing nothing over her breasts, peeling apples in a swarm of bees, and when Jubal approaches her to ask for gas, she thrusts her thumb, which she has cut, toward Jubal, as though he is expected to suck it for her, and that is what he does. She falls and they roll on the porch, entangled. When Jubal leaves Holly, he comes upon Haffner, who laughs at him insanely; then he encounters Kashperl who appears to make a pass at him. Holly, Haffner, Kashperl provoke him, and Charlotte arouses him — all four encounters, after we've looked at the first two from many angles, impinge within three pages in the middle of the novel. Appropriately, Morris filters the day's swift events most often through the pattern-perceiving mind of a newspaper editor, Hodler.

In Orbit is vision-structured in time. What Morris sees raises the rhetorical question, often repeated in his novels, "How explain it?" He demands the reader's active involvement in the answering process. "That's the picture. You might want to add a few details of your own." This is the reader's field of vision, in which time is fragmented. With immediate poetic force, we experience a single instant from various points of view and achieve a sense of simultaneity. The time scramble may seem arbitrary, but the fragmentary approach enables one to look at separate moments from different time and character perspectives, and thus we see more, and more deeply, each time. Conventional "time," says Haffner, "is for people who live on the installment plan."

Morris evokes the pathos of the isolation from each other of similar minds by showing how separate lives plug into a common current of feeling and perception unaware. Separate visions come up with the same or similar similes, as when Jubal (then Hodler) sees Holly's farmhouse porch, then later Charlotte's terrace, as a stage. Both Hodler and Alan come up with the same paradoxical question about the mystery of human perception: "Does it charm him to the extent that it escapes him?" When Holly says her assailant was a spaceman, Hodler looks up as if he might see him in the sky. This "as if he might see" motif appears in most Morris novels, a constant rhetorical reference to the importance of creative vision. Like a phantom, the boy moves in and out of the literal fields of vision of the townspeople, but he is very vivid in the private movie theaters of the characters' minds. Jubal knows none of the people he encounters, nor does he perceive the pattern of relationships among them as they meet him; each thinks his encounter with Jubal is singular.

The reader takes it all in with a glance. "Is that so funny?" asks Haffner, laughing at Pauline hosing down the cinders. "So much depends on your point of view." Tableaux and events are even funnier from the reader's complex point of view, for he sees her spray Jubal, also; and the plane that sprays the orchards gradually sprays most of the characters. The comedy in Morris is, at times, pretty broad, as when Haffner, then Jubal, chases his runaway car, calling it as though it were an unleashed pet. But in every image, Morris' is a black comic vision that sometimes sees things with a cross-eyed folksiness. Morris wants the reader to end with the "disturbingly impersonal" and timeless vision of a Holly or a Charlotte, of a child (like little Brian in *Cause for Wonder*).

The vision-structure of the novel enhances the profundity of the character relationships. The hero-witness relationships pattern that has made this vision-structure in most of Morris' novels meaningful reached the end of one line of development in *Ceremony*; a new line had

already been established in *Cannibals*, with a female hero,
the Greek, affecting change in Horter. A similar sexual
relationship was further develpeod in *What a Way to Go*
between Cynthia and Soby. In *Cause for Wonder*, the hero
was once more a man, but a very old man. Madman
Dulac's witnesses, especially Howe, are willing accomplices
to the hero's acts of lunacy. And under the influence of
Dulac and his castle, the natural impulsiveness of most of
the characters comes out. Unlike Dulac, Jubal only
appears to go berserk; it is his witnesses who, misinter-
preting his actions, surrender to impulse. In *One Day*,
Morris shows how suppressed emotions in the American
character exploded in a perverse hero, the President's
accused assassin, as a "meaningful accident." Several
such accidents occur in *In Orbit*. Most of the characters in
One Day identify with — or Morris relates them in some
way to — the assassin. Unable to understand himself, he
seemed to behave as though others would. In *In Orbit* both
Jubal, who rather closely resembles today's typical
American boy, and the twister are heroic forces affecting
their witnesses: "Is it more than a tree that falls? It falls
to give this day its meaning." The communal and personal
pasts of the town are marked off from the future by the
events of the day, "which were already being assembled
according to the needs of the survivors." "On the radar
screen" of the mind "a spaceman and a twister left the
same track. Both were in orbit, or out of it." Their effect
on the townspeople is impersonal, like the effect on
Kashperl of a man who happened to read a few chance
lines aloud in a bookstore, then "creaked off ignorant of
what he had done to Kashperl."

Thus, Jubal is unaware that he has "raped" Holly *for*
Hodler and Avery, both of whom wanted to make love to
her. In this new variation of the hero-witness relationship,
the weird behavior of the witnesses, whose gestures Jubal
misinterprets, sets off impulses in him. We see here more
clearly than in earlier novels the ways in which suppressed
but wild people affect the hero. The magnetism of their

need draws out, energizes, encourages the hero's own wild streak, authorizes his acts, then authenticates them by the witnesses' responses to them. These responses then transform the witnesses. "Hodler sees it all through the rapist's eyes," and he observes that "part of the pleasure Avery feels in this rehearsal is to see it on the face of Hodler." Each of Jubal's "victims" smiles as though enchanted. Confronted with such events, Hodler can't remember Haffner's name: "His mind is a blank. Has he lost it?" Morris shows the beneficial effects of losing one's mind now and then.

It is the mind that is most important. Even with a twister, attempted rape and seduction, and assault with a bag of wild cherries and a knife, Morris is determined to subordinate, as is his custom, the action of events to psychological epiphanies. When Hodler and Avery think a spaceman raped Miss Holly, the psychological effect on them is more violent than Holly's actual encounter with Jubal. When Jubal sticks Kashperl with a knife, "no holes or blood are visible." Morris depicts the infliction of unhealable, invisible wounds which are good for the victim because partly self-inflicted. Normally, people are too normal to be natural. Kashperl sees that "his friends have labels, they play roles, and they think they have been discovered. The shock — and it is a shock — is of familiarity. To see in a face no more, and no less, than what one knows." While Kashperl shows Jubal a knife, unaware that he is Miss Holly's assailant, the mailman's cryptic message — "Ought to leave him at large as a public service" — becomes gospel to the reader.

Each person in Morris' representative sampling of small-town people nurtures a wild streak similar to the berserk, marauding stranger's; his, however, is mostly their invention. "Bit of the mad dog in us all, eh, Hodler?" says the young intern. Morris reconceives the current idea that there's a little of Eichmann and Oswald in us all. "The mad dog in Hodler is not on the surface, but McCain knows it is there, and he finds it reassuring, almost comforting." This passage suggests the source of the witnesses' inner disposition to produce, then respond to the hero. "Did they all dream of being a man on the loose?" Hodler wonders. "Envied by inhibited red-blooded men, pursued by comical galoots like the Sheriff. He went that-a-way. With the thoughts, fantasies, and envious good wishes of them all." Morris scales this appalling thesis down to manageable, and thus more frightening, size. People emerge from certain seemingly trivial moments with something of their old selves missing. "A dozen or more people are known to be missing. Are Hodler, Charlotte, and Alan three of them?"

It is Alan, the witness, who puts his wife Charlotte into orbit when he puts Kid Ory's horn on the hi-fi. "Somebody not in orbit has to lower the needle carefully into the groove." So-called normal, or successfully suppressed, people need supposedly abnormal people: Alan needs Charlotte, Hodler needs Holly, Charlotte herself needs Haffner, who seems odd to her, and on this day of the twister they all need and use Jubal. Psychologically, man daily subsists, it seems on the tiny deviations from or reversals of the generally accepted. People are adept at making a thing something of their own, something opposite from the thing's intended purpose. People also need, now and then, a violent disruption of their normal mode of life. Wild as Holly's behavior is, her life has its habitual ceremonies. "Sanford?" she always asks, hearing a man approach her from behind. One day it is not Sanford Avery, but a person who reluctantly enacts Sanford's own erotic daydreams. Hodler's response to the day's violent disruption is typical: "it scares the shit out of him, but he likes it. He would gladly take the twist out of that boy who seemed to strike in the same, irresponsible manner, but a twister had obligations that he felt this boy did not. There were these opposing forces, high and low pressures, moist and dry air in unpredictable mixtures, great heat and cold, fantastic combinations that built up like nuclear fission, and most important of all there was the element of chance that dissolved it in vapor, or brought it to perfection, a tube that dipped from the sky and rearranged most of the matter it touched." He "feels a pleasurable apprehension in the knowledge of this potential killer." Like most witnesses, Hodler discovers that "destructive elements are not merely on the loose, but some of them are rubbing off" on him. Hodler and Kashperl, feeling the impact of the hero and the imminence of the twister, perceive that "one of the problems of the twister is the vacuum at the center causing objects that are sealed up tight to explode." "Know what nature abhors, Hodler? — a vacuum. Know what a man on the loose heads for? A vacuum!" This twister-fugitive metaphor powerfully expresses the condition of the American character at this moment in the nightmare of history.

Holly is the first of Jubal's "victims." She resembles Miss Caddy in *The World in the Attic*, and Avery is like Mr. Purdy (also like Mr. Parsons in *The Deep Sleep*). Holly belongs to the Morris breed of lovable simpletons; sometimes they are young, sometimes old, and animals prefer them to the more rational adults. But by now their unpredictability has become a little banal, and only the Morris genius for embellishing the simple type keeps it from atrophying into caricature. The impersonality of such human and natural events as motorcyclists and twisters passing through is reflected in Holly's childlike, "serene unblinking gaze." To Hodler, Holly looks like "a woman patiently awaiting further visitations," because impersonal human encounters sometimes satisfy a deeper need than personal ones.

As Jubal steps up to the car window, Haffner thrusts his bag of wild cherries at him. (Jubal's crowning Haffner with the bag recalls Scanlon's dumping a cigar pot on his own head in *The World in the Attic* and Ormsby's pushing the helmet down over Lipido's head in *Man and Boy*.) "'Poy on the loose!' Haffner repeats, and the idea delights him." Haffner (who resembles Herr Perkheimer in *What a Way to Go*) is to Charlotte what Hodler and Avery are to

Holly. Unable to take care of himself, Haffner takes care of Charlotte. Like most Morris characters, he "showed special promise as a clown." He prefers "the flawed performance," and likes the idea of a sonata for one needle in, one *out* of the record groove. Happily stunned by the boy — the figurative twister — Haffner sleeps through the literal twister.

Propelled by his wild encounters with Holly and then with Haffner, Jubal runs into Kashperl. The cut Holly gave herself somehow inspires the cut Jubal impulsively gives Kashperl with the knife Kashperl is trying to sell him. Kashperl (who is like Sol Spiegel of *Cause for Wonder*) collects books, with "a preference for the fading title, or the missing author, or better yet the rare volume that proved to lack both." He prefers disorder. "The play of chance" gives him room in which to influence human events. Even in his quieter moments, Jubal affects his witnesses, as when Kashperl watches him padlock his duffle bag and guitar to a parking meter with time left on the dial. "With a gesture the meter is now a grave marker. Does it tick off the time before the dead will arise? In Kashperl's book this is style, and he is impressed. With a gesture, no more, this boy makes old things new." Jokingly responding to the boy as though he were the rapist at large, Kashperl asks him about it: "He wanted what Jubal had had without all the trouble." Jubal's comment reveals one aspect of the hero-witness relationship: "She wasn't so old she didn't enjoy it, fat man. I'd say she got more out of it than I did," for in love-making, the woman "gets most of the fun, and all the poor guy gets is the credit!" Jubal is like a natural force that people foolishly stand in the way of, and his knifing Kashperl is another "meaningful accident." "I asked for it," says Kashperl, "and I got it" — naturally, just by being himself.

"Anything at all might interest Alan. It had to be alive to interest his wife Charlotte." "After one year in Pickett she prefers creatures who don't think" — cats, and people who resemble cats, as Haffner does. "Charlotte herself is alive in a way electricity is, and it makes her unruly. On certain days, like this one, she seems charged with it." Alan "would rather live with it than do without it." Hodler makes a similar observation about Jubal, and in many other descriptive passages the parallels between Charlotte's and Jubal's natures are stressed. Like Jubal, Charlotte just seems to be with it naturally. "She does not like the thought, or the poem that submits to typing. She does not like the music until it becomes the dance." After his run-in with Kashperl, Jubal encounters Charlotte whose grocery cart, like Haffner's car, drifts away from her down a ramp (the runaway car motif is carried over from *One Day*). Just as he sucked Holly's cut, he rescues Charlotte, whose heels are caught in the doormat. Charlotte is a more self-aware version of Holly, but both experience events purely. "What next?" thinks Jubal, echoing Horter in *Cannibals*. "At the thought of it, he laughs. All this time he has been on the run from something; what he feels now is the pull of something." A woman — a natural, pure force, acts on him. While nature herself works up a dance, Charlotte, having felt Jubal's charge, whirls "in a manner of a person possessed." But just as male and female sexual forces are about to converge in Jubal and Charlotte, Morris delays this most intensely immediate moment in the novel with the longest excursion into the past — Jubal's.

At the climax of the novel, Morris moves the center of consciousness from the journalist's mind, Hodler's, to the poet's; this is the only section from Alan's point of view. In a novel poetically performed, this sensible, overly cerebral writer and teacher of poetry is the least poetic character, though he achieves the finest epiphany. If Avery arrived too late to watch the Holly-Jubal encounter, Alan witnesses the Charlotte-Jubal scene. Jubal and the twister converge simultaneously on the conceptual thinker and his wife, the solo dancer. Twister, male energy, poetic compression, the dynamics of the dance — all these forces merge for an instant, while the passive observer, Hodler, is caught in a rain drain.

While the novel's allusions are predominantly cultural, Alan offers an important literary one: Yeats's "How can we know the dancer from the dance?" concept, which Eliot developed further. Alan watches "this mute figure [Jubal] watch the dance. He wonders how it must look through the stranger's eyes." Simultaneously, he observes that a baby's legs on a porch nearby seem to move in time to Charlotte's dance music — the natural "dance that preceded the music. The beat preceding the dance." "No rhythm to it, no meaning to it, just a pointless, mindless movement." Affected by witnessing these other spontaneous creatures — the baby, the boy, the dancer — Alan experiences pure being, impersonal vision: "He hardly knows, or cares, if the flash he sees is in the air or in his head." "Is it possible to say he no longer sees the dancer, only the dance?" Such an eternal moment of pure duration is holy to Morris, and he goes beyond Browning in poetic rendering of *the moment.* But having survived the literal twister, Alan reverts to his Herzogian stupor of thought: contemplating the aftermath of the twister, he muses, "One's first thought is 'What is it like? What does it remind me of?'" Charlotte declares: "I'm not reminded of *anything.*"

Hodler is the novel's Morris-mind, but like Soby, Horter, and Cowie, he is more removed from Morris autobiographically than are Clyde Muncy, Foley, Boyd, and Howe. It is what escapes his conceptualizing that Hodler likes most about what he witnesses: "The meaning that escapes exceeds whatever he has grasped." Hodler arrives at the "scene of the crime," but he sees that the real crimes are all in his and Avery's heads; no crime, it is later discovered, has really been committed here, for "penetration" of Holly did not occur. Morris often echoes Blake: "It occurs to Hodler that the evil men do is less depressing than their vagrant, idle thoughts." Hodler is relieved to see no cuts on Avery, who "suffers from a crime he failed to commit." Hodler himself feels defensive when Avery calls Jubal a pervert. "Hodler wears no space helmet, but one might think that he had just been shot into orbit." Though he is usually the witness of the aftermath, Hodler feels as though he is Jubal's accomplice. As a man who controls his impulses, he does help create the psychological climate of restraint that finally turns boys like Jubal loose. But his collusion differs from Avery's leering delight. "Hodler is a sober man, but for this boy on the loose, free to indulge in his whims, he feels a twinge of envy. There is something to be said for impulsive behavior, although Hodler is perhaps not the man to say it. Visiting spacemen are free to act in a way he is not." Actually, we know that Jubal doesn't indulge his whims; he is driven by others, beginning with one of his own sort, LeRoy. Like the reader, Hodler is a bystander, but near the end he becomes an active observer who will give his own "eye-witness report." Having traced the signs of a human twister, he finally witnesses him in action just when the actual twister steals the show. As the boy rides on out the other end of town, following the twister, Hodler sleeps. "Something in his nature, as well as in nature, seems to find release."

Compared with all his witnesses, Jubal, Morris suggests, is stable. Ironically, Jubal is fleeing his bully buddy's violence against him when he arrives by chance in Pickett; and it is to protect himself from its citizens that he reacts violently in his encounters with them; he assaults the men because their impulsive behavior startles him; he merely attempts to control them. The Sheriff himself, having interviewed the smiling "victims," declares that it is he and the kid who need protection. In the midst of the rain that precedes the twister, Jubal exhibits the conservatism that streaks through most apparently wild men: "he waits, a remarkable example of a responsible, law-abiding citizen, until the green flashes on giving him the all-clear up ahead."

If his own appearance is bizarre, many things in

acceptable society, especially businesses, also look weird: propeller-type banners that twirl between the gas pumps of the One-Stop Diner; his exotic costume could have been provided by Kashperl's store: "Everything is familiar, in stock, and selling — except the face," smeared with soot. Hodler wonders, looking at the numerous low "camp" pictures on the wall of Holly's room: "Was a spaceman so unusual?" Like rider and motorcycle, Holly and house are equally haywire; house and inhabitant cohabit on similar planes of aberration.

Jubal decides that the movie view of life and of war is crazy; then the view of "real" life and peace that he glimpses while on the run seems even crazier. "The crazy ways of the world silence Jubal." Looking for a gun in Kashperl's store with which to protect himself, he says, "You run into some awful nutty people," and Kashperl himself proves to be one of them. People either act nutty like Holly and Haffner, or think only evil like Kashperl. "If the army is no place for a growing boy," Morris concludes, "neither is the world." Juxtaposing Jubal with the "normal" people who think Jubal is a madman, Morris shows that it is the peculiar that is normal.

Though Morris never takes his eyes off the berserk elements in the American character, the style he uses to describe disorder, chance, and contingency is the most perfectly controlled style in contemporary American literature. Everything style has been trained over the centuries to do, Morris makes it do in his novels. In this one, he restricts himself to a comparatively few images, but his mind savors them so persistently that we always feel the weather of his mind; as in old-fashioned novels — Fielding's, for instance — we are always aware of an ambient sensibility as part of the fictive experience. All descriptions are double-edged; of course, this stylistic excellence, sustained line by line, can be wearing. But though we are constantly aware that he is actively using style, the way he uses it is unpredictable.

Sometimes the author is too transparently clever, as

in dialog that echoes his own key phrases. His rhetoric sometimes so exceeds the occasion that one is too conscious of Morris' predilection for the non-event. His wit is sometimes too dependent upon rhetorical reversals, bizarre parallels, Blakean or Chestertonian paradoxes. Hodler thinks, "Cold tips often prove to be hot ones" — Morris worries this phrase, for instance, over a whole page. In revitalizing the cliché, Morris often depicts the triumph of the commonplace over the spectacular, as when Hodler perceives that the date makes more sense out of the news than he can make of it. Still, a proliferation of such reversals — Haffner carries a pipe tool but does not smoke a pipe, loses all his pocketknives, but never the sharpening stone, and is "delighted to see the healthy dogs with their ailing owners on leashes" enter the vet's — evokes chuckles that verge on exasperation. Some of his conceits are worked over in a muddy context, as when Haffner sees Jubal coming: "A white man emerging from a black man, or the two in one?" Jubal's face, blackened by his buddy with a cigar stub dipped in stovelid soot, evokes too many such speculations from the author and the characters. Some of his puns respond negatively to analysis. But the word play throughout the novel on such controlling terms as "in orbit" and "spaceman" has become quite vital by the end — the word has become flesh.

Morris' rhetorical interrogation of his raw material is a stylistic trademark. In this novel rhetorical questions elicit actual events. "And how is Miss Holly?" Hodler asks Avery, as a routine rhetorical question, to which Avery always answers, "*Who the hell would know that?*" But today, "Somebody finally knew. It is a torment to Hodler that this essential knowledge is what he once desired for himself." When the mailman reports that a spaceman raped Miss Holly, Kashperl asks Jubal a typical, kidding question: "Now why'd a boy like *you* do that?" Today, just by chance, he asks the right person. If "Hodler admits to the frailty of language," Morris forces that frailty to perform amazing feats of style and significance.

Briefer than *Man and Boy*, *In Orbit* is Morris' shortest novel. After sixteen novels, the best of which are brief, one is tempted to conclude that the long, large-canvas, many-faceted novel which so many readers have looked for may not come, that the short novel is after all Morris' forte. But mindful of what he can accomplish in the margin of unpredictability allowed by his continuing development of familiar raw material, we ought to resist that temptation.

Though he continues to be an observer of current trends in the American character, Morris is less than ever a critic; his is an impersonal vision which selects details that fascinate him. Cerebral though he is often accused of being, so much so that even in this age of criticism, of Herzogian readers, he alienates many who must still admire him, Morris strives first of all to put his reader through a pure experience. In a work of art "the transitory, illusive facts," he said in *The Territory Ahead*, "are shaped into a fiction of permanence." *In Orbit* is a work of art that, to use Conrad's phrase, carries "its justification in every line." And Morris' first task, like Conrad's, is to "make you *see*." He shows us the American landscape and makes us see into the American character. In "The Lunatic, the Lover, and the Poet" (*Kenyon Review*, Autumn, 1965), Morris could have been speaking of his own inclination: "Grown accustomed to monsters, real or imaginary, perhaps we know this new world better than Shakespeare, whose instinct was to speak his mind through the mouths of clowns and fools." Though the implications of his novels are terrifying, Morris (to use Conrad's words once more) "speaks to our capacity for delight and wonder, to the sense of mystery surrounding our lives."

gene derwood:
cassandra sane

Listening to the prophetic doom-murmuring voice of Gene Derwood on a recording, I feel as though I am standing rigid, nerve-vibrant and vision-blurred, in the gloom of the temple at Delphi, listening to the coarse, dark voice of despair, threaded with the flickering gold of hope. It is a spell poetry rarely casts, a spell at the prospect of which I willingly suspend disbelief. But when the voice on the record stops, and I have only the black cracks on the polar page to go by, I must confess to myself that I feel I have been had.

But if her poetry is not really as good as she makes it sound, it is often enough very fine. The voice of Gene Derwood, even on the page, seems to speak under "a dome of twilight hour," and she seems to say, like a female Prometheus, "I snatch the stuff of God." She had that general love of mankind that is no more intimate than a prophetess can endure. Out of her rather abstract compassion, she spoke rarely, in her best utterances, in the first person singular, but generally within the stated or implied frame of "we" — the "we," usually, of fellow victims, "lips dumb with Cassandra woe." Her friend, Joseph Bennett, in his Preface to her collected poems, said, "Her eyes were strange; Pythian." "Her poems," said George Barker, "are like gifted children answering an unholy quiz by the Powers of the Air." She spoke with Cassandra-like terror and despair at having the prophetic powers. Although it seems often to tremble on the razor's edge of madness, to gulp in fear of the gibberish of prophetic lunacy, her voice was always disciplined by the rigors of art to articulate what may have seemed "beyond the powers of art to reify." In a world in which the "bombish mentors" had strewn the lanes of civilization with human entrails, Gene Derwood, a sane Cassandra, was oracle of what she saw. And the fantastic images she saw then have become quotidian.

Gene Derwood was about forty years old when she died in 1954. Born in Illinois of English, pre-Revolutionary stock, she lived in the Middle West and in the South, but spent most of her adult life in New York in the South Ferry area of Manhattan in what she called "upper New York Bay." Much of the day she sat on her terrace overlooking the East River, the city, and "the chained bay waters." Her "gentle, quiet life" was partially devoted to her interest in flowers and in astronomy. Wife of poet-anthologist (or anthologist-poet) Oscar Williams, she was a painter as well as a poet. Among her more than one hundred and fifty oil paintings are portraits of Auden, George Barker, Max Ernst, and Dylan Thomas.

Her poems, most of which seem to have appeared in the years 1940–54, a time of almost continuous war, were published in avant- (but not too avant-) garde periodicals. A perfectionist, she delayed publication of her individual poems and of her collected works in order to improve them. *The Poems of Gene Derwood* (Clarke and Way, 1955) appeared posthumously. They were greeted with warm critical appreciation. She was likened to Herbert, the metaphysical poet, because of similarity in theme, to Blake because of visionary qualities, to Hopkins because of her imaginative use and reconstruction of language, to Wilfred Owen because of her preoccupation with antiwar themes, and to Thomas Hardy because of her view of man in nature. I feel her prophetic tone in crying out the stupidity of man's humanity resembles Jeffers'. Such categorizing is not necessarily misleading, for Gene Derwood's originality lucidly proclaims itself. But she did not welcome the critic, as no prophetess would, saying in her last poem, "Let men keep from me, and my name, | The coarse-thumbed fuss | Of schoolish talking, mongering my fame."

Original themes are hard to come by, and they are not to be found in Gene Derwood's poetry. Her level of reflection is usually somewhere among the stars — lofty. Her poems express her concern about man's estrangement from the universe, from nonhuman forms of nature. War is the prime form this estrangement takes. Most of the fewer than forty published poems refer to some kind of organized violence and cruelty of men against men, never of two individuals against each other. As in "A Conversation," scientific reason is culpable above all causes: reason and imagination, science and art, logic and intuition conflict, and "bombs speak their prodigious blasphemy." Viewing the war as a female outsider, she was lacerated into indignation and invective by her own imagination. "Her innocence," says Joseph Bennett, "was so radical that it astonished one — the full force of a purity of soul which had a certain fury, it was so strong." But her innocence was tempered with mature awareness of evil. Man's estrangement from nature is in proportion to the extent that his logic, his vast knowledge, enable him to control, exploit, and despoil it, and to utilize it for war purposes. She explores the ambiguities of human perception and feeling and the convolutions of suffering.

But her themes are not entirely gloomy, although even the hearts of her love poems are laced with bitterness — toward her lover, toward herself, or toward general dehumanizing aspects of civilization. In "Spring Air," she can go into ecstasy over the coming of spring, as poets have always, without much persuasion, been able to do.

One is most aware of the wonder of Gene Derwood's imagination in her eccentric use of language, in the rhythms, the nuances, the sensations conveyed by her rare sensibility. She seems to have constructed a grammar, a syntax, that makes sense only in the contexts and for the sensations *she* creates and communicates. Language itself seems to have entranced her. Standing in awe of the mysteries and in horror of the cruelties of life, she forged a language that is vigorous, intense, splendid, rich, and that reaches new dimensions of expression. Her imagery is fabulous, often surrealistic, recalling Rimbaud and the French imagists, and she welds words as Hopkins and Thomas do. Her awareness of form and technique, her use of color, and her vivid, striking images owe something, no doubt, to her work as a painter. Her poems exhibit a high frequency of omission of words, omission of punctuation, and of inversion. She seems to make spontaneous use of what she has assimilated in her reading of all kinds of poetry; she is an eclectic poet, who uses archaic and esoteric words, giving them new connotations in special contexts. She makes witty puns on clichés, but most of her humor is rather grim. She often uses the terminology of astronomy, painting, music, science, and of horticulture. Like many modern poets, she raids the storehouses of myth for analogical and allegorical material, and she, like Hart Crane, makes poetic statements about abstract or philosophical ideas by analogy with popular entertainment forms, such as the circus and the movies. Her vision is often complex, sometimes confused, causing certain images or perceptions to burst bright in the reader's mind as though they broke suddenly free of murky entanglements.

Most of the best qualities of Gene Derwood's poetry are exemplified in "Elegy on Gordon Barber," one of the most moving elegies I know.

elegy on gordon barber

lamentably drowned in his eighteenth year

When in the mirror of a permanent tear
Over the iris of your mother's eye
I beheld the dark tremor of your face, austere
With space of death, spun too benign for youth,
Icicle of the past to pierce her living sigh —
I saw you wish the last kiss of mother's mouth,
Who took the salted waters rather in the suck
Of seas, sighing yourself to fill and drench
With water the plum-rich glory of your breast
Where beat the heart escaping from war's luck.

Gordon, I mourn your wrist, your running foot,
Your curious brows, your thigh, your unborn daughters,
Yet mourn more deep the drought-caught war dry boy
Who goes, a killer, to join you in your sleep

poetic image in six genres

And envy you what made you blench
Taking your purple back to drought-less waters.
What choke of terror filled you in the wet
What fierce surprise caught you when play turned fate
And all the rains you loved became your net,
Formlessly yielding, yet stronger than your breath?
Then did you dream of mother or hopes hatched
When the cold cramp held you from nape to foot
And time dissolved, promise dissolved, in Death?
Did you cry "cruel" to all the hands that stretched
Not near, but played afar, when you sank down
Your sponge of lungs hurt to the quick
Till you had left the quick to join the dead,
Whom, now, your mother mourns, grief-sick.
You were too young to drown.

Never will you take bride to happy bed,
Who lay awash in water yet no laving
Needed, so pure so young for sudden leaving.
Gone, gone is Gordon, tall and brilliant lad
Whose mind was science. Now hollow his skull
A noble sculpture, is but sunken bone,
His cells from water come by water laid
Grave-deep, to water *gone*.
Lost, lost the hope he had
Washed to a cipher his splendour and his skill.

But Gordon's gone, it's other boys who live afraid.

Two years, and lads have grown to hold a gun.
In dust must splendid lads go down and choke,
Red dry their hands and dry their one day's sun
From which they earthward fall to fiery tomb
Bomb-weighted, from bloodying children's hair.

Never a boy but takes as cross Cain's crime
And goes to death by making death, to pass
Death's gate distorted with the dried brown grime —
Better the watery death than death by air
Or death by sand
Where fall hard fish of fear
Loud in unwetted dust.

Spun on a lucky wave, O early boy!
Now ocean's fish you are
As heretofore.
Perhaps you had sweet mercy's tenderness
To win so soon largesse of choice
That you, by grace, went gayly to the wave
And all our mourning should be to rejoice.

While the poem is a beautiful and moving elegy on the death of Gordon, it ends up as an even more eloquent threnody on the horrible death of young soldiers. What begins as a lament for a personal friend soon moves simultaneously toward a lament for unknown young men. And what starts as a lament over the death of Gordon soon moves simultaneously toward an invocation to rejoice over the manner of his death, which is desirable over the manner of the deaths of young soldiers. Unlike a soldier, he did not go "to death by making death," passing "Death's gate distorted with the dried brown grime — | Better the watery death." The first stanzas focus on Gordon, and then in stanzas five and six the perspective has shifted to "other boys who live afraid."

When the mother bends her head over the coffin to gaze upon Gordon's face, the poet sees "the dark tremor" of his face reflected in the tear "over the iris" of his mother's eye. The momentary tear mirrors an image that is permanent in the memory of the mother; and the poet will always be able to see Gordon's face in the mother's eye. The face is made austere by the space between the living and the dead. It has the look of older, wiser men, a look spun by death "too benign for youth." "Dark tremor" suggests not only the way his face may have looked under water as he drowned, but the look, too, on the mother's face as she gazes at him. Made cold by death, his face is like an "icicle of the past," piercing "her living sigh —" The dash enhances the effect of "pierce" and of "icicle," which is Gordon's face, frozen by death in water. "Wish," in "I saw you wish the last kiss of mother's mouth," is almost too ambiguous, but with the emphasis on "mother" in this stanza "kiss of mother's mouth" is very effective, coming just before the image of Gordon taking "the salted waters rather in the suck of seas." Gordon, going back to mother ocean, the source of all life ("his cells from water come by water laid | Grave-deep"), dying by drowning in undefiled water, contrasts with the filthy deaths of soldiers. In the first stanza, Gordon goes from his mother, who nursed him not too long ago, "back to drought-less waters," sucked down by the eternal mother ocean. The juxtaposition of "kiss" and "suck" is effective. He himself sighed as he filled and drenched with water "the plum-rich glory of [his] breast," and "your purple" in the next stanza ironically suggests perhaps the purple heart awarded by the military.

The poet mourns Gordon's wrist, his running foot (both of utilitarian value in war), and his "curious brows," his thigh, his "unborn daughters," but she mourns "more deep [suggesting deep ocean again] the drought-caught war dry boy," the boy caught in the drought of human feeling that is war, who dies on dry land, "who goes, a killer, to join you in your sleep." Such a boy would envy Gordon what made *him* blench, for it took Gordon's "purple back to drought-less waters," in contrast to the ghastly manner of a soldier's death. The questioning method makes the poet's monologue with the dead boy more intimate

In the next four lines, the poet wonders how Gordon felt when some "choke of terror filled you in the wet | What fierce surprise caught you when play turn fate | And all the rains you loved became your net, | Formlesly yielding, yet stronger than your breath?" "Fierce surprise" reiterates the icicle image and is like the sudden impact of bullets which the young soldiers feel. Just as children play war and only a few years later are embroiled in the real thing, Gordon passed immediately from play, swimming, to fate; fate seems a more ennobling cause of death than the human machinations of war. The many rains that

Gordon loved and which because part of the sea are now the net that chokes him with terror, pulling him down; the water yields when he struggles, but formlessly, being nothing he can hold onto and resist, so that it is stronger than his breath and he yields. Derwood conveys a keen sense of what she imagines it is like to drown, a feeling made more palpable with "When the cold cramp held you from nape to foot." Gordon's dreams of his mother and of "hopes hatched" ceased when the "wet" dissolved time and promise; the repetition of "dissolved" conveys a sense of the dissolving process, with the slow sureness of the rhythm and the s sounds. The pathos of the drowning is further conveyed by the third question: "Did you cry 'cruel' to all the hands that stretched|Not near, but played afar, when you sank down|Your sponge of lungs hurt to the quick|Till you had left the quick to join the dead." The lines may apply as well to young soldiers who die, like children drowning, on the dry land, while others, at home, "play afar."

It seems to me that the last two lines of the stanza — "Whom, now, your mother mourns grief-sick.|You were too young to drown" — are rather trite, especially the latter, but the former rounds out the thought by keeping the mother in the picture, and the latter, by its simplicity after much complex language, does catch the reader off guard. The implication is that he was too young to drown not just because he was young, but because he was some-one special.

What will never be for Gordon may apply as well to the young soldiers. Gordon will never "take bride to happy bed," because the sea has taken *him* to its bed. "Who lay awash in water yet no laving|Needed" emphasizes the purity and innocence of Gordon (which contrast later with the foul death of boys who go as killers to their graves). The rhythm of the *g* alliteration of the next five lines gives a sense of threnody: "Gone, gone is Gordon . . . grave-deep, to water *gone*." and "lost, lost" sustains the dull rhythm of grieving. Gordon was tall and brilliant, his mind was science, which, when not used to destroy civilization (as Gene Derwood usually sees it and as it now does in war), is pure as Gordon himself. The skull that held that mind is now as hollow as a used bombshell, the head, once "noble sculpture," suggesting the Greek statues of young lads, is now "but sunken bone." He is reduced to what he was at birth, "cells from water come by water laid." All his youthful hopes for a future such as *humane* science could shape, "his splendour and is skill," are "washed to a cipher," to a zero.

In one line, the poet emphasizes her major concern, which is for the "other boys who live afraid" (formerly the title of the poem). Gordon did not live afraid, for he was playing when he died. "Gordon's gone"; no use weeping for him when others will die after a prolonged fear of death, after having themselves killed others.

"Two years, and lads have grown to hold a gun" — two years since the war began (or perhaps since Gordon's death). Perhaps these are like the other lads who played afar when Gordon drowned, and now they are old enough to kill in war, and now, instead of in the laving ocean, "in dusk must splendid lads go down and choke." On their hands is the dried red blood, their own and their victims'. They die under the dry sun, which seems the only one they have seen. In airplanes, they fall earthward, crash, "bomb-weighted," and lie in the sudden, brief, "fiery tomb," the plane. This plane dropped bombs that bloodied "children's hair." Children because their victims, soon after the time when they were children themselves

Since the beginning of human life, boys have carried the cross cut from Cain's crime. Boys go "to death by making death," and pass "Death's gate distorted with the dried brown grime" of their own and their victims' blood, mixed with the general filth of war. Better is Gordon's way of dying "than death by air | Or death by sand | Where fall hard fish of fear | Lord in unwetted dust." The young soldiers are transformed by fear into hard fish that fall loudly into the dust amid the loud bursting of bombs and gunfire. In their sudden leaving, they do need the laving of sea water because their purity and innocence have been defiled by their own actions and by the general atrocity of war even though they were forced into it.

"Spun on a lucky wave, O early boy!" Dying early, before the other kind of dying that comes of making death, Gordon Barber was lucky. Because all life came from the ocean, because he died a natural, clean death in the ocean, he is still ocean's, not fear's fish. "Perhaps you had sweet mercy's tenderness | To win so soon largesse of choice" — mercy was sweet and tender to him, for he won, in the manner of his dying, the gift, by mercy's choice, of a clean death. It was by grave that he went, in the spirit of play, gayly to the wave," unaware that play would turn fate. Because he was saved from murder and the death of a wholesale murderer, as young soldiers were not, "all our mourning should be to rejoice."

"cassandra singing"—on and off key

After my freshman year at the University of Tennessee in my hometown, Knoxville, I set out to encounter Life in New York, made the Greenwich Village scene in the pre-beatnik days when Maxwell Bodenheim in a trench coat was still peddling his poems. I worked as a mail clerk atop the Empire State Building, hopped the counters of numerous White Tower hamburger stands on the night shift, and finally signed as a messman on a ship out of Edgewater, N.J., thus satisfying a long-fermenting urge to take to the sea. While we were in port in Texas City, a leather-jacketed relief messman from nearby Galveston came aboard and couldn't stop talking about a wild girl, leader of his motorcycle gang. When her brother was killed in a smashup, she joined the gang and proved herself a more fearless daredevil, a more vicious brawler, than he had been. Out of this conversation came, thirteen years later, in 1966, my three-act play, *Cassandra Singing*, depicting the strange relationship between a motorcyclist named Lone and his invalid sister Cassie in Harlan, Kentucky. It had its out-of-New York tryout at the Albuquerque Little Theatre.

I give the impression of a lovely leap. Actually, the process was a prolonged and agonizing series of leaps and drags. I tend to look upon the three hundred letters, critiques and reviews concerning the play, together with the numerous telephone calls and personal encounters, as constituting a bizarre combination correspondence-tutoring course in playwriting conducted by a battalion of teachers over the course of more than a decade.

After fourteen years, *Cassandra Singing* is still with me. At thirty-three, I stand on the finish side of the ninth major revision of the play and the eighth major revision of a novel that is concerned with the same characters. Every playwright or novelist has that one work on which he really gets hung up, and *Cassandra* was mine. But since I have dealt with the same raw material in two radically different forms and over such a long stretch of time, I think my experience, though possibly unique, may offer exaggerated illustrations of certain creative problems which every writer encounters. In my writing classes, I preach against the kind of waste I indulged in. So my account and evaluation of the *Cassandra* experience may be read as a cautionary tale which urges the young writer to avoid a similar immersion in his raw material.

Traveling, shifting from job to job, and writing in most of the other literary forms, I created a dynamic context of distractions and inducements for the play's evolution. Before analyzing the play itself, then, let me begin with a chronicle of the composition of *Cassandra Singing*, play and novel.

1954: During the McCarthy investigations, I refused to sign a loyalty oath in basic training; while being investigated, I was assigned to a holding company at Fort Jackson. The nervous tension created in this situation contributed to the intensity and fullness of vision that produced the one-act version of *Cassandra*. Even then, the novelistic implications of the long one-act began to work on my imagination. The play won third place in a state contest at the University of Tennessee.

1955: The C.I.C. decided I wasn't a security risk, so I was on a troop ship to Alaska the night the play opened at Carousel Theatre. It created a controversy, the vibrations of which are still felt in Knoxville, the play's original locale. In Anchorage, I planned the novel version in Joycean detail.

1956: From Alaska I went to Iowa State Teachers College, where I met my wife in the college radio station. For my radio show, I directed the one-act *Cassandra*; the morning after the closed-circuit broadcast, the station's faculty adviser sent me a long list of "obscene, indecent and profane" words and expressions from the play, but without mentioning whatever good qualities the play may have had. While taking a playwriting course, I worked simultaneously on the long play and the novel versions of

Cassandra. A high-school friend showed the one-act to Ed Shade at the Irene Kaufmann Settlement House, Pittsburgh. I revised the play and hitchhiked through a snowstorm to see it performed. The settlement house serves a Negro-Jewish slum area. A Negro boy portrayed Gran'paw and Jewish and Catholic kids portrayed the other Anglo-Saxon Protestant characters. *Cassandra* followed an evening of amateur vaudeville, and the audience was one of the most receptive the play has had.

Back in Knoxville as a senior at the University of Tennessee that summer, I finished two hundred pages of the novel and the first complete version of the long play (and got married). My agent, Ann Elmo, returned the long version, but tried to sell the one-act for television. When Nolan Miller accepted the one-act for *New Campus Writing* #2, I once again revised it; Margaret Mayorga listed it in her *Best One-Act Plays of 1959*.

1957–1958:   Both the play and the novel opened up several graduate fellowship possibilities, but Kenneth Rexroth's articles on the San Francisco Renaissance seduced me. I intended to finish the novel while taking creative writing courses with Walter Van Tilburg Clark at San Francisco State College. Even at eighteen, I couldn't take much of Greenwich Village; at twenty-three, I could take even less of the unearned poses of North Beach. Disenchanted in one of the world's most enchanting cities, I produced out of a profound depression an additional one hundred pages of the novel, five short stories, five hundred pages of literary criticism, two one-act plays, several poems, and another novel — besides three revisions of the play. (I am often tempted to return to San Francisco.) Ironically, my M.A. thesis novel was not *Cassandra*, but *The Beautiful Greed*, published three years later by Random House.

In San Francisco, the play endured its most protracted, excruciating, and discouraging baptism in amateur theater. Jules Irving rejected the long version as a major production at the college. But the one-act, staged as a directing class project, was well done. I made extensive revisions for a Players Club production at the college, but a lavish musical finally preempted it, and a reading at North Beach's Fugazi Hall was scheduled instead. Opening night, the actor playing Lone got a Hollywood call and the play was never heard. Encouraged and intelligently advised by Herbert Blau, I rewrote several scenes, hoping to obtain an Actors Workshop production, but the final decision was No. Two separate groups in Berkeley came close to the tryout stage. Four other groups considered it in San Francisco. The most agonizing experience came from the Ensemble Theatre, a creation of young directors inspired by the Group Theatre concept of the thirties; early in rehearsals, the director discovered that he lacked the various resources to mount and perform a play consisting of twenty-five characters, sixteen scenes, five sets.

After a year of serious consideration, Studio M in Florida (which premiered several Tennessee Williams plays) reluctantly returned *Cassandra*. It won third place in the national contest at Baton Rouge Little Theatre under the title, "Children of a Cold Sun." When Collin Wilcox, a friend of the days when I acted in productions at the University of Tennessee, wanted to play Cassie at Carousel Theatre, Knoxville, with her husband directing, she was told that Carousel, a joint university-community venture, had to operate on a commercial basis and so was unable to risk doing full-length new works. That summer my wife and I returned to Knoxville, where we lived in a mansion by the river lent to us by friends vacationing in Europe, and I revised the play once again.

1958–1959: That fall, high in the mountains at Boone, North Carolina, I began a teaching career. At Appalachian State Teachers College I taught five courses, directed three major productions and four one-acts, and wrote very little. A group at McGill University performed the one-act *Cassandra*; but Aaron Frankel, who intended to produce the long version at the Margo Jones Theatre in Dallas, was overruled by the board.

The next summer on an old farm outside Boone, I worked during the day on an entirely new version of the novel (while my wife wrapped meat in a supermarket), and at night I was a disc jockey in Boone.

1959–1960:   My new agent, Monica McCall, showed the long *Cassandra* to John Gassner, who gave me a John Golden Playwriting Fellowship for twenty-five hundred dollars at Yale Drama School. I worked on the play again, hoping it would be produced at Yale so its problems could be detected and dealt with under such ideal conditions. Neither student nor faculty directors chose to do it. Instead, I was asked to adapt Plautus' *Casina* as a modern musical satire of the beatniks. One of the worst plays I have ever written, it was finished in a week; audiences loved it, students loathed it.

Back in Boone for the summer, living in an even more remote and primitive farmhouse, I worked every day on the Cassandra novel. At night I acted in and helped stage-manage the outdoor spectacle *Horn in the West*. The one-act *Cassandra* was movingly performed on one of the outdoor theater's three stages.

1960–1961:   Teaching four English courses at Centre College in Kentucky, I became so keenly involved in the life of the college that I had only the two weeks at Christmas in which to do a complete revision of the play. But during those four consecutive summers in the mountains of North Carolina, I got caught up in writing bouts that often extended to thirteen hours a day. That summer, I was financially in a position to concentrate on writing alone. I wrote six hundred pages on the novel version of *Cassandra*; that summer, too, I began teaching in the writing workshop at Morehead, Kentucky, where I have since taught several summers. Shuttling scripts of *Cassandra* among agents, foundations, and contests, I recklessly rushed a reading at *First Stage*; the editor suggested a few general cuts and revisions and invited resubmission.

1961–1962:   Back at Centre, I revised the play during Christmas vacation, and *First Stage* accepted it for publication. In May, I received a dramatic telegram from a director friend who had found an eager producer for *Cassandra* — the actor, George Segal. I never heard from either of them again.

At Boone, I wrote two hundred pages of the novel version. The cast of *Horn in the West* gave a fine studio performance of the long version of the play in an acting space not much bigger than the commedia dell'arte roadside plank-stages. At least (and at last) I knew what the play looked like; I saw immediately many of its problems; I was able now to revise it drastically.

1962–1963:   It was while teaching only two courses, both in creative writing, at the University of Louisville that I found the time to develop the routine and the discipline that I had longed for; since then, I have written at least four hours every day. In Louisville, I wrote fourteen hundred pages of a completely new version of the novel. That summer, I moved to a farm outside Louisville where I revised the novel; my publisher, Random House, wisely rejected the fourteen-hundred-page version.

1963–1964:   In a Greenwich Village bookshop, Hale McKeen, a New York producer, bought the issue of *First Stage* containing my play. If I would shorten it and make other revisions, he would direct and produce the play. I agreed, and he took an option. Over several months, I completely revised the play three times. We sent tape-recordings back and forth, and McKeen made several trips to the farm for conferences. Finally, in January, 1964, I went to Albuquerque for rehearsals, and the play was performed January 31 through February 8.

The theater — a community venture devoted mainly to the production of Broadway comedies, with one drama permitted in its season of five plays — had been especially successful under the two-year direction of

Bernard Thomas, an old friend of McKeen's. But it took more than friendship to persuade Thomas to take a chance on a new play, particularly one like *Cassandra* — it took courage, as the predicted reaction of his patrons proved. While there was little choice in the casting, there was a tolerable balance between poor and good performances, and three were very fine. Susan Rieselt, a New York television, stock, and road-show actress, played Cassie; the other actors (and technicians) were amateurs. (The terms "amateur" and "professional" mean little to me; there are only convincing or unconvincing productions.) Although the set designer responded adequately to the tasks imposed upon him by the play, I was able to see the fallacies in my conception of the large, multi-unit set. Only one scene was completely rewritten — the day after my arrival; the production situation was not intended to be ideal for rewriting, but lines were cut or revised and brief scenes within scenes were cut every night of the run. At first, the actors had difficulty understanding the characters, but one of the most gratifying aspects of the various productions of this play has been that the actors nonetheless fervently believe in the play and love its characters.

The publicity was surprisingly full and dazzling. The play was subjected to severe audience reactions, unused as most of them were to seeing, or enduring, such a play on their stage. Most were shocked, outraged, mystified, bored; many others were, for various reasons, impressed, and reviews were enthusiastic. Audiences laughed in all the right places in this serious drama, and most of the scenes seemed to hold. Unusually foul weather and unusually vociferous grapevine activity were reflected erratically in ticket sales, which were in the end a little below average.

1964–1967:   What I learned from the Albuquerque experience went into the final revision several months later. In the spring of 1966, while I was teaching at Kenyon College and working as assistant editor of *The*

Kenyon Review, that version was tested at the University of Oregon — and I saw that I could finally turn loose of the play. It is a good play; it is not the great play I was trying to write, perhaps because the raw material with which I began should have been transformed only into a novel.

In its thirteen-year career, *Cassandra* has been considered by approximately twenty-five Broadway and off-Broadway producers, twenty major groups out of New York, forty community theaters, thirty-five universities and colleges. Though I was director of plays at Appalachian, I don't believe that playwrights should take advantage of such situations; on the other hand, it's depressingly ironic that while I taught at Centre, Louisville, and Kenyon, *Cassandra* or another of my plays was being done half a continent away. The play has won awards or made a good showing in twelve regional and national contests; on the basis of this play, I've been nominated twice for a Ford grant. Six major agents have handled the play. It has been published in one-act and three-act form; twelve magazines and play publishers have considered it. Out of the various productions, publications and contests, the play has earned $475. (By contrast, one of the better-known literary magazines has just paid me $560 for a novella, written in three days, one of the best things I've ever done. Again by contrast, I worked four solid months on a recent play, *Fugitive Masks*, and received $15 royalty for nine performances at world-famous Barter Theatre; Ohio University produced the same play this spring — 1968 — and paid the standard royalty fee.)

I should be horrified if this account made people think I had written nothing but endless versions of *Cassandra Singing*. During the prolonged struggle with its massive raw material, I was able, fortunately, to write and publish many other things. I wrote six one-act and three long plays which have won prizes, production, and publication; I wrote three novels, two of which were published; fifteen poems — ten published; twenty short stories — thirteen published; a book-length critical study of the novelist Wright Morris — also published; thirty essays and articles — most of them published; and fifty long book reviews. Obviously, Thomas Wolfe was my childhood hero; but James Joyce is the aesthetic hero of my maturity; and the gargantuan, cannibalistic impulse to consume the raw materials of life struggles with the aesthetic impulse to which I am intellectually committed. Yet I cannot explain why some of this work, including the most aesthetically finished, was written quickly and with ease; in that respect, the creative process remains a mystery to me.

A survey of the criticism of early versions from various theatrical groups and other readers will suggest why *Cassandra* was so long getting staged. The whole body of criticism, oral and written, has been extremely helpful. The contradictions within groups and among the various commentators is only momentarily annoying, for contradictions create a tension which further stimulates me to reconceive. While I have gotten some very good detailed criticism, I often suspect that most people don't know how to give it in the little time they can devote to it. For theater people there must seem something rather futile about critical reflection without direct consequence, because the theater is a place where most thinking is worked out in the glare and sweat of the theater's physical immediacy. In recent years, I have felt that present opportunities and an exciting future for playwrights lie outside New York, in the community, college, and repertory companies. While I myself have no great cause for complaint against these theaters, my experiences with them indicate alarming irresponsibility in their handling of new plays. Within the last few years this situation has gotten depressingly worse. At conferences and in publications, groups loudly proclaim the importance of encouraging new American playwrights and their intention of doing so, but their sincerity is to be doubted when they hold scripts as long as eighteen months, then return them without even the very basic decency of a printed rejection slip — something not even the crassest Broadway producer would dream of doing. All the playwright can do is *write* plays; the rest is up to others.

Many groups came close to producing *Cassandra*, intending to work out the play's problems with the author. Several contest judges, however, felt the play needed more work before it would be ready even for rehearsal testing, though one allowed that it was "the most powerful piece in the contest." Having read only half of it, one director was eager to produce it, but a complex of factors unrelated to the play's quality resulted finally in a negative decision. Often, other powers vetoed directors who wanted to do the play.

Some groups decided that their theaters were physically unable to accommodate the play. The availability of actors posed another problem; some groups lacked enough skilled and mature actors to handle convincingly the many fully-developed characters. A financial or psychological reluctance of certain groups to do an original was another hindrance. In a season planned for other large-scale shows, usually musicals, there was no room for another "big" production. Often, the decision was that, "everything considered," the play was too "difficult."

But some said simply that the play wasn't their "cup of tea" — too grim, violent, and raw for their own tastes or those of their particular audiences. Some felt the play structurally unfinished, and they were thus dubious about its playability, despite its power in the reading; on the other hand, one editor of *New Campus Writing* considered it a weak reading experience, but a strong theater piece. Some said the play was too imitative, comparing it most often with Tennessee Williams, and in passing with Carson McCullers, Erskine Caldwell, and Eugene O'Neill; but others found it "fresh, individual, underivative." One experienced judge pointed out that the reasons people give for not doing a play, especially an original, are seldom the real ones.

On the generally negative side, some said that the play is consciously strident and abusive, too heavy and morbid, that it piles one scene of agony on top of another, and lacks humanity. One producer was put off by its "objectionable matter." Another "couldn't put it down." Those who were impressed cited the play's substance and conviction, precision and clarity, vigor, power, and excitement. But for differing reasons even sympathetic readers and viewers agreed that it was "overlong, overwritten, overdone." Albuquerque audiences concurred in some of these reactions; whole rows walked out on a play that was "just an excuse to use foul language and ridicule religion." The best audience was the one that braved the decade's worst snow for the sole purpose of seeing a play; having heard about the production, they knew what to expect.

Almost all agreed that "the author has talent" or is "extremely gifted," although one pointed out that the play is unworthy of the talent expended upon it. Unable to produce it themselves, most agreed it deserved a production, preferably a university tryout first, and in most instances new scripts from the author were welcomed. Although all who read the play in various stages agreed that its problems diminish with every revision, achieving greater unity, sturdier construction, and stronger impact, the criticism outlined below applies in varying degrees to almost all versions. Who made the criticism, and when, doesn't matter much.

Comment on the play's theme ranges from "the author has something to say" to "greater emphasis on theme is needed." Admittedly, the play's premise has always been rather unclear. For instance, not until Albuquerque did I clarify in my own mind one of the subordinate themes: incest. One critic felt that the theme (which he didn't enunciate) is too weak to justify the debased characters and their crude language. Members of one reading committee reported that the author wished to portray forms of human degradation; fortunately, the group's director read the same play the author wrote.

My own statements of theme have varied radically as the play itself has taken strong new turns. Although the play has always attempted to convey an existential attitude toward life, growing out of Lone's and his sister Cassie's involvement in their dilemmas, not until Albuquerque had I been able to see the theme lucidly: To live fully, one must balance the forces of action and imagination. Lone's life is an exaggeration of action, Cassie's an exaggeration of imagination, and this polarity is seen clearly when their roles are reversed by a combination of suicidal will and chance — Lone's accident on his motorcycle. A subordinate theme is the inability of people to distinguish between love and hate, to see that in a dynamic interplay each makes the other possible. When the operation of these forces is revealed to Lone as a consequence of his own actions, he makes an existential response to life.

Most of the play's problems point to a lack of focus, as reflected in the charge of thematic confusion; but lack of focus is nowhere more apparent than in the aspect of character. The play has long been overpopulated: originally, the full-length version had twenty-five characters; in Albuquerque, it had nine; it now has six: Lone, Cassie, Coot (the father), Charlotte (the mother), Virgil (Charlotte's faith-healer brother), and Blackie (Lone's motorcycle pal).

Some of the raw materials of the play were ready to respond when that messman came aboard ship in Texas City and told me about the wild girl in his motorcycle gang, while others accumulated over the years. The character of Cassie, for instance, is a rather strange mixture. When I was fourteen I hitchhiked to New York to see Carson McCullers' *The Member of the Wedding*; backstage I told Julie Harris that I would write a play for her some day. Frankie in that play (and in the novel *The*

Heart Is A Lonely Hunter, which I once adapted to the
stage) partly inspired Cassie. Another literary inspiration
was Cassandra, the Greek prophetess of doom, who was
condemned never to be believed. There were the brother-
sister relationships in the *Oresteia*, O'Neill's *Mourning
Becomes Electra*, Sartre's *The Flies*, Cocteau's *L'Enfant
Terrible* (the movie version), and Jean Stafford's *The
Mountain Lion*. There were the people I knew in life. One
of my most intriguing friends in Knoxville was the
daughter of a composer who lived in a mansion by the
river; she had raven-black hair and pure white skin and
was often ill. While in the army, I met the only genuine
bohemian I know: Hope Savage, the daughter of the mayor
of a small South Carolina town; immersed in Shelley and
Swinburne, oblivious to the twentieth century, she lived
in a fabulous white Greek-style mansion. She expressed a
desire to be a gypsy; today she wanders somewhere in
India, expressing a desire to be God knows what. All these
girls, real and fictional, are transformed into Cassie
McDaniel, in whom none of them would recognize herself.
Conceived before *The Wild One* and James Dean, her
brother Lone is pure invention, though he resembles both
Brando and Dean, and several other real persons whom I
met after I had written the play.

If your characters are unlikeable and fail to evoke
compassion, there's no play — unless another raft of
people think that the author excels in creating characters
who are well-developed, exciting, and moving. But despite
the fact that my characters are real and worth-while and
that their "dark and tangled emotions" are engrossing, in
the early version the spectator got lost in the complexity
of relationships. I had hoped that this richness of character
would make any play more interesting; that hope is best
realized, I now see, in a novel. Unsympathetic readers
found the characters stark and inhuman in their vice.
Some said the characters are too self-aware, but others
observed that they lethargically indulge in complaints,
never comprehending what's happening to them; con-

trolled as they are by their weaknesses, they are never in command; they only react. Given the setup at the final curtain, some have said, one imagines absurdly melo-dramatic and fatal futures for the characters, who are deluded by hope in the face of continual misfortune. Close to the enduring problem is the observation that the author feels too deeply for his characters, and thus reveals their thoughts, actions, and reactions, too fully. Since the play continued to lack focus, balance, and proportion, one may well wonder at my failure to ask basic questions about playwriting: Whose play is this? What does he want? What is he willing to do to get it? And so on. Well, I did ask them, of course, but although few of the characters derive directly from actual people in my life, I was so immersed in the life of these people and the "novelistic" dimensions of their experiences that I failed to see clearly certain absolute dictates of the theater.

It was early pointed out to me that, of the secondary characters, Gran'paw McDaniel was powerful but in-essential. Even in the long version, the question of his function remained a problem: a weak character in Act I, he became a strong character in Act II and sent the play in a new direction. In Act I, his effect on the family was felt mainly from a distance — the ancestral home in Cades Cove in the Smokies. (Until Albuquerque, the play was set in Knoxville.) His coming to the house in Knoxville had little direct effect until I forced one — one that became disproportionately strong. He disappeared from the play four versions back.

My attitude toward Gran'paw never changed basically, but a radical change occurred in the character of Virgil Stonecipher, a faith-healer. A few years ago, an intimate association with a real faith-healer caused me to present Stonecipher sympathetically, as a sincere evangelist. Thus, what began as a street corner scene, one of the most theatrically effective in the first versions, became, for more profound dramatic reasons, one of the strongest scenes in the printed version; yet it was eliminated from the Albuquerque production because its very power caused an imbalance, a diffusion of focus. In radically altered form, it reappears in the present version. Virgil is now the mother's brother.

Coot McDaniel, the unemployed father, a lovable old drunk, has remained essentially the same. Repeated revision has only made audiences like him more, and many regard him as the play's most appealing character; it was Coot who drew director-producer Hale McKeen to the play. Aunt Reba, the mother's sister, was almost as likeable as Coot. An aging strip-tease artist in a small-town theater, she was loud and boisterous; both Lone and Cassie were fond of her. But she was one of the first major characters to be cut, proving finally too rich a distraction. Her hypocritical sister, Aunt Maud, of the Salvation Army, meek and mild in the beginning, took on some of her sister's lines and dramatic functions, and later even those of the excised Gran'paw. Now, she, too, has gone the way of all splendid irrelevancies. Originally, Uncle Troy, a city detective, was a callous bully, but certain thematic changes necessitated a more sympathetic stance. Now he, too, is gone, taking his chances in the novel. Charlotte, Lone's mother, has been one of the most difficult characters to get in focus; vague in the one-act version, only repeated revisions, new situations and relationships brought her out; yet her motivations are still unclear. Blackie, too, has undergone a radical change from a showy, theatrically dynamic villain to a person of more dimension; the audience, unfortunately, is now inclined to sympathize with Blackie almost as much as with Lone. In Albuquerque audiences liked Blackie most; he was, however, for reasons beyond the director's control, much better cast. (Lone has always posed a casting problem.) Members of Lone's gang, the Hellhounds, have changed little. Many lines and bits of business have been swapped around from Bluetail to Cowboy to Mavis to Gypsy. Lone's sweetheart, Gypsy, remained the same; but, in Albuquerque, I realized finally, reluctantly, that the gang, including Gypsy, had to go. Now Blackie alone has the burden of linking Cassie's and Lone's world in the bedroom to the world outside.

The play has long suffered from an ambiguity of character focus. Even the two main characters, Lone and Cassie, have been two too many; the emphasis has shifted back and forth from one to the other; at times it has even been a group (family) protagonist. There is a division of opinion as to whether the play should be either Lone's or Cassie's or should focus on them together. Most agree, though — and I finally faced this necessity in the revisions for Albuquerque — that if the emphasis is to be on Lone and Cassie, as it must, the other fully developed characters (all four of them), each with his own compelling story, must be strictly subordinated.

The initial character inspiration was Cassie. The audience was to witness the effect on her of her brother's life outside the room. Having shown Lone's effect on her in the first half, I killed him off (in earlier versions) so I could show the transference of his character to Cassie. Thus, the character relationship seemed to dictate a structural split. But I did not develop Cassie enough in Act I to enable her to take over the play in Act II. Readers couldn't accept her quick recovery; I had depended too much on general knowledge of the nature of rheumatic fever. Some, unable to believe in her as a character anyway (she's rather bizarre), totally rejected the physical and psychological transformations. Some felt she was too passive, "not really a force in the play." When I decided to cripple Lone in a motorcycle accident and let us watch his reaction as Cassie lived out his former life, I solved, or seemed to solve, the split-focus, split-structure problem. Despite the now bothersome (but lovely) title, the play was his. One confusion in his character is still not clear enough: how suicidal is he? One thing is certain: he has always been a little too pure and has grown increasingly saintly; sadistic audiences side with Blackie in his efforts to soil Lone's lily-whiteness. Now that the play has shifted around to face Lone, attentively, squarely, it makes Lone worthy of focus.

I finally faced the theatrical fact that character motives are especially diffuse, vague, and confusing when too many lives and conflicts interweave (no matter how interesting the pattern) and when no single dramatic force impels the characters' action, or compels inertia. Several of the play's reversals are difficult to accept, as for instance the change in Coot (in a middle-phase version) when he effects a reconciliation with Lone. My intimate (novelistic) knowledge of the characters often blinded me to the necessity of revealing them clearly to the audience. On the other hand, I caused confusion by letting the characters analyze each other regarding actions occurring outside the immediate setting; the world of these significant actions can be conveyed only novelistically.

Many readers and viewers praised the dialog as being vigorous, authentic, "hard-hitting," realistically poetic. Yet some of the best scenes are those with little dialog. Again, while individual speeches have generally proved too long (a problem almost solved before Albuquerque), other effective scenes are two recent ones in which characters have long arias. Several versions back, I decided that the dialect was slowing up the reading of the play, so I put the burden of authenticity and regional expressiveness on typical and representative phrases.

Some readers have had difficulty accepting the resolutions of the characters' dilemmas. Events result in catastrophe rather than a solution. The conflicts are resolved neither in the structure of the play nor in action between characters. Certain characters appear to have found solutions, but are merely escaping, one reader contended; she summed up with the disturbing observation that characters, atmosphere, and situation are not used for revelation, but for the sake of violent contrasts to the norm, and that this exaggeration is used to evoke emotional fascination for the characters. The problem of resolution has produced a new ending for almost every revision. To make the resolution inevitable was one of the main tasks of the final revision.

Most critics agreed that the play is "damned theatrical"; the indications for music and sound are "excellent"; it is a colorful play; its style and mood are consistent. But while the author is clever in his use of motifs, in planting little touches, these get lost before they have issue. And there are too many subtleties for the theater; the author depends too much on the actors and the director to flesh out things subtly hinted. The transitions, unprepared for in preceding scenes, are too abrupt. On the other hand, the writer is too inclined to give lengthy set and action description in the script. Although he demonstrates great technical skill, some of his devices are clumsy, as for instance the "remember when" device in the scenes between Cassie and Lone. Certain elements have become outmoded over the years: the motorcycle gang and the folk-song element (there are twelve songs, one original); and so on. It is little consolation that the songs were used long before the current folk craze.

The play has always needed structural reconceiving, pointing up, clarification. While most readers agreed that the construction of individual scenes was excellent, the scenes were too disjointed, lacked integration: compression of time and action and locale was needed. Although the scenes generally create dramatic tension, too many melodramatic scenes piled up in alarming fashion, and there seemed to be an incredible number of tragedies. (Most readers failed to see the play's humor, charging that the misfortunes were unrelieved; with each revision more humor has come into the play, even with the excision of comic characters such as Aunt Reba and Aunt Maud.) Most agreed, however, that the play does move, although one said it moved too ploddingly. The proliferation of scenes stems from the abundance of characters and stories. Even so, some critics said I run a well-ordered plot, and that I achieve unity in spite of the complications of character and narrative. The present version has eleven scenes, three acts. Another cause of spread-focus was the multiplicity of sets, so that the play wandered physically. I now agree with those who insisted that unity of place would give the play greater impact.

This question brings up what I consider the major problem, if not of the play, then of my attitude toward it — the early locale: Knoxville, with its mountain background. My infatuation with my hometown is similar to Thomas Wolfe's with Asheville, and like Wolfe I look homeward but live elsewhere. A reading of James Agee's *A Death in the Family* will suggest how excruciating one's nostalgia can be for an apparently drab town like Knoxville. So I wanted to get it all in — thus the many characters, the many stories and places, to achieve an epic quality. Some readers thought the play was set in a backward Southern community; but North Lonsdale is on the outskirts of Knoxville, a neighborhood in which I have never lived.

One of the most impressive regional elements has been the mountain background which the characters only talk about, so that readers spoke of the decay of the folk cultural aspects, the feeling for Southern sounds, attitudes and artifacts; one reader saw it as a partly folk, partly realistic play. John Gassner often warned me not to get too infatuated with the folk, regional raw material. Actually, the folk element and the mountains were always intended to be background only. Although they were not of my direct experience, I perhaps projected those elements too strongly.

This imaginative, rather than autobiographical, response to the mountain element has, in an indirect way, solved many of my problems, in so far as they stem considerably from my actual involvement in Knoxville. For I have become imaginatively seduced by the Eastern Kentucky Cumberland mountain region, and the play is now set in a little coal mining town which combines aspects of Harlan and Hazard, in the depressed area. Being imaginatively, but not personally involved, I could select more consciously the most expressive elements and avoid inessentials. The Eastern Kentucky elements also seemed to have greater significance both in themselves and for the play's purposes. The problem, indicated at Albuquerque, was to avoid the impression that I intended to present a mere picture of abject misery, of a kind of social disease.

All the factors causing lack of focus forced excessive length, as well. Several readers thought the one-act version the more effective length — that the play had been merely lengthened, not filled out. In Boone, the play ran three hours, and in Albuquerque forty-five minutes overtime. A two-act play most of the time, it became a three-act play in *First Stage*; a two-act as the play opened in Albuquerque, the first act was arbitrarily broken in half on opening night to rest the audience. I have now made a more logical three-act break, and at Oregon the play was within average playing time.

I cannot discuss briefly the subtle effect my writing in many other forms had on the development of *Cassandra*. But working on the novel version simultaneously with the play almost from the initial conception has certainly had traceable effects, and I know that I have learned about the one medium by writing in the other. Some readers felt that *Cassandra* would be better as a novel. The criticisms of the nine versions of the novel parallel those of the play; probably the complicating factors in the play were spawned in the novel. But novel and play have both hindered and enhanced each other.

At Ohio University for the past two years, I taught creative writing and interpretation of drama. Because of my involvement with *Cassandra Singing*, my approach to plays is purely theatrical, nonliterary, nonthematic. I want my students to look at the elements that make plays act on audiences as *theater*, and to speculate on the playwright's awareness of the nature of the theatrical experience and his means (some quite mechanical) of using the elements of theater to control audience response. O'Neill's plays, for example, often reveal the presence of novelistic elements and aims which obstruct the implementation of his extraordinary theater sense; on the other hand, Tennessee Williams, in *A Streetcar Named Desire* (though it has eleven scenes) is not at all novelistic; everything he attempts, he achieves in purely theatrical terms.

In the end, and despite all my experiences that might point to the contrary, playwriting is a solitary creative act. The prolems arise in the play itself, and the writer's first obligation is to make his work playable. That is always the main business at hand. But it is a long and futile business when the playwright is so immersed in his raw material that he is more inclined to be in awe of the infinite richness of his world than to select those fragments which, under the pressure of controlled form and intense vision, most forcibly express the essence of his world. As Mark Schorer has said, technique is discovery. The writer's temperament compels him to embrace his raw material, but his technique enables him to discover deeper meanings, feelings, and patterns which his mere bemusement by uncoordinated details persists in obscuring. Technique is, of course, detachment. That was the song Cassandra was singing to me. And, in true classical fashion, I did not heed it.

bibliography of cassandra singing, play and novel

Play:
One-act version, *New Campus Writing #2*. New York: Putnam and Bantam Pocket Books, 1957; three-act version, *First Stage*, Vol. II, No. 2, Spring 1963.

Novel:
Chapters published in *Windhover*, Vol. I, No. 1, North Carolina State College, Raleigh, N.C.; *Southwest Review*, Vol. LI, No. 3, Summer 1966, Dallas, Texas; *Lillabulero*, Vol. I, No. 1, Winter 1967, Chapel Hill, N.C.; *Transfer*, Vol. I, No. 22, Summer, 1967, San Francisco State College; *North American Review*, Vol. 252, No. 4, July, 1967, Mount

poetic image in six genres

Vernon, Iowa; *Cimarron*, Vol. I, No. 1, Sept., 1967, Stillwater, Oklahoma; *South Dakota Review*, Vol. IV, No. 4, Winter, 1967–68, Vermillion, South Dakota; *Ann Arbor Review*, Vol. I, No. 1, Fall, 1967, Ann Arbor, Michigan.

(This turns out to be a possible success story after all. While this book was in preparation, Crown Publishers accepted *Cassandra Singing* — novel version — for publication in the early fall of 1969. Revision problems center on scenes carried over from the play version; fuller, novelistic description is needed.)

theater without walls

A springlike climate of theatrical experience pervades this country, but not all nor the most exciting of it is created in theaters — much of it is non-theater, even anti-theater — theater outside the theater. Poets give theatrical public readings of their poems, inspired a decade ago by the San Francisco Renaissance that vibrated to Ferlinghetti's, Rexroth's, and Ginsberg's jazz-poetry readings; of course, jazz itself is public music, a theatrical event, as is much of the new "serious" music: John Cage's theatrical music replaces harmony with duration and calls upon a vast repertoire of theatrical effects, including egg beaters; electronic music also is theatrical, breaking up the static form of classical concerts by introducing machines into the concert hall. The latest sculpture is not a static presentation, but a continuum of happenings — it moves, it is always in process, creating and destroying itself simultaneously in front of the spectator's eyes. It performs. The Black Gate last year subjected prone spectators to the theater of light, with events entitled "The Proliferation of the Sun" and "Blackout" (as I, finally, got up and sneaked guiltily out, I looked down upon a floor carpeted with tightly shut eyes). This new sculpture invites the spectator to become a performer; in Europe, there is a giant statue of a prone woman; families visiting the museum on Sunday may enter her through the orifice of their choice. The work of art as an environment enclosing the spectator is a flaming fad at the moment. Long ago, Jackson Pollock's instant painting techniques inspired the action painting that one may now witness in a theatrical atmosphere, sometimes right on stage, sometimes as part of a more embracing theatrical event. Op art and pop art, whatever else they reach for, are theatrical gestures. While squares and straights cover the walls of the nation with paintings by the numbers, hippies and yippies in the Village, inclining toward the more theatrically immediate, stop off at multi-paint vats and pull out instant color explosions that look the way the new beat sounds. Café events such as folk singing are theatrical, involving audiences in the way some new plays attempt to do. This climate helped to produce the phenomenon called Happenings and the coffeehouses that offer psychedelic experiences. Even preachers are getting into the act, introducing drama into the church itself, as sponsors, or carrying the church, in dramatic dialogs or monologs, into the ambience of theaters and cabarets, as the Reverend Malcolm Boyd does. Theater, outside the theater, is in fashion. The long hair, the beards, the beat garb, mingling with the mod fashions of the teeny boppers, the exotic buttons — all proclaim that the curtain is always up on the theater without walls. This theatrical *back*ground moves, with every rapidly passing day, closer and closer into the *fore*ground.

So in many ways theater groups, formal and informal, are taking to the streets, setting up at the crossroads, reaching out for the common man, even, at times. For several years, many playwrights, directors, actors saw more possibilities in film than in theater; but now the two media are rampantly cross-fertilizing each other. The *Tulane Drama Review*, one of the inside-dope voices of the outs, recently published a thick, special issue on the use of film in the theater. Film is used in Happenings, Environments, psychedelic atmospheres, and other non-matrixed events. Poets, composers, dancers, painters, sculptors, and underground film-makers are thrusting onto the low-budget stages of the new avant-garde theater a dynamic interplay of media: new music effects, new sounds, symbolic speech, electronic devices, engineering apparatus, new architectural forms, stylized movements — art in process. They seek new dimensions to assault all the senses.

As a young playwright of seventeen, with one university-produced play behind me, I set out from my hometown, Knoxville, Tennessee, in the spring of 1949 to New York, for my first exposure to professional theater. The off-Broadway phenomenon was only just about to make theater history. The Broadway plays I saw — *A*

Streetcar Named Desire, *Death of a Salesman*, and Carson McCullers' the *Member of the Wedding* — inspired me to a fierce determination to become a playwright. I admired the actors, the directors, and especially the playwrights, and I knew the audience for which I would write.

Last spring, as a playwright with some twenty out-of-New York productions behind me, as a teacher of playwriting and of a course called Interpretation of Drama, and as a theatergoer, I made a similar trip. The strongest urge was to see Bergman's, Resnais', and Antonioni's latest movies, not to see plays. But out of both a sense of professional obligation and a fervent desire to immerse myself in the new theater, I saw one Broadway play, Pinter's *The Homecoming*, two off-Broadway plays — Norman Mailer's *The Deer Park* and Alan Arkin's production of *Eh?* — and five off-off-Broadway plays — four of which I want to comment on now: Jean-Claude van Itallie's *America Hurrah*, Sam Shepard's *La Turista*, Ronald Tavel's *Gorilla Queen*, and Barbara Garson's *MacBird!* The fifth, presented at Caffe Cino, was a forgettable musical. I also saw twelve movies anyway.

At the American Place Theatre, which is sponsored by and housed in an Episcopal church, I saw *La Turista*, by twenty-three-year-old Sam Shepard. My agent assured me that *La Turista* was the most experimental, far-out play in New York. The youthful audience rambunctiously enjoyed Shepard's expressionistic, absurdist satire of American tourists in Mexico. Especially "liberating" was the unrestrained use of expressions of sexual emotions and descriptions of bodily functions. One seemed to have an encyclopedia of space-age bawdy at his nose, ear, and tonguetip.

At the intermission, a very elderly priest made an unsteady exit, assisted by a younger priest, smiling condescendingly behind his back. The old priest appeared to have been reduced to gibberish by what he had witnessed in church. One of the most theatrically vivid moments of my immersion in the drama of the moment was that tableau —

the old priest climbing the aisle in very slow motion past the long-haired playwright and the walrus-mustached director, walking out on the antics of "the new mutants" — playwright and director, hip to hip, wiggling almost hysterically in satisfaction, jeering and pointing at the priest as he tottered out into a snowstorm. Playwright and director had achieved — if only in this one refugee from the theater of Lady Gregory — their highest aspiration: to violate their audience.

The point of this anecdote sticks in me. There, I mumbled to myself, but for the grace of my youthful disguise, go I. At thirty-four, this is a bitter identification to make.

That theater is truly the American Place, if not of this moment, surely of the next. To get some impression of where we are, so that we may know how we came here, why we are here, and how far *out* we are going, let's look at three other American places. This theater is anti-literary, almost defies critical assessment, is extremely audience-oriented, and thus provokes a gut response. That is mainly the kind I will make.

Jean-Claude van Itallie's *America Hurrah* is composed of three one-act plays: "Interview," "TV," and "Motel." "Interview" satirizes the job interview as symbolic of many other negative aspects of America's electronic civilization. We see abstracted onto the stage the psychological machinery that makes victims of us all. Like much of modern literature, many of the new plays lovingly depict a whining victimhood. Van Itallie dramatizes the impersonality of technology: the four interviewers wear shiny, plastic, smiling masks; they make mechanical movements, machinelike sounds, and repeat superficial questions, all of which turn the four applicants into automatons named Smith. The play's action explodes in a brightly lighted, simple box set with a slanted stage; squares of a glinting, aluminumlike material cover the walls and ceiling. A few severe boxlike shapes, placed about the stage, serve numerous functions. Van Itallie employs an interesting verbal device to set these events at a Brechtian distance: the applicants speak to the interviewers, then in an aside to the audience say such things as: "I said, apologetically." At one point, all four interviewers are questioning the applicants simultaneously: here van Itallie strives for satirical counterpoints and expressive juxtapositions. When the applicants leave the interview situation and move about the city, they encounter other forms of impersonality. The interviewers assume the roles of priests, psychiatrists, politicians.

Van Itallie uses many styles — realistic, expressionistic, impressionistic, symbolic — to touch on many of the standard themes of modern literature and theater: superficiality, alienation, and so forth. The actors seldom act. Instead, they use their bodies to perform "tasks" and to engage in "activities." Without transition, they go from impersonating real people abstractly to expressing, as a well-trained ensemble, extreme human emotions — love, hate, despair, ennui, lust, violence — to objectifying abstractly the internal energies of machines or natural events. Lighting, music, and sound effects are not used to enhance or stress human events, but have an impact equal in importance to the actors' tasks. Thus, on this stage, the biological organisms and the machinery function in harmony to project a unified theatrical effect. Such theatrical values as pace and tempo are abstractly, overtly manipulated along with the lights and other elements.

This is a theater of tremendous, controlled energy. As they transpire, and then elude us, events construct their own logic. This kinetic technique is supposed to affect the audience viscerally rather than intellectually. The satirical points are, after all, simple and familiar. It is the strange method that traumatically disorients even the most knowledgeable theatergoer. The audience's effort to avoid becoming totally disoriented and to make sense of what's going on proves futile. Ideally, the audience experiences the impersonal forces, human and mechanical, which constitute the process of dehumanization that we daily undergo — the audience experiences the impossibility of making sense of a process such as that.

We see and hear the gear-jamming of human robots desperate to transcend themselves. At times they emerge from this frenetic activity as individual human beings, though coldly isolated from the others, who are frozen in attitudes expressive of machinelike nonsentience. Then we get Albee- or Williams-like arias, or long realistic speeches, as when the girl who dies in an automobile accident comes to the party where she is expected and apologizes for being dead. "Excuse me. I'm sorry" are oft-repeated verbal motifs in the play. This moment of pathos is heightened by its occurrence in the midst of abstract theatrical dynamics.

In most of the new plays, story is cannibalized by theatrics, but this new theater makes possible an infinite combination of human actions and patterns of movement, intricately choreographed, and a great variety of electronic utterances, colors, and lighting effects.

"TV," the second one-act play of the evening, is less abstract, though it uses similar techniques. It demonstrates the way in which the clichés and gross, low-level distortions of human behavior in an affluent culture as presented on TV actually depict, expressionistically, the rituals, ceremonies, holiday celebrations, and stock situations of our everyday lives. Van Itallie stresses this theme by having a young woman and two men, whose job is to watch TV eight hours a day as program evaluators, represent the so-called realistic level. The setting for this level is the viewing room of a TV rating company. The events are simple and episodic: both men lust for the girl; a birthday party is given for one of the men; one man chokes on a chicken bone, while the girl and the other man watch indecisively. Simultaneously, fragments of television programs of various kinds are acted out all over the stage, significantly juxtaposed with the trivial events on the realistic level. The progress of the play is toward an increasingly violent merging of the two levels of action, which are equally real.

The play's humor depends upon a rather obvious appeal to the cultured audience's prejudices against TV. The satirical jokes are banal. To see one's own attitudes stylized on stage and feel oneself among like-minded people is to feel as though one is in a nightclub, womblike situation. In many of the new plays, character portrayal is usurped by such special in-group attitudes, or by propaganda of some sort. This play is influenced, as van Itallie has said, by Marshall McLuhan's insights. In much of the new theater, the medium *is* the message. (And like many of the avant-garde theater's tactics, McLuhan's concept strikes me as an hysterical discovery of the obvious, transformed into a catch phrase worthy of a niche in some Madison Avenue hall of fame.)

"Motel" is the shortest, least abstract, most genuinely original of the three one-acts. It is also the most successful. The first two plays grew directly out of improvisations, class exercises in the Open Theatre (a workshop for actors, playwrights, and directors). But here, van Itallie's own voice speaks, and he is in complete command of the theatrical elements used in the production. The play is so simply conceived that nothing extraneous, however effective it might be theatrically, can be imposed by the director. His job is to present well what the playwright has so fully realized.

The scene is a motel room, and the play is an absolute theatrical expression of how that peculiarly American phenomenon the motel reflects American character and civilization. Many of the plays in the new theater suffer the presence of the actor unwillingly. To declare an idea that real faces and bodies would tend to weaken, van Itallie encases his actors in eight-foot-tall papier-máché figures. The three characters are monsters, robots, dolls, elephantine puppets without a master.

The only speech in the play is a twenty-minute monolog delivered over a public address system, but apparently coming from the giant figure of the woman who runs the motel. There she stands, swaying, broom in hand, as she delivers her insanely protracted commercial on the wonders of her motel, which has the latest of everything — to flush the toilet, merely get up off the seat — and a sentimental touch of the old. She is talking at us for a long time. Then painfully bright car lights shine in our eyes, suggesting the sort of people about to enter. Since the motelkeeper never talks directly to the two typical customers, also giant dolls, we are to infer that we are the customers. Her voice, calm and realistic, not stylized, becomes increasingly louder as the man and woman dolls occupying the motel room enact contradictions of her commercial claims. As she recites a litany of those typical American commercial artifacts that are obsolete upon their appearance, the man and woman, who came here to make love, immediately rip off each other's vulgar, tourist-like clothes, then set about demolishing the motel room, including uprooting the toilet, decapitating the motel-keeper — merely another fixture — finally scrawling la-trine-type graffiti on the aluminum walls (which are the same as for the other two plays) and then dismantling the walls, too, as the sound is turned up to the threshold of pain. The audience is so assaulted by the theatrical effects — the sounds, smells, sights (as palpable as the new action sculpture) — that it does not discern theme intellectually, it experiences it physically. Van Itallie projects allegorical, didactic, grotesque images, which are modeled after the banal objects of everyday life in a consumer culture (the ambience of which is mass media), fit only for brief use and abuse, and swift and violent disposal — including ourselves. Made in the image of our products, we resemble cheaply manufactured dolls. "Motel's" techniques, including a sensational use of obscenity, are justified.

Sam Shepard, on the other hand, also a product of the Open Theatre, and of such cabaret theaters as Cafe La Mama and Caffe Cino, appears to have written *La Turista* out of the conviction that Aristotle was a fascist. The first act, or action, of *La Turista* is set in a hotel room in Mexico, the second in a hotel room in the United States, probably in Texas. The decor of both rooms, like a pop art painting, assaults the audience.

A young married couple, dynamic Salem and effeminate Kent, fugitives from cigarette commercials, are tourists who have come to Mexico to rest, who then return to America to recover from Mexico. The play opens with the couple sitting on separate narrow beds in stiff postures, painfully immobilized by sunburn, viciously snapping through the pages of glossy American magazines. Kent has a severe case of dysentery — an impoverished country's revenge upon the biologically unfit, pampered, parasitical American. (In Act II, in America, he has sleeping sickness, which may have any of a number of simple meanings.)

A young Mexican peon invades the hotel room while Kent is in the john, and usurps his place in bed. Without transition, Kent emerges from the john as a C-grade movie cowboy and acts out his childhood fantasy role; thus in cartoon style, Shepard parodies the American male's masculine notions. The Mexican boy brings in two bizarre witch doctors, who kill two chickens and spread the blood over Kent's body, from which the Mexican has stripped the cowboy outfit. As the witch doctors chant and incense smoke, smelling like burning human excrement, fills the theater, the Mexican puts on the cowboy outfit and struts among the audience, which obliges him by feeling his muscles. That pleasure was mine.

The director of *La Turista* is Jacques Levy, who also directed van Itallie's "TV" and "Motel." We witness here, too, the director's preoccupations with biomechanics: agonized slow-motion, acting-class calisthenics, frantic physical outbursts, actors running, screaming about the theater among the spectators, climbing over doors. In the play's final action, Kent, the antihero, runs down a ramp from the center of the audience and leaps through the high rear wall of the room, leaving a stylized outline of a man for the audience to gape and wonder at. As with many such moments in the new theater, we think: Man, that was an effective stroke! But it might as well have been another. In such plays, the quality of inevitability in art is missing.

The toiling of the actors, the great strain their tasks and group activities, verbal and physical, exact of them is contagious; the audience must sympathize with the actor-character — characters are never presented separately from the actor as a "task" performer — and end up exhausted, too, if it is to *experience* the forces released on the stage. The audience responded to separate theatrical moments, touches, stunts in this action play, though it could not follow the *a*logic of the play. It did follow the play's drift, its strident tone, its attitude of abuse, rebellion, and anguished confusion.

In its presentation of the fragments of the author's confused response to the complex society against which he is reacting, the production makes a kind of eclectic free use of elements of the avant-garde theater, and of films such as Truffaut's and Godard's.

If Ionesco only appears to bombard the audience with obscure talk, Shepard literally floods the theater with verbiage, some of it naughty-boy stuff. Like van Itallie, he offers several long arias. Sitting on the bed, immobile, Salem recites in a monotone, in great detail, an episode of her childhood in which she spat on her father. One point of Shepard's theatrical demonstration is that this generation spits on the banalities, deceits, hypocrisies of its parents. Onstage, backstage, in the wings, out in the audience — the presence of Mom and Dad is felt. These plays are mired in swampy attitudes toward Mom and Dad. Their main line of reasoning seems to be that if Mom and Dad's middle-class values are false, that if they and the institutions they uphold are complacent and indifferent, the only alternative is some form of outlaw behavior or ideology. Thus, actual social outcasts like the thief-pervert Genet and the psychotic Artaud, and political outlaws like Brecht, are enshrined as saints. But one also senses a strange, perverse sentimentality in these plays — the result of their strident attack on or avoidance of middle-class sentimentality.

If van Itallie makes expressive use of silence as well as noise, Shepard's relentless verbiage and sound effects suggest a recent adolescence submerged in rock, and other racket music — a din appropriate, I suppose, for our urban civilization. We sense with theatrical immediacy that this young man writes out of a milieu of psychedelic coffee-house environments, of outlandish costumes. The author wore one himself. I spotted him immediately, though I had never even seen a picture of him before.

Except for the superficial, obvious, cliché targets of Shepard's rebellion, I don't think the play solicits thematic interpretation. This is a theater of pure experience. It's like taking part in any of the vast number of theatrical activities outside theater walls that are a part of our everyday lives now. What did the killing of Oswald on TV mean — in that moment? This new theater simulates that kind of senseless, "everyday" happening.

Like *La Turista*, Ronald Tavel's *Gorilla Queen* was presented in a church — the venerable old Judson Church on Washington Square. Presented by Judson Poets' Theatre, this production was mounted (and sexually, everything was mounted) in the choir loft, appropriately enough, since a Greek chorus of apelike creatures commented from their perches in the junglelike center acting area on the absurd human happenings that occurred on the little stages left and right. As in all four of the productions I am describing, the stage was exposed as the audience — here, a homogeneous, in-in-group of one hundred subscribers — trailed in. Ironically, the young homosexual who sat next to me, and who lives in the Village, had never before heard of the group, which had for years been making theatrical history — for instance, the first Happening was done there (a generation ago, it

seems). On the left of the shallow stage, about as big as a
commedia dell'arte stage set up at a crossroads, sat a
zoo-type cage. Near it stood the Venus Fly Trap, a girl
bizarrely painted up, chewing gum — surely Juicy *Fruit*.
On the right were a fireplace and an outdoor café. On the
walls, two movie posters set the play's tone and intent:
one, circa 1933, showed a synthetic King Kong carrying a
girl in a sarong; the other circa now, showed an obscene
King Kong, abducting a nude girl with flaming red nipples.
Working the lights in full view was a girl in a black lace
slip and a top hat, who called light cues rather ostenta-
tiously.

Behind us, the ape creatures entered the theater area
from the gutted, cavernlike center of the church below,
climbing rope ladders. The apes climbed, that is, up into the
trees where the audience sat, squeezed into three long rows,
like cypress limbs. The first ape was dressed partly in
motorcycle hoodlum garb, fur around his face — which,
like a baboon's behind, was red. Making ape noises, he tried
to mount a few folks in the front row. Suggesting the
process of evolution, he toiled through ape noises into human speech, like one who has a chorus to lead. Then eight
or nine other apes climbed up, and scratched, ate lice, and
fornicated onstage.

Clyde Batty is the hero of this piece. His amorous
intentions toward a lady in a Scarlett O'Hara costume are
frustrated by the dark designs of a character in black called
the Chimney Sweep, but early in the charade he is embraced
by the nymphomaniacal Venus Fly Trap. Taharahnugi
White Woman, looking like Hedy Lamarr, wants to lie
with Clyde. Meanwhile, Sister Carries, the effeminate witch
doctor, wearing a nun's headgear and polka-dot shorts,
attempts to sacrifice to Queen Kong at the fireplace
Claudette Colbert, a sloppy, tall girl in a silver bikini, who
chews gum, talks Brooklynese, and proves to be a virgin
lesbian. This sacrifice is frequently interrupted by Clyde and
various counterintrigues. Anticipation for the entrance of
Queen Kong is worked up. When *he* finally appears, he is

indeed *Queen* Kong, who immediately exhibits a lech for Clyde. Taharahnugi is unmasked as a transvestite; and it is later revealed that he is really Queen Kong in human form. One of the high points of the evening comes when Queen Kong in the cage commits sodomy in full view of the audience on Clyde Batty, the play's main link with the audience's pretensions to humanity. The evening, a very long evening, ground on like the delayed orgasm of a eunuch.

Just as the Broadway hit *The Odd Couple* offers a laugh a minute, *Gorilla Queen* offers an asinine sophomoric pun a minute, and the audience laughed at every smutty one of them, whether bisexual or homosexual. But I'm glad to report that early in Act II, the audience, extremely fatigued by Tavel's endless ramifications of the tired old reversal formula, laughed on cue rather reluctantly. (On a popular-culture level, of course, we have the movie, *Planet of the Apes*, in which the apes are superior to "man." The old "how-it-looks-from-inside-the-cage" routine.) Shouting blasphemies and obscenities, taunting clichés at the audience, and striking pornographic postures — the production underestimated the audience's ability to adjust readily to every conceivable shock technique.

That was certainly the most unusual night I've ever experienced in the theater, but despite my disgust, I sense that *Gorilla Queen* is the vanguard of tomorrow's theater. This play would be pure camp were it not tainted by the ideological assumptions the author and others insist underlie the play. Having crowned Mae West America's greatest playwright, Ronald Tavel — who wrote scripts for Andy Warhol and sued him for part of the take from his movie *The Chelsea Girls* — assures us that he is in straight earnest, that his play deals with dream, myth, and the roots of poetry, that his parodies are a kind of atomic age voodoo, that his travesty of the camp movies of the early forties expresses modern man's frustrated craving for ritual. But until his medium transmits *that* message, the audience experiences things nearer its heart and groin.

Turning to the young homosexual sitting next to me, I chose a four-letter word from the play's own limited vocabulary to sum up my judgment of the play. In hushed, cathedral tones, not inappropriate to the building in which we sat, the swish hippie assured me that the play was more than that. Then giving me a smug in-group look that excluded *me*, he said, "If you only knew how *true to life* this play really is."

The new-theater people seem influenced by Broadway musicals. *Gorilla Queen* has three production numbers: "Cockamania," "Freakadelic," and something about sniffing bicycle seats. The dirty phrases scrawled on the motel wall in *America Hurrah* come out of the mouths of the characters in *Gorilla Queen*, as in most of the other plays I saw. Sex and profanity are presented as freedom from, with no indication of what the freedom is for. The new permissiveness allows the homosexual playwright to deal now directly in public with his world. But haven't some of the best plays of the American theater since the twenties been the sublimations of homosexual playwrights who disguised their frustrations? The new playwright finds himself in a theater more and more obviously dominated by a homosexual, camp, or aberrant sensibility in open expression.

Encouraged by the success of that chaotic triumph of sophomoric thinking and feeling, Barbara Garson's *MacBird!*, other playwrights must be digging into their files for the outrageous satire they wrote in college that no one would produce. We have had non-books; it is to be expected that we would get non-plays by non-playwrights. The protest movement has produced a non-playwright — *MacBird!* was written for protest rallies. Thus, this play, even more than the other three, demonstrates the in-group origin and appeal of much of the new theater. *MacBird!* is a satirical attack on abuse of power in government, using Shakespeare's *Macbeth* as a structural referent. Among the play's gratuitous fantasies is the depiction of President Johnson (MacBird) as engineer of the assassination of John F. Kennedy.

The new theater, in some ways a theater of revolt, is often merely revolting; it is a theater of political, economic, sociological, and cultural opposition, of fanatical icono-clasm — arbitrary opposition appears to have mastery. There is little joy in this theater, except in attack; there is little celebration, and little balanced perspective. In four days I saw four satirical plays in an age that lacks the common conventions and conditions for satire — thus, the plays in this theater, particularly *MacBird!*, are often empty raving and smug self-aggrandizement, not satire. At worst, off-off-Broadway reveals in its attitudes, its con-duct, its choice of plays: hypocrisy, lies, fraud, irresponsi-bility, and self-deceit. It is snafued by confusion of purpose, intention, and performance.

Liberal intellectuals like Elizabeth Hardwick of *The New York Review of Books*, Dwight MacDonald of *Esquire*, and Robert Brustein of *The New Republic* (who, as the powerful new dean of Yale Drama School, brings to Yale protest plays like Megan Terry's *Viet Rock* and Arnold Weinstein's *Dynamite Tonite*) are thrilling to the theater of intellectual masturbation as *MacBird!* hovers over the heads of the squares, the system, the Establishment. The image-conscious *Tulane Drama Review* recently asked: who and what *is* the New Establishment? They had to conclude that it is created from the avant-garde almost on its appearance.

We see a similar paradox in the reception of *Marat / Sade*. The play sets out to shock the middle-class Estab-lishment into turning itself inside out and changing its life, one lived by lies. But as Leslie Fiedler has pointed out, assimilation is the secret weapon of the Establishment, and almost overnight the avant-garde's latest outrageous message is transformed into midcult clichés, becomes profitable fodder for Madison Avenue, and its startling new forms have become the workaday elements of

Establishment theater. The middle class is so eager to absorb the latest radical theater that the avant-garde artist (Albee, for instance, and Pinter) wakes up famous and rich. With a tone of great disappointment, Brustein observes that *MacBird!* is *not* being harassed by the government — despite ready pretexts: for, as everyone around me nervously observed, the Village Gate is a fire-trap. *MacBird!* may not be changing people's minds, but it is making money, with its well-to-do, middle-aged audience crammed behind tables as large as a napkin.

Another paradox lies in the fact that most of these plays, especially *MacBird!*, speak to the convinced. This is so obvious that after I had been arguing this point for months, I heard a lady from Brooklyn, behind me, even before she had seen the play, say: "The people who need this aren't here." Those who come feel superior to those who don't, and the writing and the production encourage in many ways this kind of in-response. Thus, between the production and the audience occurs a mutual moral massaging. The liberal audience hears and sees yet another confirmation of its own convictions about the others. The audiences these plays attack don't come to the theater; rather, people of like mind with the playwright nod in smug assent to every line and gesture — as did the audience for *Gorilla Queen*, especially. But even middle-class audiences go to a performance of *Marat / Sade* in the same frame of mind as they go to *Hello, Dolly*, and they go away in much the same spirit — while among the elite one observes an atmosphere around *Marat / Sade* that resembles the snob-sentimentality one usually associates with people who adore Broadway musicals. This self-indulgence can be theatrical, but it is mystery-cult, not humanistic, theater.

These plays set out to change the lives of the audiences, but the audiences usually think they have done that, else they wouldn't be here; they would put in the time at *Luv*, that perfect product of midcult bohemia. The plays I saw were written to shock Aunt Sally's world back home in Columbus, but Aunt Sally doesn't go to La Mama or Village Gate cabaret theater — only people formed by Aunt Sally in childhood go to these plays, to get their revenge on Aunt Sally: the result is rather obscene.

We write plays to shock segregationists out of their inhuman attitudes, knowing full well that Lester Maddox and the Ku Klux Klan don't go to the theater. Instead, the rigor mortis of self-righteousness sets in on the already convinced audience, or some, out of a generalized guilt, masochistically endure the abuse of Negro playwrights (whose own people can't afford the theater). If avant-garde theater weren't the glorified opposite brother of a Shriners' convention, as I've suggested, we would see not only plays that examine the whore in the housewife (though Ibsen did that long ago) and the killer in the judge, but also plays revealing the sentimentalist in the rebel, the spiritually dead in the protester. If they really want to disorient and shock us into new perspectives on old problems, playwrights might make liberals and radicals the target of that intention — since the assumption is that it is we who really care — by attempting plays written securely from the point of view of a Bull Connor or of the LBJs of this world.

What facilitates the assimilation I observed before is the fact that the protest and commitment in our theater is transformed by the nature of the theatrical experience into pure theater. Though what one talks about after the show is ideas and convictions and the stupidity and inhumanity of the people who didn't come, what one experiences during the play is pure theater. The theater has built-in means for taking revenge on those who would use it as a platform. Garson wanted to demonstrate to us that Johnson is ridiculous and contemptible, but in the theater itself, Stacey Keach's portrayal of MacBird is so entrancing that we end up liking the man, and all the elements of theater conspire to achieve that reversal of Mrs. Garson's intention. Audiences may be bored by the philosophy of *Marat / Sade* (the elite has heard all this existential cant before), and Peter Brook's theatrical direction declares with every overwhelming stunt the fact that he is obviously, and perhaps hysterically, trying to compensate for the static tedium of the play. The play finally appeals not to the intellectual, responsible adult in us, who might act on its message, but to the self-indulgent child in us who loves, for instance, the spectacle of the cross long before he understands anything about Christianity. It would be difficult in reading these four plays to tell how good they are (even Brustein was skeptical as to whether *MacBird!* would *play*), and it is perhaps too easy to *see* how bad — but the new theater techniques can substitute pure experience for the inadequacies of the play itself; theater schools like Yale are turning out frighteningly expert technicians, while few playwrights of godlike power are in evidence. The playwright's function is little more than to provide a scaffolding for the director's brilliant theatrical ingenuity.

In responding to this new theater, I know from experience that one must guard against hasty reactions. I lectured on the new American playwright in March of 1967 at the University of Dayton, and my diatribe, my harangue, was based so much on reading these new plays and reading about the productions of them and about the purposes of the theaters that did them, that I felt I ought to see more plays. So I went straight from Dayton to New York and saw the plays I've just discussed; I read more plays later, and now I find I am less hostile, though basically my observations still seem valid.

These plays demonstrate that as film is a director's medium, theater also is becoming a director's medium. And Roy Levine's production of *MacBird!* is the best demonstration, along with the others I've described, of this vigorous trend. This director's theater confuses the traditional roles of actors, playwrights, audiences. This new theater, which we have few opportunities to see outside New York, but which will probably become the theater of the next generation, is a theater without actors, a theater without playwrights, and finally, perhaps, in its desire to theatricalize the multifaceted theater of everyday life in our culture, a theater that dispenses with the audience.

approaching
autobiography as art

"There is properly no history," declared Emerson, "only biography." With subjective authority, Thoreau pointed out that there is no biography either, only autobiography.

In 1967–68, a revolution in American literature began in the suburbs of autobiography. This genre took decisive turns that vigorous trends in fiction and in other non-fiction had prefigured. Fascinating biographies of writers perhaps inspired novelists to focus more directly upon their own lives. Norman Podhoretz's *Making It* (Random House), Willie Morris' *North Toward Home* (Houghton Mifflin), and Frank Conroy's *Stop-time* (Viking) are autobiographies with uncommonly strong conceptual, technical, and stylistic characteristics of fiction. The greatest detonation in this explosion of form is, properly enough, Norman Mailer's doing. In *The Armies of the Night* (New American Library), he pushes journalism-as-autobiography far beyond James Agee's lyrical *Let Us Now Praise Famous Men*. I haven't read enough Mailer to be able to agree with reviewers who declare that this is his finest work, but one thing is certain: neither journalism nor the novel nor autobiography can ever seem quite the same.

With our public concern — quickly becoming every citizen's private anguish — over ruin and riot in those great cities that seduced talented men and women of the rural areas and small towns, American writers feel compelled to turn the harsh light of their creative vision, unfiltered by aesthetics, upon the way the past has both nurtured and poisoned the present. In public contexts, nostalgia curdles into nausea. Until recently the novel was a major force in the education of middle-class attitudes and aspirations, but it has lost ground to "the article as art" (Podhoretz' phrase). Novelist Truman Capote's *In Cold Blood* is not so much imaginative journalism that explores the meaning of a violent event as it is a biography of two young killers and a submerged autobiography of the biographer. Jean Stafford's account of her interviews with Lee Harvey Oswald's mother, *A Mother in History*, leaves Stafford the novelist almost equally exposed.

Advertisements for Myself is one more aggressive instance of Norman Mailer's compulsive self-scrutiny; his novels corroborate autobiographical claims.

James McConkey made his major bid for fame with *Crossroads* — frankly labeled "An Autobiographical Novel." A somewhat younger man, thirty-one-year old Frank Conroy, went further: material that normally appears in a first novel as disguised autobiography, Conroy presented in *Stop-time* as an unabashed memoir, his implied justification for such audacity being, apparently, that he had once been an American adolescent. Who would dispute, in the late sixties, the authenticity of such a claim to fame? *Stop-time* raises the question, What is an autobiography? Compared with the question, What is a novel? that question has always been as simple as, What is a biography? But at a time when the creative vigor of nonfiction occasions repeated, though premature, autopsies on the novel, redefinitions are urged. Autobiography gets a new lease on life with *Stop-time*, for despite its shortcomings, this audacious memoir heralds a new literary subtype in America: the adolescent autobiography (in Holland in 1964 a somewhat similar book appeared, *I Jan Cremer*, by a young man of twenty-five, but it was presented as an autobiographical novel). Still, in American life-studies, the technical achievements of autobiography have gone little beyond *The Education of Henry Adams* and Gertrude Stein's *Autobiography of Alice B. Toklas*, for the creative possibilities have not yet been adequately recognized by readers nor imaginatively explored by writers. A closer look at these four recent autobiographies may provide some sense of where the form is going.

The literary lives of Podhoretz, Morris, Mailer, and Conroy are almost as intimately related as the nature of their literary products. Morris and Podhoretz are friends; Midge Decter, Podhoretz's wife, is on the staff of *Harper's*, which Morris edits. Podhoretz and Mailer are friends (Mailer defended *Making It* in *Partisan Review*). Morris made publishing history by devoting almost an entire issue of *Harper's* to *The Armies of the Night* (under the title "On the Steps of the Pentagon"). Haunting the periphery of this group is Frank Conroy, who contributes reviews and stories to *Partisan Review* and *The New York Review of Books*, publications within what Podhoretz calls the New York Literary Intellectual Establishment or Family.

In the sixties we have seen the "dirty little secret" of SEX liberated from the latrine. We may also see the "dirty little secret" of SUCCESS liberated from the ivory tower. What Hedy Lamarr in *Ecstasy and Me* did for sex in 1967, Norman Podhoretz does for success in 1968. Lamarr swore by her experience that sex, even dirty sex, is fun. Podhoretz testifies by his intellect that it is possible, even desirable, to live with the "Bitch Goddess of Success," enjoying and using fame, power and money, without expecting Mephistopheles to knock at the door any moment. Lamarr and Podhoretz deserve our gratitude.

In *Making It*, Podhoretz analyzes his long "blind" journey from the provincial slums of Brooklyn to the literary towers of Manhattan. Looking back from his present eminence as aggressive editor of *Commentary*, Jewish journal of liberal social criticism, he sees that he has moved through a series of "conversions," facilitated by certain institutions and their exemplars: conversion to culture (via Columbia and Cambridge, tutored by Lionel Trilling and F. R. Leavis), to intellectual power (via *Partisan Review* and *Commentary*, tutored by Philip Rahv and Elliot Cohen), and finally, unashamedly, to cash and status (via Paradise Island, tutored by Huntington Hartford). Fame he had always pursued, consciously and uninhibitedly, though first as poet, rather than as critic and editor.

The conversions constituted a process of becoming; *Making It*, written out of a state of being, delineates Podhoretz's final realization at thirty-five that, all contemporary literary intellectual opinion to the contrary, it is better to be famous than obscure, powerful than subservient, rich than poor — a success than a failure. "The best of everything is good enough" for Podhoretz.

Little Podhoretz's family and teachers praised him — a brilliant boy, bristling with promise. He began in high school to perceive the mysterious relation between class structure and cultural taste, by which, according to the "brutal American social contract," he was transformed from a "filthy little" Jewish "slum child" into a "facsimile WASP." In his college days he earned a reputation for aggressive, ostentatious, and opportunistic ambitiousness. Product of the late forties, of the "Age of Criticism," he later built a reputation as a book reviewer who showed a preference for creative nonfiction over fiction, and a tendency to attract attention by attacking "inflated" reputations. He accepts the charge of "critical overkill" and "strident negativism." But he has always been committed to the supremacy of literary standards; his personal ideals have frequently been abused by reality; and his self-scrutiny reveals some rather staggering moral niceties for such an avowed egomaniac.

Finally, the New York Literary Family adored and adopted him. As he presents his pantheon of heroes, praise becomes portraiture. In an age of victim-worship, Podhoretz repudiated his Willy Loman heritage and pursued, Gatsby-like, his "platonic conception of himself." But despite the many traits he shares with Fitzgerald, Podhoretz's *Making It* is the obverse of *The Crack-Up*. Like most heroes, he takes a risk, the greatest risk of all for a writer — ridicule on a grand scale. But Podhoretz achieves a balanced estimation of his own talents; he thinks no more highly of Podhoretz than I do. And his writing this book strikes me as an act of magnanimous selfishness.

Podhoretz tells of the many things he has learned in academic, military, occupational, and literary contexts. "It was the American in myself I stumbled upon while trying to discover Europe." In the army and later as a resented subeditor at *Commentary*, he learned that position is power, autonomy, and freedom, and that "those who fail to demand always get nothing." In the "intellectual ghetto" of New York, he learned that men trained in the humanities hate their "jobs," their "second environments," because they are forced to make a living in an inhumane system. He learned that Babbitt's gospel of success is perversely allied to the Intellectual Family's doctrine of failure. He perceived that frustrating contradiction in American society which preaches that it is virtuous to succeed, but venal to enjoy the fruits of worldly success: money, power, fame, and social position. The lust for success is the "dirty little secret of the well-educated American soul"; it motivates, in many instances, liberals and serious writers who publicly declare a loftier purpose. The betrayal of this "secret" is a violation of taste, but also a weakening of its power to shame. He learned that success doesn't corrupt — it only rots the already tainted. Having learned that the cause-monger's most cherished cause is often himself, he rejected many assumptions behind both the "tired middle-aged language of skepticism, pessimism, and resignation of the fifties" and the "uncritical celebrations" of the arbitrary oppositionism of the sixties; he made the "new" *Commentary* the evangelical voice of the youthful, adventurous spirit of reform, and thereby laid up gold in the Ivory Tower.

Podhoretz offers a fascinating and complex, though lucid, delineation of three generations of the New York Literary Intellectual Establishment, or what he calls the Family (whose tree is Jewish in all but a few goy twigs). Consequently, we derive an understanding of the origins, ideals, inner workings and malfunctions, shifting political and cultural perspectives from the thirties to the present of such magazines as *Partisan Review*, *Commentary*, *The New Yorker*, *Show*, *The New York Review of Books*. He attacks the intellectual's sometimes brutal insensitivities, betrayals, superstitions, hypocrisies, reversals, and his opportunistic use of fashions in artistic taste and political issues as arenas for moral competition.

Though partially inspired by Norman Mailer's *Advertisements for Myself, Making It* is more ethnocentric than egocentric. For Podhoretz uses distinct stages in his life as occasions for insights that transcend self. With admirable candor, wit, intelligence, and charm, he throws his entire personality into analyzing the nature and mode of operation of ambition, creative energy (analogous to the sexual drive), power, fame, and intellectual paranoia, masochism, envy, guilt, impotence, self-doubt, vanity ("Jewish variety").

To absorb the shock of Podhoretz's insights, the intellectual might easily dismiss *Making It* as inflated literary gossip or impose upon the author's testimony a pattern of rationalization — but he does so at the peril of self-delusion. From the general judgment of this deliberately provocative exposé, I dissent. What most reviewers and readers seem to resent is that Podhoretz has published their own intellectual autobiography under his name — without their permission, nor yours, nor mine.

At the opposite pole of American experience from Podhoretz is the conforming middle-class gentile growing up in Mississippi. Willie Morris' *North Toward Home* describes the emotional, intellectual, physical odyssey of a young southerner from childhood in Yazoo, to young manhood in Austin, where he edited two of the most admired and despised newspapers in America, and on to Manhattan, where he became editor of *Harper's*, America's oldest magazine. The book depicts the "Yankeefication" of a southerner who finally, though reluctantly, comes to regard North as home.

Still, the friendships Morris has formed in New York are with such southerners as William Styron, whose *Confessions of Nat Turner* is the first-person testimony of that rare thing in the Old South, a Negro insurrectionist, and Ralph Ellison, whose *Invisible Man* is as much a work of art as it is a plea for Negro rights. But generally, New

York friendships contrast brutally with those Morris formed in Mississippi and Texas, where "You shared certain things: a reverence for informality, an interest in what other friends were doing, a regard for geographic places, an awareness of a certain set of beloved landmarks in themselves important to one's everyday existence, a mutual but usually unexpressed sense of community." On the other hand, in New York, "'We lunch twice a year,' a native . . . once said to me of a good friend of his, and without a trace of irony." The only New Yorker with whom Morris feels affinities is Norman Podhoretz. They talked about the places they had come from, about home, about people from their pasts. "We told stories. . . . I felt here, as I had perceived before, a certain electricity between Eastern Jewish intellectuals and white southerners when the mood is relaxed and the pretensions gone, a certain élan in the casual talk about great characters, about comic moods, about Waspish Easterners more 'inside' than we, and even, perhaps, an affinity in the historical disasters of our ancestral pasts." Morris and Styron, southern whites; Ellison, southern Negro; Podhoretz, Brooklyn Jew — in such relationships, with paradoxical, ironic, comic, and tragic roots in the cultural and geographical past, examined autobiographically, Americans are beginning to suspend bitterness to understand the past as it lives or languishes in the present.

Willie Morris' testament is a major document in this process of understanding because its primary inspiration and motivation is not ideas, except as they inhabit images charged with human emotions and a sense of time and of place. "Each street and hill was like a map on my consciousness." The third of the book devoted to Morris' childhood in Yazoo consists of a predictable recital of excruciatingly typical middle-class small-town events related to school, church, family rituals, Negro-white relationships, baseball and other sports, hunting trips with dog and dad. His affectionate tribute to a tough, demanding high school teacher balances his earlier unforgiving

portrait of his severe fundamentalist grammar school
teacher. (Podhoretz, also, includes a prolonged portrayal
of one of his teachers.)

Too often he forces his childhood memories into
occasions for grown-up, snobbish wit (aggravated by
four years at Oxford as a Rhodes Scholar), cutely con-
descending in tone, as when he describes fundamentalist
religion, perennial target of sophomoric southern
liberal self-righteousness. The proffering of truisms as
wisdom — this is one of the traps inherent in the autobiographical mode, for the author must scramble desperately to justify offering his life to posterity (as what, if
not as exemplification of one thing and another?). His
description of a mountebank rural sports announcer
suggests his own inadequacies as autobiographer in the
early sections: "After the usual summaries, he mentioned
that the game had been 'recreated.'" Like many auto-
biographers, Morris allows his summaries ("we would"
do such and such) to deceive him into thinking he has
recreated on the page what remains vivid enough in his
own mind. The art of American autobiography has yet to
keep pace with its vigor and audacity.

But transcending these faults is the feel of place that
the reader absorbs into his own consciousness forever:
lazy Yazoo and neighboring towns and cities, including
Jackson (where he visited his venerable grandparents)
and Vicksburg (where he played trumpet for the funerals
of boys killed in Korea); Austin, and numerous Texas
towns where he searched for the latest news about ordinary,
foolish humanity; and though his targets are predictable,
even his responses to Manhattan, "the Big Cave," are
suffused with a feel for place peculiarly southern. But more
than cityscapes, one comes away with a profound sense
of landscapes and of the human and natural weathers that
fluctuate over them. Characteristically, he gives to the
three sections of his book simple geographical names:
Mississippi, Texas, New York. "Only retrospect would
tell me that I was to take something of these things with

me forever, through my maturing into manhood. . . . I
still suffer from the pain of that alienation."

Morris provides indispensable insights into the men-
tality of Mississippians and Texans of every class, race,
and attitude. At thirty-three, he has an incredibly intimate
knowledge of practical politics. A vocal member of the
silent generation of the fifties, he fought cultural and
political narrow-mindedness and cruelty as editor of the
University's *Daily Texan* during the McCarthy era of
radical right-wing hysteria, and later as editor of the
weekly liberal *Texas Observer* during the state's transformation from an agrarian into an industrial giant. The
insanity, inextricable from the twisted humanism, of
Texas politics is lucidly explicated through a gallery of
character profiles that spawns anecdote after anecdote,
many of which hurt while one laughs. "There were the
Texas stories, extravagant, reflective, ironic, boisterous —
but always relevant, and exuberantly alive."

Morris offers a less informative and insightful view
of the New York intellectual and literary world than
Podhoretz does. Podhoretz's power lies in the explication
of ideas, appropriate for a New York intellectual; Morris'
power lies in character study and storytelling, appropriate
for a southern intellectual. The young Jewish intellectual
fought for the supremacy of one set of ideas over another;
the nascent southern liberal had first to awaken to the
mere "acceptance of ideas themselves as something worth
living by." Mean, verbose, the New York literary world in
the sixties was given to backbiting, "polemic and broad-
side" and to "extravagant claims and exaggerated dis-
missals." He discovered the "considerable limitations of
intelligence" among isolated, emotionally crippled people
who "cared little or not at all for human beings." About
New Yorkers, low-, middle-, and high-brow, he concludes:
"I had never run up against people so lacking in the
human graces." But he recognized the dangers for the
"Mississippi exile . . . alienated from home yet forever
drawn back to it, seeking some form of personal liberty

elsewhere yet obsessed with the texture and the complexity of the place from which they had departed as few Americans from other states could ever be." One had to resist the inclination to turn one's back deliberately upon the time and place of one's childhood "for the sake of some convenient or fashionable 'sophistication.'" Yet Morris is one of thousands of southerners who yielded to the "catastrophic wanderlust" of his generation and found a second home in the North — a "stark removal," while one's "deepest loyalties" belong to another time, another place.

All questions raised in an autobiography flow from this primary question: who is speaking? Sometimes the answers go beyond the speaker's control. When Morris tells about the time he threw out of his apartment a German girl who was bad-mouthing Jews, he expects us to respect him as a moral person among monsters. Self-righteousness as the disguise of hypocrisy and the balm of guilt is not one of Morris' subjects, but it is certainly one of the reader's. Enslaved to small-town mores, so that he tormented Negroes without remorse, Morris was liberated by his professors at the University of Texas, after a transitional humiliation in a fraternity. For those early enslavements of the mind, Morris has punished numerous intellectually defenseless people with ridicule. Like the unreliable narrator in fiction who deceives himself in the manner of his telling, Morris tells more about himself than he realizes. In his shifting environments, he seems to have conformed to the most powerful influences. His objectivity is directed mainly toward "the others."

Among the recent autobiographies that reflect social conflicts, *North Toward Home* provides a special vision — of the land rather than of the cities. On the South's own vision of American Dreams and Nightmares, Morris quotes his friend C. Vann Woodward, a southern historian, as though summing up the spinal theme of his reminiscences: the national self-image is one of "innocence and moral complacency." But "the Southerner's preoccupation . . .

was not with innocence but with guilt, not with the ideal of perfection but with the reality of evil." The Jew's assimilation into "modern America" seems less painful, for he rises to equality from a thousand years of persecution as a victim with abstract ideals founded on innocence; but for the other two great minorities acculturation is anguish, for southern whites and Negroes enter the space age entwined together in the reciprocal guilt of master and slave. "To Woodward these realities had provided Southerners with a different point of view from which they might, if they would, 'judge and understand their own history and American history, and from which to view the ironic plight of modern America.'" And that is the task that Willie Morris accomplishes.

Frank Conroy is less comparable to Podhoretz and Morris than to Russian poet Yevtushenko who in 1963 published, at thirty, a mere 124-page *Precocious Autobiography*; the title was not a little coy, since he had published a good deal of poetry, risked the censure of Khrushchev, and thus earned (or failed to earn, depending on one's criteria for evaluating a literary reputation) the adulation of the United States, where he promoted himself as a young poet internationally on the make. But compared with *Stop-time* — the first book of an obscure young writer — Yevtushenko's testament is insipid. Frank Conroy has nothing to offer but his American boyhood and adolescence. Frequently, it is enough; occasionally, more than enough.

Conroy's problem as a young autobiographer seems to have been how to avoid the same me-rack fallacies that characterize most autobiographical fiction and nauseate creative writing instructors. His solution was to abandon fiction altogether. But to throw off the artifices of art entails risks which Conroy has not so much confronted as eluded with sheer verbal talent. When a writer opens or stumbles into new territory, he either explores the possibilities or, like a lost explorer with a machete, hacks a straight path from here to there. Conceptually, Conroy is a hacker. Stylistically, he is a weaver. If he fails to use "technique as an agent of discovery," fails to find a pattern, impose a shape (as the novelist is obliged to do), he succeeds in creating unforgettable moods, conveying painfully keen impressions, conjuring lingering atmospheres. Autobiography requires Conroy to express insights overtly; they are often banal: "it came to me that the world was insane. Not just People. The world." Crudely aware of the need for some sort of conception, he imposes the flimsiest imaginable: driving home from London drunk to his wife in the country at four A.M., he works up speed, in the course of which he reviews his life (leaping over an apparently gray decade from 1954 to 1964) in "stop-time" — "measured, punctuated musical silences" (he is a self-taught jazz pianist). In the middle of the book, he alludes to this conceptual frame and rounds it off at the end with a few feeble strokes as his Jaguar stops at a small-town fountain. Now and then, in a parenthesis or a brief episode, he jumps backward or forward in time to establish parallels, but the effect is only a slight enhancement, not a conceptual revelation.

But the energy of Conroy's reminiscing vision triumphs over errors of strategy and omission. If the book sometimes seems to read like "I Was a Teenage Zombie," it is because Conroy is generally sullen, resentful, stodgily bitter; though he creeps frequently to the verge of self-pity, he usually backs away in time. But what saved him then and makes his youth interesting to the reader now is that he had the imagination to grow up among interesting people. Dagmar, his vulgar, sensual, Danish mother "was a courageous woman who refused to let life break her." Jean, his quixotic stepfather, descendant of New Orleans aristocrats, though reduced to driving a cab in New York, "deeply believed that the good things in life were given to one." Frank's superficially adjusted sister, Alison, finally has a picturesque nervous breakdown in Paris. He remembers his father as the bedridden victim of cancer who told him a story about a man "who sat down on the open blade of a penknife embedded in a park bench." Living in Dagmar's New York apartment off and on was Donald, a pale, sexless piano accompanist who felt compelled to hurt defenseless people with words; he conned his way into Dagmar's good graces and earned Frank's and Jean's hatred. On the white country roads of Florida, Frank's buddy was Tobey, whose wild spirit sparked latent sources of energy in Frank's sluggish mind and body. While Dagmar was visiting her home in Denmark, Jean befriended Nell Smith, a skinny suicidal drifter who made Frank's and Jean's life exciting for a while. In Denmark, Frank meets Christina, Scandinavian small-town love goddess; he wins her, then deserts her, along with many girls whose paths and bodies he crosses by chance.

If, free of the constraints of fictive form, Conroy often becomes ensnarled in unexamined consequences, he achieves enough advantages to justify the experiment: he conveys a sense of awkward adolescence as vividly as most of our best novelists; few succeed quite the way he does in evoking a sense of time and place; and though generally the episodes of his life are presented in a gratuitous fashion, many are masterfully recreated. In the chapter entitled "White Days and Red Nights" he cringes in fear alone in a rural Connecticut cabin during the winter weekends while his mother and Jean work the night shift as wardens at a home for the feeble-minded; one midnight he visits the worst of the wards. Donald plays a subtle joke on Jean one Christmas Eve in "Hate, and a Kind of Music": "I began to have that worst of all feelings for a child, that more was going on than I could grasp." Frank loathes the chore of cleaning out Jean's kennels, but to get away from Dagmar's and Jean's endless squabbling, he sometimes sleeps with the dogs: "Faintly dizzy, half-asleep, and beyond time, I slipped gradually out of the world." In "Hanging On," Frank's antics in the chemistry lab where he works after school get him fired, but, ingeniously, he redeems himself. "Nights Away from Home" and "License to Drive" chronicle his attempts to escape

to Florida from malaise in New York. In "Losing My
Cherry" he relates one of his many feeble sexual adventures. "Going to Sea" and "Elsinore, 1953" tell of
his voyage to Europe and his experiences in a special
Danish high school, where he began to write short stories.
Before entering Haverford College, where the story ends,
he loafed in Paris. "Haverford College would give me a
chance to start with a clean slate, and that was all I'd
ever wanted . . . to destroy my past, a past I didn't understand, a past I feared, and a past with which I had
expected to be forever encumbered."

It is difficult to suspend judgment of Conroy while he
is so easily inclined to judge others. Despite his smug
allusions to the mystery of human brutality, his participation in the kangaroo court beating of Liggett, fat outsider
in a progressive school, is contemptible. Like much
contemporary literature narrated by the antihero with
only a navel to contemplate, *Stop-time* is turgid with
unearned assumptions which may be summed up this
way: My life is dull and meaningless because everybody
around me is phony. The implication, reiterated with
intimidating monotony, is: I am therefore superior since I
know how meaningless all our lives are. So did Thoreau,
who observed that most men "lead lives of quiet desperation," but his own life — of the mind, at least — was so
fascinating that he recommended it on good authority to
others. All a boy like Frank has to offer is the authenticity
of his situational agony as a case in point. In literature,
life revenges itself against such an attitude: the lifeless
victim's heated testimony breathes life into his tormentors.
It is, of course, this surviving love of life that inspires
Conroy's consciousness to endow his anemic private
experience with a luminosity he can share with others.
He learned early the transforming power of the written
word, whether it came from James M. Cain or Albert
Camus. Style is the man, and Conroy's style contradicts
the criticisms of human sterotypes implied in his vision.
Though in life he hardly seemed more than a shadow, life

and literature conspire to give substance to the Conroy of *Stop-time*.

If within the past few decades a trend toward auto-biography has gathered force, it is as a strong thrust in that trend that *Stop-time* is an important, unique book. Two trends converge in *Stop-time*: the literary tendency since the forties to render the subjective life of kids (*The Member of the Wedding*, *Other Voices*, *Other Rooms*, *A Catcher in the Rye*); and the cultural tendency to indulge, if not worship, youth as a virtue in itself. From *Look Homeward, Angel* to "Look Inward, Hipster" we have come a short way by a long route. "Why pretend?" the young voices seem to say. "Don't put people on. Tell it like it is. Do your own thing." Write a book distinctly labelled: "This is my bag." "Don't call me Ishmael, call me Herman. The Adventures of Sam Clemens, not Huck Finn." The new twist is to tell it while it's fresh. "Don't wait to look back. Look into your own heart, *now*, and write." All the frontiers of the American outer experience are defunct. One has only to compare the classic pro-letarian novel of the thirties, *The Disinherited* by Jack Conroy (no relation to Frank), with *Stop-time*, to see the degree to which the old problem of the cult of experience in American literature has shifted from landscapes to inscapes. (In ways that are increasingly astonishing, the depressed thirties are resurrected in the affluent sixties.) Still, Frank Conroy's adolescence was not ordinary, and it was certainly geographically mobile. He speaks out of a transitional sort of consciousness, for the inner life of the younger Frank who grew up in the postwar forties and the early Cold War fifties does not differ much from the unromantic agony of the typical product of the New Frontier and the Great Society. But ironically, Conroy is over thirty and the kid who still haunts his six-foot-tall body probably doesn't trust him.

Though Norman Mailer, like Henry Adams, speaks of himself in the third person, *The Armies of the Night* (a 1969 National Book Award winner) is not "The Education of Norman Mailer" but the continuing and relentless education of Americans *about* Norman Mailer, and here we graduate into deeper subtleties. Fortunately for us, it is Mailer who studies the American character more honestly than any other American — by looking into his own heart and mind — and thus sees through the Dream into the Nightmare. The intellectual as tough guy, doing his own thing, Mailer is where it's at, this instant. His bag is himself, and nothing goes in that does not come out again in one of his five novels, numerous stories, poems, plays, essays.

Mailer's powerful style gives a powerful thrust to the simple narrative (reducible to an anecdote), and the power of the style is in the man — a man so unique there is no room in America for another like him. It is no wonder then that in writing about himself, while purporting to describe an historic public event — the October, 1967 peace assault on the Pentagon — he should achieve an innovation in literary form. The book is subtitled "History as a Novel, the Novel as History" — neither a put-on nor a put-down.

The American writer loves to present himself as the man who was there and who has come back to report to the stay-at-homes. If you want the inside dope on Mailer's "outrageous" words and deeds and to know what happened within the immediate radius of his navel (sometimes mistaken for the hub of the universe) during those three days of protest and play, this is your book. If you want Mailer's opinions of Paul Goodman, Dwight MacDonald, and Robert Lowell (along with the lesser lights who did all the actual work), this is your book. But in addition to all that, and to yet another bracing swim in the swift currents of Mailer's stream of consciousness, there is one thing that only this book offers: insights into the psychological wellsprings of the political activism of certain artists and intellectuals. To pass it off as mere exhibitionism is to be self-indulgent. But what emerges from Mailer's book is a depiction of the use of public arenas as showcases for private neuroses and psychoses, as well as for healthy forms of sublimation.

Mailer begins his candid exposé with himself. His attitude is ironic and paradoxical, his tone is both self-congratulatory and self-accusatory. He finds himself interesting, often fascinating; and he is not a little in awe of the many Mailers he observes. He sensed then — at the Ambassador theater rally, at the party afterwards, during the march, in jail — and demonstrates now that all artistic and intellectual endeavor, even in a "noble" cause, is to a great extent play. Not mere play. But play of a profoundly psychological, spiritual, even metaphysical sort. One should not expect him to go on to scrutinize the dangerous consequences of an idealistic, anarchic, radical blindness to the way private psychology and group play operate in public events. For if Mailer's half-playful march on the Pentagon became a pretext for a forced march — lightened by wisecracks — into the dark night of his own soul, the next move, Right and Left, is ours. Aren't the best autobiographies those that turn out in one way or another to be our own?

In a work of fiction, whether it is based more or less on the author's imagination than on his life, the relationship between the writer and the audience he assumes for his work is usually indirect. The autobiographer normally speaks more directly to his assumed audience, working from a dominant attitude toward his life (lyrical, intellectual, and so forth) and a dominant perspective. The four autobiographies I have discussed offer some variations on this pattern that suggest future possibilities for both writers and readers of autobiography. In Podhoretz's autobiography, the perspective is that of intellectual recall consistently inseparable from a larger social dimension; Morris' is the perspective of lyrical recall with asides about the larger social dimension — and each of these books proceeds chronologically with an emphasis on the events of a life. Mailer's book is an intellectual and lyrical self-scrutiny, *implying* a social relevance much larger than he overtly delineates, with an emphasis more on style and sensibility than on events. Conroy offers a

totally lyrical recall of childhood, with little direct relevance to his contemporaries, through the vision of a
basically imaginative or fictive sensibility, revealing itself
in style, characterization, and selectivity.

In "The Self Recaptured" (*Kenyon Review*, Summer,
1963), a discussion of the autobiographical novel (taking
Proust's *Remembrance of Things Past* and Wolfe's *Look
Homeward, Angel* as principal examples), Louis D. Rubin,
Jr. offers a back door approach to the problem of studying
the autobiography itself as art. He quotes Northrop
Frye, the great theorist of form in fiction, as saying that
autobiography "merges with the novel by a series of
insensible gradations." Of course, the gradations are more
sensible in some autobiographies than in others. Is it true,
though, as Frye states, that most autobiographies "are
inspired by a creative, and therefore fictional, impulse to
select only those events and experiences in the writer's life
that go to build up an integrated pattern"? The best do,
but as Rubin points out, most autobiographies and
biographies follow not the imaginative logic of fiction but
the chronological logic of life, and the details are, from a
fictive point of view, unselective. But more important than
selectivity for the autobiography that approaches art is
the treatment through conception and technique of what is
selected.

Rubin argues that an autobiographical interpretation
is relevant for certain novels "not because of any biographical or psychological insights it may give into the
author," but because it is a commentary on the "*formal
experience*" of the novel. "From the way the story is
written, by the kind of details, by the value placed on
certain events — very unimportant events, often, which
nevertheless are obviously being remembered, recaptured,"
we sense "the mind of the authorial personality" and "that
is what is important." (This is certainly true of Mailer, in
both his fiction and his nonfiction.) The author's "perspective is built in; it is an essential dimension of the
narrative. It is the interplay of past and present, or, more

particularly, the seeing and understanding of the past through and with the eyes of the present, the experience of time and memory itself." The reader's "essential experience of the novel" is his awareness of the author's shaping activity as he attempts "rediscovery and redemption in time." " *The teller of the tale* . . . does not exist dramatically as a person, but rather as an instrument of perception, the authorial personality. This personality is part of the form of the novel." He converts his life, which was "full of flux and impermanence, into an ordered and meaningful reality in language, complete and permanent in itself. The process is the form." Mr. Rubin's commentary on autobiographical fiction suggests a few approaches to a deeper understanding of autobiography itself.

The serious study of autobiography (indeed of many other kinds of creative nonfiction as well) has been too long neglected. While an examination of Yeats's autobiography as art has just appeared, we ought to go beyond literary figures, not only to examine the classic autobiographies but to discover concealed aesthetic values in lesser-known lives. We may discover or rediscover a number of works that may be evaluated and appreciated by more meaningful criteria than "literal faithfulness to 'real life.'" In the future, one of the tasks of the autobiographer as artist will be to avoid missing opportunities for transforming the transient formlessness of life into the permanent forms of art. The study of autobiography as an art ought perhaps to begin with two major questions: First, what aesthetic qualities are involved in the way the author has shaped his life, or what is the function of the conceptual imagination in the writing of one's life story? Out of this question will come a continuation of Rubin's examination of the way some fiction writers involve their own lives in their work. And the second major question is, What transcendent significance does a man's life have for others, and to what extent does that significance flow from the form he has given it in literature?

index

index